ST. MARY'S CITY, MARYLAND 20686

Aesthetics

EXPLORATIONS IN PHILOSOPHY
James H. Fetzer, Series Editor

EXPLORATIONS
in philosophy

Aesthetics

James W. Manns

M.E. Sharpe
Armonk, New York
London, England

Copyright © 1998 by M. E. Sharpe, Inc.

All rights reserved. No part of this book may be reproduced in any form without written permission from the publisher, M. E. Sharpe, Inc., 80 Business Park Drive, Armonk, New York 10504.

Library of Congress Cataloging-in-Publication Data

Manns, James W.
Aesthetics / James W. Manns.
p.   cm. — (Explorations in philosophy)
Includes bibliographical references and index.
ISBN 1–56324–953–7 (hardcover : alk. paper). —
ISBN 1–56324–954–5 (pbk. : alk. paper)
1. Aesthetics.   I. Title.   II. Series.
BH39.M385 1997
111′.85—dc21   97–21723
CIP

Printed in the United States of America

The paper used in this publication meets the minimum requirements of American National Standard for Information Sciences— Permanence of Paper for Printed Library Materials, ANSI Z 39.48-1984.

BM (c)   10   9   8   7   6   5   4   3   2   1
BM (p)   10   9   8   7   6   5   4   3   2

To Syham

For filling my life with beauty

Table of Contents

Series Preface   ix
Preface   xi
Acknowledgments   xiii

1. The "Elusiveness" of Art: Questions of Definition and Delimitation   3
    Art: A Word Like Any Other Word   7
    Art: A Word Unlike Any Other (A World Unlike Any Other)   11
    "Two Different Worlds"   13
    Institutional Irregularities   15
    Danto's Infirmities   18
    Summary and Conclusion   23

2. Theories of Art: Representation   26
    Representation Theory: Its Origins in Ancient Greek Thought   29
    Pictorial Representation During the Renaissance and Beyond   38
    Pictorial Representation, Recently   43
    Truthful Representation in the Narrative Arts   47

3. Theories of Art: Form   52
    Formalism   54
    Organicism   61
    The Gestalt Approach: General Theory   67
    Gestalt Theory and the Visual Arts   70
    Gestalt Theory and Music   74
    Final Thoughts   78

4. Theories of Art: Expression   80
    Thomas Reid   84

Leo Tolstoy   89
R.G. Collingwood   92
A Pause for Reflection   97
"Wiser"(?) Approaches   100
Wisdom Renounced   105

5. Intentions, Intentionality, and Artistic Communication   109
The Intentional Fallacy   110
Inside and Outside a Poem   113
The Inside-Outside Distinction Evaluated   114
Originality   118
Art's "Tragic Demise"   123
The Human Factor in Art   127
Treating Works of Art as Persons   129

6. Universality, Objectivity, and the Claim of Taste   133
The Problem   134
The Subjective Approach: David Hume   140
A Case for Objectivity and Universality: Thomas Reid   147
Subjectivity Universalized: Immanuel Kant   156
Universality Revisited, and Revised   168
A Final Thought   175

Notes   177
Bibliography   183
Index   185
About the Author   191

Series Preface

The series, *Explorations in Philosophy*, is intended to provide undergraduates and other readers with quality introductions not only to the principal areas of philosophy, including traditional topics of investigation—epistemology, ethics, and social and political philosophy—but also to contemporary subjects of importance such as critical theory, feminist studies, and the ethics of reproduction. In each case, the editors have chosen authors who could not only explain the central problems encountered within their respective domains, but who could also propose promising solutions to those problems, including novel approaches and original analyses.

The present volume, *Aesthetics,* focuses upon and evaluates the most important theories of art—formalism, expressionism, and representationism—and explores issues that are central to the nature of art, including the problem of definition, questions of taste, the role of intentions, and the prospects for universality. While the author, James W. Manns, has emphasized "classic" sources, he has attempted to provide sympathetic interpretations of views he discusses to ensure that his critiques and recommendations are directed at serious rather than imaginary targets. The result is a lucid and fascinating exploration of both art and aesthetics that should appeal to beginners and experts alike.

James H. Fetzer

Preface

This book aims to provide the reader with a sense of the abiding issues in aesthetics. It embodies a deep respect for tradition—tradition in the arts and in the theories of art that have been formulated across the centuries. Artistic fads come and go, and have come and gone as long as there has been art, but the works of some artists have somehow managed to preserve their august rank amidst all the comings and goings of artistic styles and approaches. This is a basic fact that any responsible study of aesthetics must take into account.

Philosophy, too, has seen its share of fads over the years; but certain philosophies, like certain monumental works of art, have succeeded in holding fast to their position of importance, despite endless fluctuations in the surface texture of the philosophical enterprise. I have endeavored to acquaint the reader with a number of these promontory approaches to the philosophy of art. To be sure, there are gaps and omissions. One book cannot do full justice to all who have made significant contributions to a field as extensive as aesthetics without sacrificing readability and severely compromising analytic depth.

I have chosen to pursue in some detail certain issues that form a cluster about the core of aesthetic analysis, though make no mistake—many a weighty volume has been written about each of the topics focused upon in successive chapters here. Still, rather than string together a series of hasty allusions, I have settled on one issue, then the next, for what I hope proves to be a long enough time to hatch a sense not only of the importance of these issues, but of their immense complexity as well.

Having contemplated for many years the questions examined here, it is inevitable that I should come to hold an opinion or two of my own, and that I should hold certain of them rather strongly. And yet I only wish that I might one day reach the point where I could lay down dogmatic pronouncements on all the major issues of aesthetic interest—happy are they who have risen above doubt! However, an ever-broadening exposure both to the objects included in this field of study—works of art—and to the theories of art propounded by others, combined with an ever-deepening inquiry into what art means *to me,* seems to leave me in a state of permanent transition. If I had written this book twenty years ago, it would have been a radically different book; and in twenty years' time further metamorphoses would likewise be apparent.

Certain convictions will not change, though, among them the following:

1. Art is a most serious matter. A few recent trends in both art and aesthetics, it seems to me, conduce to or actually embody a flippant approach toward artistic creation and appreciation. It can only be hoped that such trends run their course and vanish finally beneath the imposing shadow of a nobler artistic tradition. My conviction in this regard runs throughout the present book, but comes to the surface most noticeably in Chapter Four, where expression and artistic communication are dealt with, and Chapter Five, where the intentional structure of art is examined.

2. Artistic creativity and discernment are apportioned in different degrees among us. To deny this, I suggest, would remove aesthetics from the realm of philosophical inquiry and reduce it to a psychological study of minor importance. To account for it adequately, on the other hand, is an immense and daunting task. Chapter Six, dealing with the question of taste, aims to circumscribe the parameters and convey a sense of the nature of this task.

3. Progress is possible in aesthetic analysis—there is sense to be made of the activity of art. Some theories are simply more fruitful than others, some theoreticians more insightful than others. One humble example of the kind of insight that leads to progress is offered in Chapter Three, where a psychological theory is applied to the realm of aesthetic response. And in Chapter One, pursuit of a definition of "art" is infused with the conviction that such a pursuit can in principle be rewarded.

4. That tradition is of vital importance to art and aesthetics has already been stated. The longevity of certain aspects of this tradition comes out most clearly in Chapter Two, in which the lineage of perhaps the most venerable of all aesthetic theories—representation theory—is traced from its beginnings in ancient Greek thought to its twentieth-century manifestations.

In the end, this book reflects one man's journey across the field of art and into its depths. For better or for worse, a careful reader will come away not only with a sense of what is important in aesthetics but also with an insight or two into the character, the attachments, and perhaps even the prejudices of its author. It is hoped that this element of the work, far from rendering it private and idiosyncratic, will lend it a certain air of poignant individuality, such as that by which art itself enlivens the truths it enunciates.

Acknowledgments

I should like to offer thanks to Professor James Fetzer for providing me with the opportunity to write this book. I deeply appreciate the trust he has shown in me and hope my efforts adequately repay this trust.

Thanks also go to Professor Edward Madden for carefully reading the manuscript in various stages of its development and making numerous suggestions that have strengthened it greatly. In addition, his continuing encouragement proved vital to sustaining the effort necessary to bring this work to successful completion.

And lastly, I thank Amy Goff-Yates for carefully reading and editing the manuscript. Her numerous corrections and suggestions have contributed immensely toward making this work more accurate, readable, and philosophically competent than it would otherwise have been.

Aesthetics

— 1 —

The "Elusiveness" of Art: Questions of Definition and Delimitation

It is hard to imagine a subject matter being more capricious and elusive than aesthetics. It is easy enough to characterize it as the philosophy of art—or, to capture a greater portion of the aesthetic tradition, the philosophy of art and beauty—but once said, we right away find ourselves face-to-face with the slippery question "What is art?" (or the equally slippery question "What is beauty?").

A long tradition in philosophy, reaching back at least as far as Plato and receiving continual reinforcement across the centuries, has it that when we use a single term in a multitude of situations, there must be some common element shared by all the individuals properly designated by that term. Of the virtues, for example, Plato says, "Even if they are many and various, all of them have one and the same form which makes them virtuous."[1] Otherwise, the term would be ambiguous, and our speech would be confused. In the distinctly aesthetic domain, we find Diderot, in the eighteenth century, proclaiming:

> *Beauty* is a term we apply to an infinitude of beings; but whatever differences there may be among these beings, it must be the case either that we falsely apply the term *beautiful,* or that there is in all these beings a quality of which the term *beauty* is the sign.[2]

More recently, we find Suzanne Langer judging that "if 'art' means anything, its application must rest on one essential criterion, not several unrelated ones";[3] and Clive Bell expresses the same methodological commitment somewhat more trenchantly, contending that "either all works of . . . art have some common quality, or when we speak of 'works of art' we gibber."[4] Whether these concepts are capable of living up to demands of this sort is the principal question we will be pondering in this chapter. Perhaps I can allow myself to say at this point that I am hopeful, but we must give serious consideration to the many obstacles that stand in the way of realizing such a goal. Certainly one of these obstacles lies in the very subject matter itself that aesthetics must deal with.

In the natural sciences it seems reasonable to expect the phenomena under investigation to "hold still" long enough to be examined. Entomology, for example, unambiguously declares itself to be concerned with insects, supplies an account of the characteristics that combine to constitute an insect, and sets about to find and study insects. Perhaps we lose some insect species here and there as mankind encroaches deeper and deeper into their areas of habitation, perhaps we discover some new ones, but the central concept that defines the parameters of entomology remains unchanged: an insect is an insect. Should there be borderline cases, they can be perceived as such because of the basic clarity of the central concepts defining the subject area.

Within physics itself, the most fundamental of the natural sciences, profound changes have taken place and continue to take place in the very matter of how scientists conceive the foundations of physical reality. Their task is further complicated by a certain indeterminacy factor, wherein attempts to isolate and examine bits of nature at the microcosmic level wind up altering the phenomena under examination.* Yet there is never any question of nature actually altering its behavior: theories change, but not nature itself. And if direct observation of certain particles proves out of the question, then scientists must content themselves with indirect observation, the observation of effects, and the like.

Sciences dealing with human behavior, such as psychology and sociology, are decidedly more volatile than physics and entomology. Human subjects are less docile than insects, and more unpredictable when placed under scrutiny than any subatomic particle will prove to be. While mutations resulting in new species do occur in the insect realm, never in the

---

*"[I]magine ourselves trying to see one of the electrons in an atom. . . . We must use fine-grained illumination and train our eyes to see with radiation of short wave-length —with X-rays in fact. . . . Now . . . watch, whilst I flash one quantum of X-rays on to the atom. . . . [It] has hit the electron. Look sharp and notice where it is. Isn't it there? Bother! I must have blown the electron out of the atom." A.S. Eddington, *The Nature of the Physical World*, p. 224.

history of entomology, nor (thankfully) in its foreseeable future has an insect willfully mutated purely and simply to register its disrespect for an unjust or constraining taxonomic system. That would be a distinctly human gesture.

There is no small measure of overlap between aesthetics and these behavioral sciences, for after all, human emotional response falls squarely within the domain of psychology, and emotional states prompting and prompted by works of art cannot resist inclusion into this domain. And to whatever extent we might judge art to be a social phenomenon, it would overlap similarly with the region assigned to sociology.

Beyond its participation in these two rather indeterminate realms, however, aesthetics is complicated by the very nature of its principal subject matter—art. For art, at least as it has been practiced in the West, is by nature restless, fluid, prone to stylistic transformation, ill-disposed toward stasis. This has been especially the case over the past few centuries, and the tendency accelerates the nearer we draw to the present. Indeed, sometimes it seems as if each new gallery opening announces a new artistic style. The quest, common among artists, for an individual idiom through which to express themselves, or by which, simply, to "make their mark," commonly leads to the exploration of novel artistic terrain or to various modes of experimentation within the different media. Attempts at formulating rules of procedure that, if widely accepted, would at least retard somewhat the transformation of styles are met more often with hostility than servility: it is said that Gainesborough painted his famous *Blue Boy* in response to a critical pronouncement to the effect that an excess of blue paint deadens a canvas.

During at least the past couple of centuries, artists and theoreticians alike have insisted on the importance of artistic freedom, and freedom likewise appears antipathetic to systematization. It is true that in ethical theory what looks to be a similar link between moral behavior and freedom is often affirmed, yet in ethics this connection leads to radically different theoretical results. The freedom of choice deemed necessary for the ascription of moral responsibility is one that, even on a weak interpretation, would put the individual moral agent *in touch with* reason—would make *one* of the agent's alternatives the rational one—while the strong interpretation has it that we are only free to the extent that we *are* rational. Since rational behavior is essentially rule-governed behavior, ethical theory therefore inclines toward connecting freedom with rule-governed behavior in either of these two ways: either we are free to obey rules dictated by reason (the former position above), or (by the latter) we are free only when we obey such rules.

In art, however, freedom implies a willingness, an urge to contravene rules or stylistic conventions. Behavior of a sort that morality would rule out, art is eager to encourage. And this hardly makes for theoretical purity and simplicity.

Even so, this emphasis on the freedom of the artist is a rather recent intruder onto the aesthetic scene. For many centuries a more technically oriented approach to art prevailed in the West. The very term "art" itself derives from the Latin *"ars,"* and when translating, *"ars"* is as appropriately replaced by "skill" as it is by "art." Thus, the sculptor's art would be grouped together with the physician's, the blacksmith's, the musician's, the vintner's, and so on. Seeing art keeping such company as this does not encourage us greatly in our search for that one component, or complex of components, that all works of art, properly so called, are to share.

If the determinants of art become shadowy and suspect as we allow our search to drift into the past, toward the roots—etymologically—of the term, then it might be hoped that a concentration on more recent claimants for the label "art" would provide us with somewhat firmer footing. Yet this hardly proves to be the case. Indeed, the long-standing association of art with skill seems appropriate at least to the extent that any great artist who comes to mind will also immediately qualify as an individual possessing great skill in the manipulation of one artistic medium or another. While skill does not seem to be a sufficient condition—one the presence of which would allow us to refer to someone as an artist—it may well be a necessary condition, one the absence of which would warrant withholding the characterization "artist."

However, any number of recent creations that would have themselves referred to as art—indeed, that have been referred to as art—give very little evidence that any skill was employed in bringing them into being. Some years back, an art gallery in San Francisco offered as an exhibit a number of boxes filled with rotting cheese, cheese that had been allowed to decompose to the point that it swelled and split open the boxes. (The artist responsible for this "show and smell" demonstration, coincidentally, was named Dieter Rot.) While some ingenuity may have been employed in coming up with the idea for this particular exhibit, less skill than fortitude seems to have been required to actualize it (in fact, perhaps the greatest amount of skill was needed to convince some gallery owner of the worthiness of the undertaking).

John Cage's famous "4 Minutes and 33 Seconds of Silence" likewise required little in the way of skill to compose or to perform: *not* playing a piano for a certain period of time is something most of us manage to accomplish most of the time. A flash of insight, a sense of a tradition (not necessarily a very deep sense), and a knack for getting under the skin of that tradition—these are the prerequisites for an artistic production of this sort, not skill.

Another recent artist fired a gun into various parts of his body—taking care, of course, to avoid striking bones or vital organs. Then he took impressions of the wounds, photographed the impressions (in black and white), and displayed the photographs. Yet another, seeking perhaps to improve on Jackson Pollack's "dribble" technique, swung on a rope above a canvas, defecating on the canvas and capturing his "efforts" on videotape (here it is obscure whether the work of art consisted in the performance, the end product, or the video record of the two). In these latter cases little more seems to be involved than a will to do something different—*radically* different. And yet all of these works/performances/stunts were both presented and reported as artistic endeavors; in fact, the one by Cage has by now taken its place among the classics. It would appear that a definition of art that succeeded in capturing the element common to all the above works, as well as those of Praxiteles, Dante, Bach, and Balanchine, might have to stretch this element so thin as to render it transparent.

Let us begin by taking a close, critical look at a contrasting pair of theories pertinent to the defining of art. Each has captured a good bit of attention during the past generation; neither accepts the model of definition that we presented early on in this chapter; both aim to establish a more open-ended interpretation of art. My aim in this opening chapter is not to proclaim one of these positions to be the victor, nor to reject both and offer instead a substitute definition of art; rather, it is to open up the possibility of providing some meaningfully restrictive definition of art. Perhaps the succeeding chapters will suggest some lines along which such a definition may be drawn.

Art: A Word Like Any Other Word

"Art" is surely not the only concept to be troubled by problems of definition. So many terms deeply rooted in our language have resisted efforts to wrap their essence in a neat package that alternative strategies for characterizing their meaning have been adopted. One of these strategies is put forward by Ludwig Wittgenstein in his *Philosophical Investigations*.[5] One of the most influential philosophers of the present century, noted especially for his probing reflections on the relation of language to the world, Wittgenstein rejects outright the enterprise of searching for essences of terms and recommends instead a more flexible approach to the question of meaning.

Certain limited domains within language, Wittgenstein contends, may be organized in a relatively clear and unambiguous fashion, much like the

rectilinear street pattern of many an American town: the science of geome-
try, for example, defines its terms precisely and adheres to these definitions
strictly. But the "living" language—the one that has grown up alongside us
over the centuries and has served our needs for communication in a myriad
of ways—resembles more an ancient city, with neighborhoods that blend
into one another, alleys that follow paths once trodden by meandering livestock, avenues brutally carved out by military strategists or (more insidious
yet) city planners—here wide, there narrow, leading where the expedience
of one era or another dictated. In an old city of this sort, one cannot give the
kind of expeditious directions one can in New York: "Go three blocks over,
then turn right and head uptown for eighty-nine blocks and you'll be there."
We should understand that it is not rudeness but desperation that leads the
Parisian from whom we have just asked directions to gesture vaguely with
his hand and tell us *"par là,"* shaking his head and muttering to himself as
he proceeds on his way. He might have just come from where we want to
go, but it would be easier to retrace his steps than to capture them in words.

Having drawn such a parallel between linguistic ambiguity and urban
sprawl, Wittgenstein then reaches for another image to capture what he
takes to be an apt approach to conceptual analysis: the family reunion.
Imagine a gathering of numerous members of the same family, coming
from several branches and spanning several generations. At this gathering,
it is only reasonable to expect that certain people will bear a definite resemblance to one another: Uncle Henry's cheekbones will be discernible in
several faces; Grandfather's bandy legs will hold up a few other folks; and
perhaps Aunt Edith's raucous laugh will clatter across the reception hall,
first from one direction, then from another. Search as we may, however, we
will find no one feature manifest in each and every individual present. Yet
numerous resemblances are apparent, so we will think of these as family
resemblances.

Turning now to language, pick any term virtually at random—Wittgenstein
focuses on "games"—and we will find various elements repeating themselves in various places. Thus we have board games, card games, simula-
tion games, ball games, and so forth, but no one feature will be found to
persist through all the instances to which that term applies. As a consequence, he claims, we should abandon the illusion that has tyrannized philosophy for so long: one word, one meaning, "or we gibber." Instead, we
should expect to find no more than family resemblances among the various
instances in which a term is applied.

Since this notion of family resemblances was thought by Wittgenstein to
apply to most general terms, especially those with some longevity to them,
it stands to reason that it would apply to "art" also. Wittgenstein never made

mention of such an application, but it was not long before someone did, that someone being Morris Weitz. In a much celebrated article, Weitz argued that traditional aesthetics has long been asking the wrong question. "The problem with which we must begin," he judges, "is not 'What is art?,' but 'What sort of concept is art?'";[6] and to determine that, we must carry out an "elucidation of the actual employment of the concept of art, to give a logical description of the actual functioning of that concept, including a description of the conditions under which we correctly use it or its correlates."[7] This elucidation, or logical description, reveals that "art" is no different from "games," in that "if we actually look and see what it is that we call 'art,' we will also find no common properties—only strands of similarities."[8] And Weitz calls this feature of both of these terms their *open texture,* wherein "certain (paradigm) cases can be given, about which there can be no question as to their being correctly described as 'art' or 'game,' but no exhaustive set of cases can be given."[9]

From this perspective, the various theories of art that have been forwarded over the years (several of which we will be examining closely in succeeding chapters)—"Formalism, Voluntarism, Emotionalism, Intellectualism, Intuitionism, Organicism"[10]—are helpful in calling attention to telling features of certain works of art, but can only prove misleading when taken to specify the *essence* of art. Open-textured concepts, of which "art" is just one humble example, expand and contract, shift and relocate from culture to culture and epoch to epoch. We must learn to make our way, and we *do* learn to make our way about them in much the same manner that we come to find our way around an old city: by plunging into the streets and allowing them to lead us until such time as we gain control over them.

Questions of correctness aside, this view is appealing if only because it makes the task of philosophy ever so much simpler than it had long been taken to be. Freed from the necessity of squeezing an essence out of a diverse assemblage of phenomena, we need only keep abreast of the linguistic dispositions of our culture (or whatever culture is in question), however meandering or fluctuating these dispositions may be, and note their various points of concomitance and divergence. Philosophy from this point of view takes on the appearance of linguistic geography; no analysis is required: "Philosophy may in no way interfere with the actual use of language; it can in the end only describe it. . . . It leaves everything as it is."[11]

Though widely applauded, Weitz's importation of the family resemblance model into the aesthetic domain did not meet with unanimous approval. An adroit reply came from Maurice Mandelbaum a decade later, questioning not just the applicability of a family resemblance model to the concept of art, but the very notion of family resemblance itself.[12] He correctly observes that in any collection of people certain resemblances can be detected, but these resemblances become *family* resemblances only when there is some actual genetic connection involved, and where this obtains, "there is in fact an attribute common to all who bear a family resemblance to each other: they are related through a common ancestry."[13] After all, if we look closely at any roomful of unrelated people, we will detect numerous points of resemblance—some will be thin, some fat; some will have prominent noses, and so on—but in this case there would be no reason to speak of *family* resemblances.

Wittgenstein tells us, "Don't just say there must be [some common element]; look and see!"[14] But Mandelbaum points out the fact—surely one that Wittgenstein would have acknowledged, if pressed—that "looking and seeing" are hardly simple, naive activities. Ten people can look at one object and see ten different things, depending on the perspective each brings to the experience. The common feature, therefore, that unites a collection of objects under one concept may well not be a "surface" quality, but may instead be relational or intentional in nature. Thus two boys fighting and two boys boxing may in some sense appear to be doing the same thing, and yet the activities are very different in nature, by virtue of the vast intentional differences that separate them.

And, I should like to add, we must look hard for these similarities. Even looking at "games," we can detect (a) a certain suspension of real modes of conduct—"Don't get angry; it's only a game"; war games versus war, and so on—and (b) conduct that is generated by one set of rules or another (playing a game is different from just playing). In short, "Wittgenstein's emphasis on directly exhibited resemblances, and his failure to consider other possible similarities, led to a failure on his part to provide an adequate clue as to what—in some cases at least—governs our use of common names."[15]

Where art is concerned, Mandelbaum suggests it is entirely possible that art possesses some essential attribute that could be found subsisting in some form of relation. Nor is it out of the question, as I will propose later on, that our experience of a work of art involves a response to some *intentional* element. Intentionality, in fact, introduces a complex of relations—between artist and work, artist and audience, work and audience—not at all apparent on such a "surface" as Wittgenstein describes. And these relational or intentional features may well be found to be shared by works or objects of the most apparently diverse natures.

Furthermore, to declare one concept to be open-textured and straightaway close the book on it does not do justice at all to the flexibility embodied in closed-textured concepts. Much in the way of novelty can readily be incorporated into firmly established categories with a minimum of violence. Mandelbaum mentions the concept of representation as it has been employed in the plastic arts, and suggests that we have witnessed profound transformations in techniques of representation over the past several decades, all of which, nevertheless, are legitimately brought within the general framework of pictorial representation. And indeed, from Bouguereau to Monet to Bonnard to Manessier, from Cézanne to Braque to Picasso to Vieira da Silva, from van Gogh to de Staël, a link with representationality is retained in the face of stunning transformations in the method by which it is achieved. In short, "Professor Weitz has not shown that every novelty in the instances to which we apply a term involves a stretching of the term's connotation."[16] The game (as it were) is still afoot.

Art: A Word Unlike Any Other (A World Unlike Any Other)

Not long after the above dispute transpired, the term "artworld" was coined and put to use in a theory that endeavors to render intelligible the ever-broadening and ever-diversifying collection of artifacts and events that beg to be called "art." It is a theory that emerges not from philosophico-linguistic analysis, as does the Wittgenstein-Weitz approach, but from a variety of sociological, critical, and art historical considerations. Arthur Danto is the philosopher who first brought this "artworld" before the philosophical public in 1964, having had his aesthetic impulse piqued by a then notorious and now famous exhibit:

> I recall the philosophical intoxication that survived the aesthetic repugnance of [Andy Warhol's] exhibition at what was then the Stable Gallery on East 74th Street, where facsimiles of Brillo cartons were piled one upon the other, as though the gallery had been pressed into service as a warehouse for surplus scouring pads. . . . Some irrelevant negative mutterings aside, "Brillo Box" was instantly accepted as art; but the question became aggravated of why Warhol's Brillo boxes *were* works of art while their commonplace counterparts, in the back rooms of supermarkets throughout Christendom, were not.[17]

The difference between art and nonart, Danto came to conclude, derived from the fact that only one collection—the one displayed by Warhol, of course—was offered to the public in the company of a *theory* of art, a theory that oriented itself toward other preceding or competing theories, and perhaps earned a measure of acceptance, or at least agitated a fair number of artistic spirits. Furthermore, this theory would not stand alone, like a rocky promontory jutting out of a sea of sand, but would take its place within a historical continuum, bolstered by certain theories, flanked by others, at odds, in all likelihood, with yet others.

The boxes that remained "in the back rooms of supermarkets," on the other hand, stood alone, mute and uninterpreted; they were never called upon to assume an alternative identity. In short, "to see something as art requires something the eye cannot decry—an atmosphere of artistic theory, a knowledge of the history of art: an artworld."[18] Or again, "What in the end makes the difference between a Brillo box and a work of art consisting of a Brillo box is a certain theory of art. It is the theory that takes it up into the world of art, and keeps it from collapsing into the real object that it is."[19]

Art is not, on Danto's view, just one among many phenomena that we come across in the course of our experience and for which we seek to supply some explanation, an explanation that ultimately takes the form of a theory of art. Rather, "terrain is constituted artistic *in virtue of* artistic theories, so that one use of theories, in addition to helping us discriminate art from the rest, consists in making art *possible.*"[20]

Danto's reflections inspired what is known as the institutional theory of art. This theory, put forward by George Dickie, attempts to provide a definition of art by placing "the work of art within a multi-placed network of greater complexity than anything envisaged by the various traditional theories. The network or contexts of the traditional theories are too 'thin' to be sufficient. The institutional theory attempts to provide a context which is 'thick' enough to do the job."[21] Referring to this network or context as the framework of a theory, Dickie claims that the most salient constituents of any framework are the artists who create and the public who receive their creations. While virtually all theories assign a central position to the creative artist, the elevation of the public to a position of equal importance is special to the institutional theory. Supplementary roles, such as "critic, art teacher, director, curator, conductor, and many more" are also mentioned, although it appears they could readily be included in the concept of a public without doing any great violence to the theory. And this public shares responsibility with the artist in the production of art: the artist, to be sure, must produce some artifact, but this artifact, in its turn, must be "a thing of a kind which is presented to an artworld public."[22]

This artworld, then, on Dickie's interpretation, is a vast and tangled set of individuals, roles, institutions, and conventions that stand in some hierarchic relationship to one another. Just what that relationship may be, however, defies specification, for it will vary from one artistic medium to another, from one geographic location to the next, and so forth. More concretely, once a play is written, a producer is sought out, or a publisher; a theater group, including a director, actors, and stagehands, then takes charge of the work; other employees market it, some advertising it, some *selling tickets* for it; eventually the play makes its appearance before an audience, is reviewed by critics, their reviews are published in newspapers, and so on. A painter is obliged to work within a different network: the gallery owner replaces the producer; no intermediaries involved with production are required, et cetera. A poet will have a different network yet. In this manner, then, the framework woven out of these multifarious elements receives and sustains the artist's creation, and indeed shares equal responsibility with the artist for seeing to it that a given creation is received as a work of art.

In these very elements, then, Dickie finds all that he needs to fabricate a definition of art: "a work of art is an artifact of a kind created to be presented to an artworld public."[23]

Clearly, this definition is capable of accommodating the generally acknowledged set of conventional works of art, but it is crafted in a way to make room, as well, for the unconventional: Warhol's *Brillo Box,* Cage's "Silence," Christo's wrapped buildings and bridges. They too, after all, were presented—as art, of course—to a public, and whatever reaction they might have generated from that public, from adulation to outrage, served to confirm and legitimize their position within the domain of art. Future works, undreamed of at present, can likewise be assured unequivocal status as works of art if they are but presented to and received into the framework that is the artworld.

"Two Different Worlds"

Danto himself has found his own approach to be at odds with this institutional theory, judging the latter to be "quite alien to anything I believe" and observing wryly that "one's children do not always quite come out as intended."[24] Surely both theories arise out of a concern with the status of emerging works or styles, especially those that emerge without distinct precedent in the artworld. Dickie focuses on the relation such works enjoy with (a) the artists who produce them—that they be intended for acceptance into the artworld—and (b) the public that receives them, whether readily or begrudgingly. Danto, as we have seen, emphasizes (a) their theoretical grounding—that new works be welcomed not merely with applause (or chagrin: John Cage once remarked that his favorite form of audience response occurred when people would shake their fists at him), but with a theory that could account for their rightful place within the domain of art; and (b) their historical interpretation—that the theory sanctioning the practice would itself be oriented toward the history of art, both the immediate, recent history out of which a work or event developed, and the longer history, reaching back through styles, perhaps through centuries. Danto writes:

in order to see [*Brillo Box*] as part of the artworld, one must have mastered a good deal of artistic theory as well as a considerable amount of the history of recent New York painting. It could not have been art fifty years ago. But then there could not have been, everything being equal, flight insurance in the Middle Ages, or Etruscan typewriter erasers. The world has to be ready for certain things, the artworld no less than the real one. It is the role of artistic theories, *these days as always,* to make the artworld, and art, possible.[25]

Danto's artworld might thus be termed more "three-dimensional" than Dickie's. The contemporary framework into which a work of art is introduced, which for Dickie bears principal responsibility for "authorizing" that work's status as art, can be thought of as "two-dimensional"—a plane that slices the temporal continuum at a particular point in time—while that very continuum itself adds the third dimension, a longitudinal perspective into which a current work and its accompanying theory can be seen to integrate with previous works and the theories that made them possible.

There is one more significant claim that Danto makes in contrasting his position with Dickie's.

We may, upon learning that an art work is before us, adopt an attitude of respect and awe. We may treat the object differently, as we may treat differently what we took to be an old derelict upon discovering him to be the pretender to the throne, or treat with respect a piece of wood described as from the true cross when we were about to use it for kindling. These changes indeed are "institutional" and social in character. Learning something to be an art work, we may, just as Dickie says, attend to its gleaming surfaces. But if what we attend to could have been attended to before the transfiguration, the only change will have been adoption of an aesthetic stance, which we could in principle have struck before. . . . No: learning it is a work of art means that it has qualities to attend to which its untransfigured counterpart lacks, and that our aesthetic responses will be different. And this is not institutional, it is ontological. We are dealing with an altogether different order of things.[26]

This is a claim that requires serious consideration. Danto is arguing that the explanatory model offered by Dickie reverses the proper order of events involved in the consecration of a work of art. Dickie's account proceeds as follows: (a) we begin with someone—an artist—offering an artifact to a public; (b) in this same gesture, the public is invited or incited to adopt a special or novel attitude toward this artifact; (c) if they do so, the artifact can be taken to have achieved the status of "work of art"—it has been welcomed into the artworld. Danto contends, to the contrary, that we only adopt the special or novel attitude toward the artifact upon accepting and approaching it as a work of art; in the proper order of events, (c) precedes (b).

The further consequence of this contention—that an artifact approached as a work of art takes its place among "an altogether different order of things"; that it has "qualities . . . which its untransfigured counterpart lacks"—is perhaps not as alarming as it at first appears to be, and turns on the question of what is involved in being a quality of an object. Instead of thinking of any object as possessing a finite and determinate set of properties such as its size, shape, color, and so on, it is more accurate to see it as qualifiable in innumerable ways, depending on the perspective we bring to it. To be sure, there is a sense in which any such qualities we come to focus on are already present in the object—our eyes do not burn them into its surface! Transfiguration, as Danto intends the term, is still not transformation. And yet in a more important sense, these qualities do lie in a state of potentiality until summoned forth by a particular penchant or purpose.

Institutional Irregularities

1. A number of questions clamor to be asked of these views. To begin, it may be illuminating to ask just how it is that some artifact would fail to qualify as art. The answer appears simple enough: it would have to be systematically ignored by the artworld public. Surely no particular quality or complex of qualities that an artifact might possess could alone ensure that it deserved to be regarded as a work of art. All that the various qualities inhering in an object can accomplish is to capture the eye (or ear) and the imagination of a given segment of the public; and a work that fails to do so has thereby failed to gain entry into the artworld.

It follows as a consequence of this approach, however, and a disquieting one, that the quest for inclusion into the artworld (the desire to be received as an artist) could lead one to do whatever it takes to gain the requisite attention: exposition would give way to exhibitionism. Sure enough, the splatterer mentioned earlier—he who was swinging naked over his canvases—did make it into the newspapers, and since journalism is one of the subdomains of the artistic public, we can only conclude that through his efforts he gained entry into the artworld—alongside Monet and Leonardo.

Or let us hypothesize that once upon a time there was an enterprising gallery owner who desired a bit of extra space in which to display his holdings. To accomplish this he blasted away a wall, and as he was cleaning up the mess the idea leapt into his mind that instead of calling for a dump truck to haul away the refuse, he would put the shards of drywall on display, each with a price tag of its own, and see how people react.* After all,

---

*I once entered a display room on campus thinking I was going to a photography exhibit, only to find the room filled with tarpaulins draped over and strewn between

hadn't some fellow recently created a stir up on East Seventy-fourth Street with a heap of Brillo boxes? Well, of course the New York public loved the ploy, and the gallery was sold out within days (undoubtedly to many of the same people who years later were to pay outlandish sums for personal items of Andy Warhol's, sold at auction): "A genuine *tour de force,*" announced one trade journal. "Oh, do come over and bash in *our* dining room wall," begged a Manhattan socialite.

Entry into the once sacred domain of Art becomes less a matter of a certain intense interaction between a creative mind and a recalcitrant medium and more a question of packaging and marketing: it might well have been the case that Andy Warhol took great delight in his ability to incite a gullible public to ponder ponderous ontological questions, with what was all the while a tongue-in-cheek display of Brillo boxes ("Let's see now; what can we do to get them going next time?"). Art may be able to reserve a space apart for itself, but it appears to be in grave danger of losing its honorific status.

2. Let us ask the question: Just who decides who is a member in good standing of the artworld? To attempt an answer to this question, let us suppose that one evening at dinner in the Delta Kappa Epsilon house—a house known on campus and beyond for its artistic inclinations—one of the brothers falls off his chair, not in any exaggeratedly clumsy, drunken, or melodramatic way: he just falls off his chair. But the other brothers find that there was just something "extremely right" about the fall, and take to imitating it, first within the frat house, then ultimately out in the world at large. Soon it becomes something of a trademark of Deke behavior, and given their general artistic proclivities, they lay claim to being masters of this new item of performance art—the chairfall.

No one outside the Deke house, however, shows any inclination to imitate this behavior or to "improve upon it," and despite some recognition by the media of this peculiar behavior, it is generally dismissed as just one more instance of the eccentricities of fraternity life, just one more way college boys take delight in making fools of themselves. Have the brothers any right, we now wonder, to regard themselves as practitioners of a new art? If their being "crazy college kids" is the factor that sours the artistic public toward their performance, then surely they can take some comfort in contemplating the other practitioners of one art or another whose work was at one time disregarded because they were (a) mere peasants, (b) women,

---

ladders standing here and there. "Setting up for the next exhibit?" I asked. "This is the next exhibit," came the reply.

(c) Africans. Likewise, chairfalling is no more bizarre than any number of other trends that this century has witnessed, several of which have already been mentioned in the preceding pages. The institutional theory has its reply prepared in advance: "It isn't art if the artworld doesn't welcome the performance into its domain," it will proclaim.

I am not arguing here that chairfalling does merit immediate inclusion into the performance art domain. It does not appear that the mere claim of the fraternity brothers to be recognized as artists should be taken as a sufficient condition for being so recognized, even if they happen to have a certain reputation for artistic discernment. But let us suppose further that one of the brothers has an influential uncle—a belligerent agent who owns the ears of a few dance company impresarios. Could this prove to be the factor that legitimizes their claim? If chairfalling was subsequently, through the efforts of the uncle, to find its way into the repertory of a few minor dance companies and one major one, would it now deserve to be regarded, unconditionally, as a full-fledged performance art?

Is the only condition that is preventing *us* from recognizing their stunt as an artistic performance the fact that a larger artworld public does not recognize it to be one? What, it must be asked, disposes the artworld itself against chairfalling? And if the artworld should subsequently mellow and welcome chairfalling within its confines, would the reason for this be irrelevant? Or would the fact that a certain agent saw a way possibly to make a buck or two constitute a reason as good as any other? In short, the critical question (a compound question) is: "What criteria dispose members of the artworld to accept certain works and reject certain others, and is it not these criteria, rather than the brute fact of acceptance by the artworld, that should figure centrally in the definition of art?"

Whatever is taken to constitute the general fabric of the artworld, it will always have fringes, edges, and we can hardly look to the artworld itself to determine the status of these fringes: any decision of any sort coming from within the artworld will either trim off the fringe or stitch it into the main fabric. Is a concept such as art wholly at the mercy of the lords—perhaps even the self-proclaimed lords—of this particular fiefdom? In short, if the artworld establishes the realm of art, what establishes the realm of the artworld? Dickie's prescription for establishing order in the artworld looks to be headed in the opposite direction, toward outright anarchy. It might instead be wise for us to look to the concept of art to exert a certain pull of its own, to lay down decrees of its own, to coerce the public rather than merely follow its whims.

3. Danto may well be exempt from these criticisms, since he too takes

issue with the institutional theory on this same question, claiming, it will be recalled, that the public's attitude does not determine but is determined by the artistic status of an object. We could say that his version of the artworld exhibits a considerably different topography from the one Dickie offers. For Danto a work is embedded in a theory, and the work and the theory together are embedded in a history of art. What we must ask, then, is whether these factors—theory and history—are capable of supplying what the institutional approach lacks. Let us first consider the validating role that aesthetic theory might conceivably play.

Danto's Infirmities

Art Theory

Regarding the suggestion that art theory in some respect renders art possible, the question that comes to mind is "What theory?" or perhaps "Whose theory?" I see four potential responses to this question, none of which seems adequate. The first two sections below respond to the question "Whose theory?" while the second two respond to "What theory?"

Artists Supply Their Own Theory

It is in fact only in very recent times that works of art—or contenders for that status—have sought the company of theory. Beethoven had precious little to say on the matter of art theory or music theory; Shakespeare hardly more (that the purpose of a play is "to hold, as 'twere, the mirror up to nature," is uttered by Hamlet, after all, not Shakespeare). Tolstoy proposed a theory of art, but it is one of the last works he was to write, and it so happens that it repudiates most of what he had written earlier in his career—that is, the masterpieces. One could go on and on citing great artists who seem to have been not at all preoccupied with theorizing about what they were doing, or ought to be doing, and this is far from surprising. A Yogi Berraism offers itself to mind here: "How," he once complained, "do you expect me to think and hit at the same time?"

Warhol himself, let us not forget, merely stacked Brillo boxes and left it to others to do the theorizing, which others were more than willing to do. But if it should be the case that a theory supplied alongside a work is sufficient to ensure that the work is a work of art, then anyone at all can not just claim to be an artist, but actually be one, simply by doing something—anything—then building a theory around it. This would reduce the dignity of the concept "art" to a level somewhat below that of the concept "thingamajig."

Recently, I viewed an exposition of pure white canvases, in which we the audience were invited to "see whatever we liked" within the frame. Any differentiation of the visual field achieved by applying color to the canvas would coerce our eye, hence our mind, in one direction or another, so the "artist" was obliged to leave the canvases unsullied by paint (apparently pure white is somehow noncoercive: try telling that to Louis Farrakhan *or* the Ku Klux Klan). There we had the work and its theory in company with one another, both supplied in this case by the same individual (and incidentally, it was presented in the Pompidou Center in Paris—a giant step on the way to institutional legitimization), but was I really in the presence of *art?* If object plus theory is sufficient to constitute art, then we already have the answer to that question; if we feel any hesitation in giving an affirmative answer, then object plus theory is not sufficient.

The Artist's Followers

If often enough the great artists themselves are not concerned with art theory, then perhaps someone in their community should assume the burden for them. But in truth, why should the status of an artwork *as* an artwork depend on this? When an artist and an audience are truly in tune with one another, there seems little reason for anyone within this nexus to propound theories explaining something that is too obvious to require explanation, providing answers to questions that no one would dream of asking. When people start stacking Brillo boxes and calling them art, then we feel the need to call on the theoretician, as we might summon a priest to save a soul or exorcise a malevolent demon. But when things are working right, theory remains a luxury, not a necessity.

An Adequate Theoretical Explanation

Danto may have in mind that any adequate theory is sufficient to sustain a work of art within the artworld. And yet, odd as it may be to think that artists need to articulate theories in order to ground or justify their practices, or that they need to have it done for them, it is positively unsettling to think that they, or someone else—anyone else—actually have to get it right, that is, develop an adequate theory of art, for us to regard certain works as legitimate.

To consider one important example in aesthetic theory, the past two centuries have seen considerable attention focused on the concept of "expression" as central to the artistic process. And yet there are many different versions of this theory, some holding that both artist and audience must share certain definite feelings—the artist expressing these feelings in the work of art, and the audience responding to those works with kindred sentiments—others holding that the artist expresses feelings that the audience reads off the surface of the work, still others contending that expressiveness is attributable to artworks regardless of the emotional state of either the artist or the audience.

What is more, the expression theory has come under much critical scrutiny in recent times, and not just because many trends in art have seemed ill-suited to an expressionist account. Various critiques have raised questions about (a) whether anything definite or interesting can be said about an artist's state of mind at the time of creation, (b) whether an audience must, or can be expected to, respond "in kind" in order to grasp the expressed content of a work, (c) whether the very concept of expression is sufficiently unambiguous to function meaningfully in an aesthetic theory, and so on. Are we to strike away two centuries of art—two very important and dynamic centuries—simply because theoreticians have been unable to come close to agreeing unanimously on what account is to be given of artistic practice during this time? If I had spoken of "beauty" instead of "expression," the time span would have been much greater and the confusion much deeper. If theory must be generally regarded as adequate in order to play a role in the validation of art, then it could well be the case that all art still awaits validation.

Theorists-at-Large

One hopes that Danto is not suggesting merely that theorizing about some trend or other is sufficient to ensure the status of that trend as a viable member of the artworld, although we have just about run out of alternatives. Could it be that the theory upon which *Brillo Box* was borne triumphantly through the streets of New York, thence to the world, was woven from no stronger a substance than the strident voices of a thousand theoreticians?

Despite his qualms about accepting the institutional theory, if theorizing alone is what Danto has in mind in making his "theory sustains art" claim, then this claim reduces to a version of that theory. Alongside the producers, promoters, merchants, and viewers stand the theoreticians. In New York at about the time Danto was writing, the celebrated disputes over the significance of abstract expressionist art were being waged between Clement Greenberg and Harold Rosenberg; "purity" and "flatness," "expression" and "action" became weapons wielded by each. Then came Leo Steinberg into the fray, the patron saint of Pop Art, and the field of battle shifted. Of this marvelous period, Tom Wolfe rhapsodizes:

Art made its final flight, climbed higher and higher in an ever-decreasing tighter-turning spiral until, with one last erg of freedom, one last dendritic synapse, it disappeared up its own fundamental aperture . . . and came out the other side as Art Theory! . . . Art theory pure and simple, words on a page, literature undefiled by vision, flat, flatter, Flattest, a vision invisible, even ineffable, as ineffable as the Angels and the Universal Souls.[27]

Theory, it appears, had taken the upper hand over practice. It could well be that it was in this milieu that Danto's thinking came of age—small wonder, then, that theory should be appealed to in validation of artistic trends. But in retrospect, these theories should perhaps be taken to indicate a certain interest, a desire to understand the creative processes at work, and such interest and desire demonstrate in their turn that the works in question were already accepted as art.

To sum up most broadly: if Danto, in emphasizing the role played by theory in gathering certain artifacts within the artworld, means to suggest that a theory must adequately account for the aesthetic interest we take in a work of art, then it is seriously questionable whether any objects *ever* should be regarded as art, since no theory ever has been in a position to lay undisputed claim to adequacy. And if theory need not be bound to any criterion of adequacy, then what is at issue is not the confirming of theories but the mere manufacturing of them, an institutional enterprise of the sort that Danto himself disdains, and one that normally proceeds from an acceptance of certain objects as works of art.

Art History

The other vital parameter of inclusion into the artworld, according to Danto, is that of art history. To be sure, the art historical context into which a work is introduced constitutes an invaluable component to its proper comprehension and appreciation. But can art history per se assume a share of responsibility for constituting the artworld? History, it would appear, speaks to us only of what has already been accepted into the artworld; if a particularly novel or iconoclastic trend stands before us, history is mute and noncommittal. Danto is correct in suggesting that "an object of the sort made by Tony Smith could have been made almost any time in modern times . . . but imagine one having been made in Amsterdam in the 1630s, set down where there is no room for it in the artworld of the times . . . and it enters that world as the Connecticut Yankee does the court of King Arthur."[28] But to the extent that we ourselves still buy into that artworld, (a) the sorting has already been done for us, and (b) whether or not some work or style has been accepted as viable within some antecedent historical framework is of little use, for we have before us, in the here and now, an object that gives every evidence of wanting to stray out of the established domain. *Our* question is, "What do *we* do with it?" not "What would they have done with it three and a half centuries ago?"

The fact is, at any point in time designated as the present, history stands ready to validate whatever new tendency may happen along, however eccentric it may at first glance seem. That is to say, there are innumerable directions artists may take at any moment, all of which could in one way or another be deduced from their pasts, either by appealing to some shadowy precedent, or by showing how a later technique was implicit in an earlier one, or simply by claiming that with respect to a certain practice, a saturation point was reached and a radical change was necessitated. In short, no matter what happens next, history stands ready to be appealed to as a justification for it.

In the early 1920s Arnold Schoenberg was appealing to music history in arguing that atonal music (*his* atonal music) was the only viable approach to composition available—that the well of tonal music had been drawn dry by Richard Wagner; that Wagner himself presaged atonality at various moments in his own compositions; that it was but a baby step from late Wagner to Schoenbergian atonality. The arguments sound fine, but so do those that sustain the belief that tonal composition had (has) a lot more life in it, that Wagner constituted not so much a culmination of a tendency but an aberration, that Schoenberg mistook his own lack of creativity for a historical necessity. History judges with its ears, though, not with its reason. And in this case history has tended to find against Schoenberg, as much successful tonal music continues to be written, as well as much not-quite-tonal-but-far-from-atonal music.

Furthermore, no matter what is happening now, what will happen next is radically indefinite. Current trends may sustain themselves for a time, or they may give way to one innovation or another; one style may predominate and crowd out all others, or numerous styles may coexist in relative tranquility. In certain contexts, and with respect to certain practices, it can easily be viewed as surprising that people continue to do the same thing today that they did yesterday. Retrospection invariably finds a "logic" governing the succession of artistic events, but no logic yet known enables us to anticipate succeeding events with any accuracy whatever.

Who could have said, in 1815, that Beethoven would have music in him of the sort that his late period discloses? No one but Beethoven himself, obviously, and even he had no clear sense of it at the time (if he had had a clear sense of his next phase of development, after all, he would have been in the midst of it!). If his grief over the struggles with his nephew had driven him to suicide, or if he had simply died of consumption or cholera, as so many others did at that time, we would take it that music of his middle period went as far as music in that style could go, and the entire nineteenth century would have taken on a different aspect.

It would sound rather silly to say that Beethoven was spared by fate in order to fulfill his and the nineteenth century's musical destiny, but any art historian who views the flow of individual creations as being in any way necessitated (and that this necessity is somehow fathomable) is merely dressing up sorcery in less garish clothing. We are always impressed by those who sit back and speak of "necessities," "incompatibilities," "propitious moments," and the like, but the truth is, there is no easier task than that of judging how things "just have to" turn out when we already know how they did turn out. If a work seems to us to be perfectly suited to its time, that is only because its time is the only time we have ever viewed it in—rather like seeing hair on the top of the head or five toes per foot as being "perfectly suited" to the human being. History, in short, can provide no help to us where the central question is, "How are we to categorize the radically novel?"

What is more, history only represents a particular slant on events—we might even say on what counts as an event. The history of art looks different today from the way it looked a century ago, even where it is concerned with the same time period. The "discovery" of primitive art earlier this century not only affected subsequent artistic practice, it extended the scope of historical concerns into regions and times theretofore ignored. And conversely, it may also have driven some former "artists" into the domain of "illustrators." *Our* history of art tacitly embodies our predispositions and preferences; it tells of past achievements, but it also tells of *us;* it is no objective and impersonal oracle toward which we can turn to be enlightened as to the viability of a novel artistic experiment. Only time, time and the heart, can tell.

Let us now collect and recollect the principal points made in this chapter.

Summary and Conclusion

While affirming without hesitation that the aesthetic domain positively bristles with irregularities and eccentricities uncommon to or unheard of in other areas of inquiry, we have expressed a reluctance to give up hope of finding some means of imparting conceptual order to this domain. Specifically:

1. The open-textured approach to aesthetic concepts, in which essences

are abandoned in favor of "family resemblances," was considered, but questioned on grounds that we should (a) look more closely at our area of concern, (b) look perhaps for features that do not readily appear on the surface of objects—intentional features or the like—and (c) consider seriously the possibility that the basic concepts we bring to bear on aesthetic matters are themselves more flexible and open-ended than is commonly thought.

2. The principal geographic features of two different versions of the artworld were considered. One of these versions (Dickie's) regards the responsibility for distinguishing between what is and what is not to be considered art as falling on a certain network of central and ancillary artistic institutions; the other (Danto's) stresses the contributions made by art history and art theory in drawing such a distinction.

3. Primary criticisms directed at the former include (a) wondering, if the artworld is responsible for "constituting" art, who or what is responsible for constituting the artworld, (b) asking whether all means of gaining acceptance within the artworld are to be regarded as equally valid, and (c) inquiring about criteria of acceptance into the artworld, and whether or not such criteria, and not the mere fact of acceptance, should be looked at as somehow definitive of the concept "art."

4. Primary criticism directed at Danto's version of the artworld includes (a) questioning whether or not the theorizing that supposedly can confer artistic status on certain objects must somehow be deemed adequate: if so, then far more than Warhol's *Brillo Box* awaits its day of confirmation; if not, then all we are left with is theorizing—the mere expounding of theories, nothing more distinguished than that; (b) bringing into question the confirmatory role of history, arguing first that history can only reflect what novelties have been accepted in the past, but can give no indication as to whether current novelties should similarly be welcomed into the domain of art; second, that history itself is permeated with our own preferences and predilections, hence that it already "speaks with our voice"; and third, that history involves a kind of hindsight which, as the expression goes, is always 20/20, but it offers little counsel where foresight is required.

Citizenship in the artworld, I suspect, may be too easy to come by to merit standing in line for.

From the foregoing I therefore conclude that we need not continue our analysis with the idea in mind that art lies somehow beyond definition, that its practitioners and theoreticians have succeeded, wittingly or unwittingly, in "doing it in." And yet I should not be so bold as to propound, here and now, *the* definition of art that will set all controversy to rest. That would only succeed in focusing the reader's attention down one narrow path—the path of my choosing—at a time when breadth of vision is a far more wholesome attitude to maintain. Still, it is hoped that the following chapters will contain hints and point out directions that may bring some clarity to the field of aesthetics. Chapters Two through Four, in fact, present the three theories of art that have attracted the greatest number of devotees across the centuries. Considering them closely, which we now prepare to do, should at the very least set us to thinking about how an appropriate definition of art may be formulated.

— 2 —

Theories of Art: Representation

The present chapter and the two that follow examine the principal aesthetic theories espoused across the centuries: representation theory, formalism, and expressionism. Perhaps, though, it would be better to speak of them as three *approaches* to aesthetic theory, since each one can claim numerous adherents whose individual versions of the parent theory at times differ from one another rather strikingly.

What is more, it would become apparent at some point (so why not point it out now) that these are not three theoretical approaches, each of which isolates just one dimension of art and exalts it into a position of total preeminence at the expense of the other two. Instead, each approach can be found to have versions that lean heavily on desiderata central to both of the others, to the extent that drawing boundaries among them sometimes resembles more the technique employed by imperial cartographers—straight lines coolly drawn through jungles and deserts, insensitive to local interests and stresses—rather than a natural mapping system that follows rivers, ridges, and shorelines.

Artistic expression, for example, may be said to be achieved through certain formal arrangements specific to this or that medium, or through the representation of some personage, scene, or sequence of events. In either case expression would be the dominant theoretical concept, but it would derive sustenance from its relation to one or both of the other two. Representation likewise seems only to distance itself from form in less successful works of art, where content and form fail to support one another and seem, in some respect, to "fall apart." In a successful work, however—El Greco's *Espolio,* say—the form, the subject represented, and even the style of representation can be pulled apart only for the sake of analysis; otherwise they cling to one another as an indivisible whole. And it is often the case that the term "expression" is called upon in circumstances where "representation" would fit equally comfortably, if not more so (the painting represents a grieving father; the painting expresses a father's grief).

Emotion, in one theory, is said to be produced through the representation of a certain action, in another by the action on us of certain forms. In different versions of each theory, sympathetic or empathic reactions are said to be called forth by the artwork. Or again, it may be that pleasure is said to result from a well-conceived representation, a finely executed formal arrangement, or an earnest act of expression. Reviewing these principal theories may at times seem akin to taking a ride on the bus line that circumnavigates a city: you can get on the bus that executes the clockwise route or the one that proceeds counterclockwise, but if you stay on board either of them long enough, you will find yourself passing through all the same stops.

And yet while this systematic overlapping may *seem* to be the case, I think there are nevertheless certain crucial points where one theory and another remain steadfastly opposed, certain questions to which one theory offers an answer while the others remain mute, and certain orientations toward works of art (or the art world) that one theory will foster and the other theories discourage. Consequently, they are worth examining in isolation from one another, to whatever extent that is possible.

Representation theory would appear to be the most venerable of all theories of art. Developed at length first by Aristotle, it is nevertheless treated as a theory (though not one of which he approves) by Plato, and by certain of the Sophists who preceded Plato. Indeed, a brief but bright flash of the theory may even be detectable in the *Iliad:* etched upon the shield crafted for Achilles by Hephaistos (blacksmith of the gods), among a myriad of other designs, is a scene depicting a field being worked by ploughmen, of which Homer says "the earth darkened behind them *and looked like earth that had been ploughed though it was gold.* Such was the wonder of the shield's forging."[1] The wondrousness of such a representation—that somehow gold could be made to look like ploughed earth—could well have led inquiring minds to construct a theory in which representation is singled out and offered up as the defining characteristic of a work of art.

The theory underwent something of a resurrection, not precisely at the time that Aristotle's thinking in general was reintroduced into Western thinking (during the thirteenth century), but later, when the Renaissance had begun to assert itself. It remained dominant from the middle of the fifteenth century until well into the eighteenth century, when important challenges came to be posed, and important new theoretical directions—principally those that have come to be known as expressionism and formalism—were being mapped out.

It must not be inferred, however, that representation theory had the field entirely to itself for what amounts to thousands of years. Artistic form was perceived by Plato, Aristotle, and many others across the centuries as having a special character to it; hence the roots of formalism reach back every bit as far as those of representation theory. Nor did it succumb peaceably before the advancing horde of New Ideas: like some cyborg creature of recent popular cinema, no matter how many times it has been blasted, shredded, and dismembered, it somehow has managed to reassemble itself and come roaring back with renewed fury. If we just enrich the term somewhat by speaking of "symbolic representation," a host of recent theorists will gladly join forces, and if we speak of "realism," a view that extols the virtues of realistic representation, whole movements in painting, literature, and film chime in. And each of these can find grounds for their convictions in the pronouncements of Aristotle.

If we raise the question "What constitutes a representation?" any dictionary can inform us that one thing represents another when it is taken to *stand for* that other thing. And yet there are many ways that certain things can be taken to stand for others, most of which are not the least bit artistic: an O drawn by a coach on a chalkboard can represent an offensive player, while an X represents a defensive player; a "v" in logic represents the either-or relationship; an elected official represents a constituency, and so on. Clearly, something more is demanded of an artistic representation than the agreement by certain individuals that one thing is to stand for another.

To anticipate briefly, it appears that there must be a certain intimate relation existing between the structures of the representing and represented objects, a relation captured by terms such as "isomorphism" or "congruence." Even at that, however, a great deal more precision is required, for instances of structural congruence can easily be found that do not involve the slightest hint of representation—that which exists, for example, between twin sisters.

It appears from a case such as this that some additional act of denotation is required for artistic representation to take place—that one structure is to be taken to stand for another. However, the mere specification that one thing denotes another and is congruent with it is still insufficient for such a purpose. The blueprint of a house, for instance, both stands for the house and is congruent with it, and yet it need not be considered a work of art.

Rather than impose a definition on artistic representation at the outset of our analysis, let us allow our understanding of this process, in all its richness, to expand as we proceed through the present chapter. Indeed, given the interconnectedness among the central notions in aesthetics (mentioned above), even the chapters dealing with form and expression will have important contributions of their own to make to any ultimate interpretation we place on the concept of representation.

If the question "Why?" is asked of the representation theory—"Why bother to represent anything?" "What's important about a representation, and how do we human beings stand to gain anything from one?"—two principal answers are given. On the one hand, it is believed that there is something to be learned from an artistic representation; when successful, it possesses the capacity to enlighten us. There is, therefore, a close connection in most versions of the theory between representation and truth: we emerge from our confrontations with works of art as wiser people.

Another slant on the "why" of representation, however, has it that a well-crafted representation has the power to move us, to exert an influence on our emotional lives. Since emotions are often spurs to action, and through action our moral character makes itself manifest, art therefore is seen to have the capability to make of us better people—or as Plato protests (for reasons to be examined shortly), perhaps worse people.

Let us begin with a close look at the original formulation of representation theory as it grew out of the argumentative interchange between Plato and Aristotle; then we will consider the manner in which it reappeared in the Renaissance, especially in the visual arts. Since the visual arts present an interesting slant on the matter of artistic representation, we will follow out the implications of the series of style changes that led into the twentieth century. The twentieth century likewise has witnessed dramatic shifts in how representation is seen to function in the narrative arts, and these too deserve our attention.

Representation Theory: Its Origins in Ancient Greek Thought

It bears mentioning here at the outset that while I have chosen, for the sake of clarity, to refer systematically to "representation," the Greek term used to capture this act or the product of this act is *"mimesis,"* which is normally translated as "imitation." Consequently, the Aristotelian theory of art is widely referred to as imitation theory, not representation theory; this usage was widespread throughout the Renaissance and beyond. The Greek term, however, appears to have contained a much richer set of connotations that our own "imitation" does; hence for the purposes of aesthetic analysis, "representation" seems to be a more suitable rendition of *"mimesis."*

To us, imitation, at least in the artistic domain, comes with qualifications ranging from "mere" to "criminal" implicit in the background: one painting could well be offered as an imitation of another in a most harmless fashion, if its status as an imitation is made apparent; and yet if its intent is to deceive—especially for profit—it becomes a forgery, and whoever tries to sell it could be subject to prosecution. Music that imitates birdsong, trains, or storms is never respected for "merely" doing so—we demand something more of it. And people who merely imitate such sounds, as well as the voices and gestures of other people, can be amusing, indeed at times exceedingly so, but they can never aspire to being anything more than entertainers—the label "artist" is too august for them.

From "mimesis" comes our "mimicry" and "mime," and while the name of "mimic" is often given to those who capture the movements and vocal patterns of others (hence, those who merely imitate), a mime accomplishes considerably more, through portraying not just individuals but states of feeling or modes of acting (modes of acting that normally embody certain feelings: the classic mime routine of being trapped in an invisible box, when properly performed, depicts someone who is really trapped, with all the anguish that that entails). Furthermore, not only would the portraying of a character, known to us as "acting," have been captured in the ancient Greek by the term "mimesis," but the actual development of the character by the playwright would have been so termed as well. Obviously the English "representation" sits much more comfortably than "imitation" in this context.

Interestingly enough, music, far from being restricted to mimicking animals or the sounds of nature, was regarded by the Greeks as the most imitative of the arts. It is clear that the correlation between certain musical modes and certain feeling states was quite generally accepted in Plato's time (he would have encouraged the musicians of his ideal state to play in certain "wholesome" modes, and forbidden performances in "degenerate" ones), hence it is not at all radical of Aristotle to suggest: "In rhythms and melodies we have the most realistic imitations of anger and mildness as well as of courage, temperance and all their opposites."[2]

In short, "mimesis" was understood by Aristotle and the Greeks in a much richer sense than "imitation" is now, and our terms "representation" and "symbolism" (when accompanied by an appropriate explanation) are to be called upon in situations where they can better capture the aesthetically relevant connotations of "mimesis." In the remainder of this chapter, therefore, in order to accommodate our own linguistic preferences, I use the term "representation," and where a particular translation is cited in which "mimesis" is rendered as "imitation," this latter term is to be taken in the rich sense explained above.

While Aristotle contributed hugely to the development of the notion that there is a close connection between art and representation, and his followers disseminated his teachings widely, he did not invent the concept of mime-

sis: Plato, Aristotle's teacher, devoted much of Book Ten of his *Republic* to developing a multifaceted critique of the representational artist, having chiefly in mind the epic and tragic poets. And Plato himself was offering a rebuttal to certain claims, made principally by the Sophists, that the epic poets and tragedians were eminently well versed in a myriad of topics on which they wrote, including moral education and conduct. The connection between art and mimesis had thus already been established even by Plato's time.

It was often the case with Aristotle that the view he came to develop on one philosophical topic or another emerged directly from criticisms of Plato's position on those very topics—criticisms that germinated and developed during Aristotle's twenty-year stay with his master. Hence it would be advantageous to look briefly at Plato's position with respect to art and mimesis, to gain a better sense of the direction of Aristotle's thinking. In so doing, two points in particular require special attention, inasmuch as they are directly linked to the question mentioned earlier—"Why bother to create representations?" These points concern (a) the metaphysical implications of representation, and (b) the emotional and moral effects it can have on an audience.

Mimesis *in Platonic Thought*

Plato is often taken to be scornful of poetry, or art in general, on the grounds that it offers us "mere imitations" of things and not genuine knowledge of reality. It appears more reasonable, though, simply to see him as directing his critique toward those poets or tragedians who take it upon themselves to create representations. He does, after all, suggest early on in the *Republic* that poetry "can be done either in pure narrative or by means of representation or in both ways."[3] The distinction here seems to be between writing that is purely descriptive and that which requires (as does any drama) the acting out of parts. Further, the extended critique in the *Republic,* Book Ten, begins with Socrates (Plato's narrator throughout this and most of his dialogues) congratulating himself on a rule that he enunciated earlier: "not on any account to admit the poetry of dramatic representation,"[4] while toward the end of this critique he shows himself still willing to "admit into our commonwealth only the poetry which celebrates the praises of the gods and of good men."[5] Poetry in and of itself, therefore, does not seem to be at issue as much as a certain sort of poetry—poetry that offers representations.

The problem with representation in general, as Plato saw it, was that it took us even further away from genuine reality than did the objects that were themselves represented. On his view, the furnishings of this world already stand in a certain, very special, mimetic relation to the source of their being—the forms. Things are what they are, he believed, by virtue of their participation in certain forms; hence a bed—to use one of his own examples—is a bed because it was fabricated after the ideal form of "bed." The form is eternal, immutable, immaterial; the actual bed one sleeps in is none of those, yet it is in some sense a representation of the ultimate form—much, it appears, as a sketch, or any number of sketches, offers a representation of a certain model, without ever being able to duplicate that model (the best sketch in the world cannot get up and walk away after the session is over). As odd as this view may appear to us, nevertheless there is real power in his argument to the effect that if we had no acquaintance with such fixed, immutable "entities," we could not even begin to make any sense whatever out of the flow of our experience. The forms constitute the permanent backdrop against which a fluctuating reality can alone be measured.

Viewed from this perspective, Plato's claim is that the representational artist offers an image that is at the third remove from reality—a copy of a copy—and nothing more. Far from bringing us any enlightenment, or attesting in any way to the poet's enlightened state, such representations can only deceive our intellect, and in so doing excite emotions that degrade our sense of social responsibility. It is at this point that Aristotle enters into the fray.

Aristotle's Reply: Art and Truth

Aristotle's *Poetics* hardly reads like a systematic critique of Plato's, or anyone else's, views on art. It presents itself more as being the great thinker's lecture notes on the subject of poetry or tragedy, to be developed and embellished on presentation, which may in fact have been the case. Scattered here and there, however, among many bits of advice on how to construct a successful tragedy and many examples contrasting what actually worked in the dramatic competitions with what didn't, are certain observations that convey a definite sense of his answer to Plato's charges.

Aristotle's argumentative strategy is one common to philosophical dispute: grant your opponent's premises, but show how they lead to a contrary conclusion. Instead of agreeing to regard poetic representation as standing at the third remove from reality, he contends that it is capable of providing a glimpse of reality that is in an important sense more real than the mundane realities that surround us. Instead of regarding the emotional response produced by poetic representation as deleterious to our character, he contends that it can in fact exercise a positive influence on us.

Aristotle argued vigorously against the Platonic notion that certain formal realities, more real than the things of this world, exist apart from the mundane realm. While not abandoning the notion of form entirely, he nevertheless recommended viewing form as necessarily being embedded in matter, and as determining the nature of particular objects in this fashion. Denying the separateness of form took Aristotle halfway to his aggrandizement of the power of art, for if there were no separate realm of formal realities, then art certainly could not be accused of being at the third remove from the real. This leaves us, then, with a world consisting only of ordinary things (embodied forms) and artistic representations; the next step is to reverse the position of these two remaining realities from the way Plato had arranged them, and argue that the artistic representations stand in some respect *above* mundane objects. This he does when he remarks that

> the poet's job is not to report what has happened but what is likely to happen: that is, what is capable of happening according to the rule of probability or necessity. Thus the difference between the historian and the poet is not in their utterances being in verse or prose; . . . the difference lies in the fact that the historian speaks of what has happened, the poet of the kind of thing that *can* happen. Hence also poetry is a more philosophical and serious business than history; for poetry speaks more of universals, history of particulars. "Universal" in this case is what kind of person is likely to do or say certain kinds of things, according to probability or necessity; that is what poetry aims at, although it gives its persons particular names afterward; while the "particular" is what Alcibiades did or what happened to him.[6]

For Plato, the forms played the role of universals, with particular things participating in those forms and artistic representations merely copying the particular things. For Aristotle, as the above quotation makes clear, the artistic representation is not just a copy of a particular; instead it occupies a position of priority in relation to particular things. In representing what *may* happen or what a character *may* do, the poet steps aside from the actual flow of events in the world and fabricates a situation that in literal terms is unlike any that has occurred in the world, and yet is capable of casting light on certain modes of human conduct. The dramatic work speaks, therefore, with a breadth and generality that no mere account of a particular situation could accomplish. The historian tells us what Caesar was like; the poet, while perhaps fashioning a work around the life and death of Caesar, is concerned nevertheless to tell us what *we* are like.

It is a fact, and one that Aristotle readily acknowledges, that many of the epic and tragic writings of his time centered on the lives of particular individuals (Odysseus, Oedipus, Electra) or particular families (the house of Atreus) and made reference to actual events (such as the Trojan War or the sea battle at Salamis). Still, no poet worthy of the name simply recounts the events in the life of an individual in the order in which they occurred—the whole truth and nothing but the truth. Plots, in order to produce their effect, should be unified, and no plot is unified "simply because it has to do with a single person. A large, indeed an indefinite number of things can happen to a given individual some of which go to constitute no unified event; and . . . there can be many acts of a given individual from which no single action emerges."[7] Much paring away and reshaping is necessary to bring the tragic circumstances in a character's life into focus so that they may tell their story and produce their effect upon us. Many years elapse, for example, between the incident in which Oedipus kills the man who proves to be his father and the time when he comes to recognize this fact. To be sure, certain important events do intervene, one of the more prominent of which happens to be that somewhere along the way he married a woman who turns out to be his mother, but most of his day-to-day life during this period simply does not bear repeating: what he normally would have for breakfast and when he would eat it, how much weight he put on over the course of a decade, the evolution of his taste in lyre music, and so forth.

"Well-constructed plots should neither begin nor end at any chance point";[8] rather, they should present themselves as wholes, a whole being something that has a beginning, middle, and end. Events should be selected (for the beginning) which suggest possible modes of continuation; they should be carried forward (through the middle) in ways that point toward certain definite outcomes; and they should come to rest (at the end) on one of these outcomes—in all probability, the one we feared would eventuate but hoped wouldn't. Individuals who feel their own lives to have been tightly knit wholes are as rare as they are fortunate, but that sense of the cohesion of parts and the collaboration of these parts toward a single, unified end is precisely what we expect from a work of art.

Aristotle continues: "Since the poet is an imitator just like a painter or any other image-maker, he must necessarily imitate things one of three possible ways: (1) the way they were or are, (2) the way they are said or thought to be, or (3) the way they ought to be."[9] Now from what has just been said, we can judge that the first option is not seen by Aristotle to be the primary task of the poet: that would be the primary task of the historian. To be sure, if a poet thought there was a lesson to be learned from the War of the Roses, then to the extent that it is possible, it would be desirable to capture the events of that war with some accuracy—too much falsification, and we would no longer be reading about the War of the Roses. And yet a slavish attention to detail can easily usurp the principal poetic function and draw our attention away from the necessary flow of events.

The second option is even further removed from the poet's real task than the representation of things as they are. If history proper is not poetry, then history via hearsay is even less so. Speaking again of portrait painting, Aristotle observes:

> Since tragedy is an imitation of persons who are better than average, one should imitate the good portrait painters, for in fact, while rendering likenesses of their sitters by reproducing their individual appearance, they also make them better-looking; so the poet, in imitating men who are irascible or easygoing or have other traits of that kind, should make them, while still plausibly drawn, morally good, as Homer portrayed Achilles as good yet like other men.[10]

Thus appearances and events can justifiably be tailored in order to render a particular representation more effective. Clearly, then, of the three ways suggested by Aristotle that an artist can represent things, he favors the third: an artist should represent reality *as it ought to be.*

Ultimately, Aristotle is as scornful as Plato of artists who do nothing more than (attempt to) duplicate reality as given—mere imitators. For Plato, such artists offer imitations that stand further from reality than the things represented; for Aristotle, they succeed only in representing the particular element in experience, not the universal, and in so doing, offer no more than a glimpse of reality as it is, not as it ought to be.

Furthermore, it is clear that in Aristotle's estimation, presenting the universal element in experience is viewed as a thoroughly attainable goal, and in fact it constitutes the proper task of the poet or artist. For Plato, even those artists who rise above shallow imitativeness and thereby escape his censure on that ground are not going to be in any position to represent the universal features of experience: it is necessary to step outside of space and time, to reach beyond the realm of sense, in order to grasp ultimate reality, and no one who actually performs such a feat will be able to translate that experience into shapes, colors, or words. For Aristotle, on the other hand, the everyday world offers hints and suggestions regarding certain universal truths, and it is up to the poet or the artist to seize upon such hints and weave from them a representation of these truths that will bring them forth clearly.

With Aristotle's position on artistic truth in hand, let us now proceed to our second point of inquiry—what the *purpose* behind or beyond the representation of certain human situations may be: whether a poem or a tragedy is anything more than an embellished treatise on human nature. Both Plato and Aristotle agree that such works can definitely be something more, but again they fail to agree on whether this something is for the better or for the worse.

Plato: The Moral Argument Against Representation

As we noted earlier, Plato showed concern that poets, playwrights, and performers were all capable of disrupting the delicate balance of his ideal state. "Dramatic poetry," he proclaims, "has a most formidable power of corrupting even men of high character, with a few exceptions."[11] This power exercises itself by cultivating in us a disposition to express emotions better left unexpressed:

> When we listen to some hero in Homer or on the tragic stage moaning over his sorrows in a long tirade, or to a chorus beating their breasts as they chant a lament . . . the best of us enjoy giving ourselves up to follow the performance with eager sympathy. . . . And yet when the sorrow is our own, we pride ourselves on being able to bear it quietly like a man. . . . Can it be right that the spectacle of a man behaving as one would scorn and blush to behave oneself should be admired and enjoyed, instead of filling us with disgust?[12]

Most generally, "poetic representation . . . waters the growth of passions which should be allowed to wither away and sets them up in control, although the goodness and happiness of our lives depend on their being held in subjection."[13] Poetic mimesis is thus seen to be capable of arousing strong feelings within us, and all but a few of these feelings—those that accompany courage or temperance, for example—are judged by Plato to be conducive to modes of behavior that are socially undesirable. Remember, "we can admit into our commonwealth only the poetry which celebrates the praises of the gods and of good men,"[14] but that doesn't leave us with much, and a great deal of *that* is probably stiff and pompous.

The Aristotelian Rejoinder

Rather than regard the outpouring of emotion that naturally accompanies a dramatic work as being deleterious to our personal happiness and social well-being, Aristotle sees clear to argue that in fact this exercise of our emotions in such a circumstance serves a positive function. This function is captured in his notion of catharsis.

Much has been written over the centuries as to just how we ought to interpret Aristotle's use of this term. It simply does not occur frequently enough in the *Poetics* to permit of a definitive, unambiguous reading, and as it turns out, depending on which way one takes it, radically different aesthetic theories can be seen to follow. The Greek "catharsis," it seems, can be translated either as "purification" or "purgation." Now, if one opts for "purification," then a most telling passage in which catharsis is linked with the aim of tragedy can be translated so as to speak of "a course of pity and fear completing the *purification* of tragic acts which have those emotional characteristics."[15] If, on the other hand, *"catharsis"* is captured by "purgation," then that same passage can be rendered to suggest that tragedy acts "through pity and fear effecting the proper *purgation* of these emotions."[16]

In the first of these readings, the purification takes place within the dramatic work itself. The tragic act—that of Oedipus killing his father, for example—is said to be purified by a show of remorse on the part of the doer—Oedipus's self-blinding. We are then left free to pity Oedipus, something we could not do prior to his expression of remorse.[17] On this view, the emotions that we the audience feel are incidental, contingent; what is central and necessary is the representation of the deed (in all its foulness), and the subsequent act of repentance (purifying the doer). The poetic representation here offers enlightenment to anyone who understands and sympathizes—enlightenment as to how we ought to live our lives.

The second reading, in stressing the notion of purgation, obliges us to ask, "Just what (or who) is being purged here, and how?" While the work itself, or the tragic act represented in it, might well be said to be purified, it would seem that purgation is something more likely to be performed on people, principally the audience. The tragic deed, from this perspective, would be said to provoke a sense of fear in the audience, the repentance on the part of the doer would elicit our pity, and we would, so to speak, leave our emotions behind us in the theater. Those very feelings that Plato thought it inappropriate to encourage turn out, on this reading of Aristotle, to be harmlessly discharged within an artificial, theatrical framework. We are left free of the burdens they impose on us—free to lead happy lives and be productive citizens.

The first reading, we might say, is the more "dignified" interpretation of Aristotle, in that it represents the artistic endeavor as primarily a search after truth, a truth achieved through the representation of events "as they ought to be." The grunts and guffaws of an audience can be extremely disruptive to any theory that attempts to make them a condition for artistic success. Poetry, let us remember, is more philosophical than history.

On the other hand, there are numerous passages in the *Poetics* that, while not making direct reference to catharsis, do indicate the significance that Aristotle attached to the phenomenon of audience response. A good plot, for example, is characterized by him as one in which "even without the benefit of any visual effect, ... the one who is hearing the events unroll *shudders with fear and feels pity* at what happens."[18] Of the epic plot, he judges that it "should be made ... [to deal] with a single action which is whole and complete and has a beginning, middle, and end, so that like a single composite creature it may *produce the appropriate pleasure.*"[19] Shudders and pleasures thus appear quite central to the function of a dramatic work.

Furthermore, Aristotle makes repeated reference to crowd response when recommending one procedure over another. This is not to say that he invariably allows the crowd to decide (democratically, as it were), for certain plots are judged first in the competitions "due to the weaknesses of the audience, for the poets follow along, catering to their wishes."[20] But plots of the sort that Aristotle deems best "are accepted [in the competitions] as the most tragic, *if* they are handled successfully."[21] An audience can be moved by means that are proper to the tragedy, or by means that are improper: "one should not seek any and every pleasure from the tragedy, but the one that is appropriate to it."[22] Means that are proper, for Aristotle, have to do with plot structure; those that are improper—then as now!—have to do with "special effects": "the visual adornment of the dramatic persons can have a strong emotional effect but is the least artistic element."[23] I cite these various observations to make it clear that Aristotle took the response of the audience very seriously, and while, unlike a Hollywood producer, he did not see fit either to allow just any audience to speak with authority (so long as it was a large, free-spending one) or to permit any technique whatever to work on an audience, still he seems not at all inclined to opt for an objective criterion of excellence, one in which discernment would have the upper hand over feeling.

Let us sum up briefly the results of this first part. To Plato, for whom the forms constituted the ultimate metaphysical realities, any representation (or imitation), artistic or otherwise, offered only a copy of something that was itself already a copy, hence removed us further from the realm of truth. And in all but a few cases, representations of human conduct were judged to have a negative, weakening effect on our character, by coaxing emotions out of us that we would do better to suppress.

For Aristotle, by sifting out extraneous elements and arranging events to suit a dramatic purpose, artistic representation showed itself capable of providing us with a more accurate depiction of reality than we could ever derive from contemplating everyday experience. Far from weakening our moral resolve, the emotions drawn from us by dramatic representations—especially the pity and fear elicited by the tragedy—are emotions we are better off having purged from our consciousness. And if their purgation brings enlightenment as to who we are and how we should act, so much the better.

Pictorial Representation During the Renaissance and Beyond

The alliance between representation and art was asserted in a variety of ways during the Renaissance, with Aristotle still occupying a central position in many theories, although Plato had his share of devotees as well. Much of the thinking that was done in the fifteenth and sixteenth centuries involved the attempt to generate a theory of pictorial representation from the ancient sources provided by Plato and Aristotle. Poetry and the drama, after all, were quite well covered in the *Poetics,* so the early modern thinkers had a ready-made theory in place, and a solid one at that. Momentous developments were taking place in Italy, however, in the sphere of painting, with the phenomenon of perspectival representation making its way onto canvases. Since there are only a few suggestions in the *Poetics* or the *Republic* on the subject of painting, and even they, more often than not, are employed only to highlight certain points regarding poetry, it is not surprising to find considerable effort being devoted to the search for a theory of visual art. But most of these efforts, as it turned out, remained oriented to the writings of Aristotle or Plato, and it was common for thinkers of the time to assert a general rapprochement between painting and poetry in terms of a doctrine known as *ut pictura poesis.* Let us look first at the renewed debate between Plato and Aristotle, carried on this time by their successors, and in relation to the visual arts, not the drama. Then we can give some attention to the doctrine of *ut pictura poesis.*

Idealized Representation: Neo-Platonists versus Neo-Aristotelians

The new wave of Platonists (known as Neo-Platonists) were not so concerned as Plato was to banish imitative artists from their kingdoms. Instead, within the Platonic system itself, they found a means of arguing that art is capable of representing ultimate reality—the forms—*more* accurately than do the particular things that are said to participate in that reality. In this way they offered something amounting to a rejoinder to the Aristotelian critique of Plato's harsh judgment of representation. They reasoned that it is not the task of the artist to produce a mere copy of nature precisely as nature presents itself—anyone who did that and nothing more *would* fall victim to the very criticisms that Plato leveled at such practice. Rather, the artist produces an idealized representation of nature (and of course the "nature" in question is principally human nature). This may sound a good bit like the Aristotelian theory, inasmuch as Aristotle recommended portraying nature as it ought to be, but the primary point of differentiation between the two approaches concerns the *source* of any such idealized representation.

The Aristotelian theorists contended that in portraying nature as it ought to be, the artist nevertheless derived inspiration from actual models, although the precise manner in which these models modeled nature was interpreted differently by different individuals. If a representation was to be made depicting piety, for example, it was the contention of some that one individual should be sought who projected the look of pure piety, and the artist could then work from that individual and produce a likeness or imitation that would capture the essence of the trait in question.[24] Another technique—one attributed by Aristotle himself, in fact, to the painter Zeuxis—involved selecting parts of various models and blending them together in the finished work into one ideal composite. A third approach suggested that the contemporary artist copy the exemplary works of antiquity, as the perfection attained by them had not—could not—be surpassed. This is hardly a technique that Aristotle could have recommended, inasmuch as his pronouncements emerge *within* antiquity (although his frequent references to the techniques employed by Homer, several centuries his predecessor, may indicate something of the same disposition of mind).

What all of the above approaches to idealization have in common is their empirical grounding. Each one finds some actually existing entity to be exemplary of what is to be represented: the first and the third find a single such entity for the artist to copy—a "real thing" in the first, a work already fashioned in the third—while the second derives an amalgamated ideal from several sources. The Neo-Platonic thinkers, on the other hand, contended that the ideal exemplar from which an artist produces an appropriate representation is not introduced into the mind of the artist by any typically worldly means, but is implanted there by God.[25] Plato had theorized that ultimate truth was something our soul had been exposed to in its previous existence, and that wisdom involved retrieving our connection to this body of truth.[26] Neo-Platonic aestheticians pursued this line of thinking and viewed the artist as one who offered concrete realizations of this act of retrieval. Further, there is Plato's suggestion in the *Republic* that "we are in the habit of saying that the craftsman, when he makes the beds or tables that we use or whatever it may be, has before his mind the Form of one or the other of these pieces of furniture. The Form itself is, of course, not the work of any craftsman."[27] The explicit introduction of God as the source of the ideal exemplars gives evidence simply of the Christianization that Platonism underwent (Plato himself is less clear about the ultimate source of the forms); otherwise the thinking is quite similar.

One other sense in which a painter would be said to present nature as it ought to be—perhaps the most important—clearly involves the formal arrangement of the subject or subjects in a painting. In El Greco's *The Disrobing of Christ* or Poussin's *The Lamentation,* just to mention a couple of works by these masters, there is little likelihood that the actual individuals who participated in the scene depicted ever found themselves in the positions they occupy in the paintings, or that they were attired as they are in the paintings, or even that they grimaced or gestured quite as they do in the paintings. Every inch of the canvas is *composed* in a manner that will make what the painter takes to be the strongest statement or impact, and as we know—as Aristotle points out with utmost clarity—life almost never presents itself in full dramatic regalia. Hence it is the painter's task, as Aristotle saw it to be the tragedian's, to rearrange elements "as they ought to be" for us to gain the fullest sense of the import of a moment in human history.

Well into the seventeenth century, hence beyond the Renaissance and into the Baroque era, Giovanni Pietro Bellori brought the Platonic and Aristotelian strains of thinking together, however uncomfortably, in his *L'idea del pittore, dello scultore e dell'architetto.* Aristotle ultimately appears to win out, though, since Bellori "leaves no doubt in the reader's mind that he thought of the Idea [represented by the painter] not primarily as an archetype of beauty existing a priori in metaphysical independence, but as derived a posteriori by a selective process from the artist's actual experience of nature."[28] Representation, clearly, had been successfully transmitted from antiquity to modernity.

Alongside these "enriched" versions of representationism can be found a much less exalted approach to artistic representation, such as was practiced by the Flemish and Dutch painters of the sixteenth and seventeenth centuries. There we find less idealization, a stronger emphasis on exact replication of natural phenomena, and a greater willingness to offer depictions of ordinary people and everyday scenes of village life. Many works from this period reveal a commitment to an imitation more simply understood. To be sure, there is composition, and the better the artist, the better the composition, but even a master of Rembrandt's stature is praised for the honesty of his self-portraits—for his unwillingness to perfect and idealize the face that looked back at him from the mirror. And perhaps Vermeer did heighten somewhat the contrast between light and shadow, but then again perhaps he didn't, for once we have contemplated his works, our own experience of the effects of light and shadow in the world will never be the same.

Ut Pictura Poesis

While these various approaches to representation in the visual arts were being explored, the same foundational text, Aristotle's *Poetics,* already provided relatively detailed guidelines for dramatic mimesis. In France, Corneille and Racine advocated adherence to "Aristotle's rules," and structured their own dramatic works accordingly.* And interestingly, certain suggestions from another source—Horace—led to an aesthetic doctrine noteworthy for its unification of painting and poetry: the doctrine of *ut pictura poesis*. Translatable "as is painting, so is poetry," or "as pictures, so are poems," this simple simile, a line plucked from Horace's *Ars Poetica*, brought the two modes of artistic representation into a single focus.** It helped as well that Plato had begun his critique of dramatic imitation by drawing an analogy with painting, and that Aristotle, too, offers similar analogies in the *Poetics*. The doctrine of *ut pictura poesis* reflected a concern on the part of visual artists to offer pictorial narratives, thus perhaps more often than not the gist of the formula was really "as is poetry, so is painting."

While contributing significantly toward effecting a unified aesthetic the-

---

*The theory developed, though, may be said to be more Aristotelian than even Aristotle was. The doctrine of "Aristotelian unities" was formalized, in which strict rules were laid down for unity of place, time, and action. But Aristotle himself only stresses unity of action (though it may be allowable to include under that heading the unity of character—it is the characters, after all, who carry the action). Of the so-called unity of time, he suggests in one place (only) that "tragedy endeavors, as far as possible, to confine itself to a single revolution of the sun, or but slightly to exceed this limit; whereas the Epic action has no limits of time, ... though at first the same freedom was admitted in tragedy as in Epic poetry" (Butcher, *Aristotle's Theory,* p. 23). Furthermore, Aristotle doesn't seem to fault the older traditions for their liberties here. The unity of place is not mentioned anywhere in Aristotle, though it may follow from the unity of time, since in those days, how far could one stray within "a single revolution of the sun"?

**Actually Horace's poem begins with an extended analogy between poetry and painting focusing on the need to *unify* a representation:

Should a painter join a human head
And horse's neck, add limbs from every beast
And cover them with multi-colored feathers
So that a lovely woman at the top
Ends in a black and ugly mermaid's tail,
When you saw this, my friends, wouldn't you laugh? . . .

The *ut pictura poesis* assertion speaks more to the rich variety of pleasures each produces:

As pictures, so are poems; one will charm
If you stand near, another from afar;
One needs a gloomy light, another shines
In brightness, fearing not the sharpest eye;
One pleases for a day, another will
Be sought ten times and still will please again.

(Horace, "The Art of Poetry," pp. 129, 139.)

ory, this doctrine nevertheless did no great favors to the visual arts. Had the lessons offered by Aristotle and Horace been dutifully heeded, perhaps painting would have been better served, for they likened painting to poetry only in order to emphasize such factors as the power of simplicity, the virtue of unity, or the variety of pleasures the art form can produce. All too often, however, artists took it upon themselves to turn painting into story-telling, with the result that a visual, gestural, iconographic "vocabulary" was developed, and a viewer was, in effect, invited to "read" a canvas by piecing together the semantic elements arranged upon it. The unique power possessed by colored shapes to move us often took a backseat to the "story-line," or was crowded off the canvas entirely.

It was only well into the eighteenth century that the general applicability of the *ut pictura poesis* analogy came to be questioned, and the strikingly individual nature of each of the art forms was stressed—notably in G.E. Lessing's *Laokoön*. But such a reversal of emphasis did not occur until far too many gods and goddesses had been allowed to spin their tales across insipid canvases.

Pictorial Representation, Recently

In the visual arts, the nineteenth century witnessed dramatic changes in the approach taken by a number of artists toward representation. Canvases began to shimmer and swirl as painters undertook to explore the myriad effects of light upon the surfaces that our world presents. Early in the century, the English painter J.M.W. Turner fashioned seascapes and sunsets that earned him the wrath of the artistic establishment. Satirized as nothing more than a madman who wielded a mop doused with yellow paint, Turner's paintings presented a diaphanous reality, far removed from the solid, homely one of the academic tradition. And yet it could be argued that they captured quite accurately the look of the waterscape or skyscape they depicted.

John Constable, a contemporary of Turner, offered landscapes with rich, variegated surfaces that also may be said to be true to the reality they presented, since nature is virtually infinite in the variety of chromatic shad-ings it manifests. (His works, too, required quite some time to gain accep-tance in the art world: "Take away that nasty green thing," he was once told, when seeking to have a work of his entered in an exhibit.)

Both Turner and Constable preceded and paved the way for the Im-pressionist movement that flourished in France during the last third of the nineteenth century. The Impressionists gave us a sunlit world, a world where the play of light across the face of nature became of paramount importance. Claude Monet showed a preference for immersing his subjects in full sunlight, sometimes varying the time of day at which a scene was painted in order to capture the dramatic differences in illumination that a few hours can bring. Renoir, on the other hand, seemed to prefer the dappling effect produced when the sun's rays filtered through the trees overhead or the lattice walls of a gazebo. Both (and of course others—Sisley, Pissarro, and so forth) offered a new approach to the representation of nature. Although castigated early on for deviating drastically from the chromatic solidity of the reigning establishment, they too sought to justify their pictorial adventuresomeness by claiming to offer a more faithful view of nature's surface than their stodgy predecessors. Representation, in other words, was still being employed in justification of an artistic procedure. And it could be argued, as well, that nature was still being portrayed "as it ought to be," for though Monet is frequently lauded for creating the appearance of having randomly planted his easel and started painting, this is an illusion that is easily dispelled by attending closely to the power of his composition: nature rarely presents itself in such flattering poses.

Even the radically innovative Cubist movement that followed sought justification for its procedures most frequently by appealing to, and expanding, the concept of representation. Instead of capturing on canvas a mere moment from the flow of time, the Cubists strove to incorporate into one complex image a succession of views of a single object or scene, such as one would receive if the object itself were in motion (as in Picasso's *Les Demoiselles d'Avignon*) or if one were to circle about the object oneself (his *Still-life with Chair*). In this fashion an additional, temporal element is suggested by the painting—a fourth dimension, on top of the third dimension offered by perspective. Indeed, the (by then) traditional means—the notion of deep space—was being reversed. Not only were elements painted at the level of the picture plane, they were built up to create the illusion of moving forward off the picture plane into the viewing space.

With the introduction of this fourth dimension, however, the concept of pictorial representation begins to show some rather serious stress marks. The average viewer with no pretensions to sophistication, when brought before a Cubist "portrait" (one of those ladies with halibut eyes), can be expected, after the obligatory, exasperated mutterings, to proclaim, "Who is he trying to kid? Nobody ever looked anything like that!" And there seems to be a sense in which this remark is entirely accurate. Most people are readily disposed to distinguishing between "accurate" and "distorted" representations, and they draw this distinction along similar lines, placing the Cubist version in the latter category.

Furthermore, it appears safe to judge that most of us believe that the system of representation that emerged several centuries earlier—a system firmly grounded in the faithful representation of perspective—can lay some claim to being realistic or naturalistic.[29] We believe, that is, that there are right ways and wrong ways to represent reality. The "flat" painting of the Middle Ages or the radically simplified or radically exaggerated figures one finds in the drawings of various "primitive" societies, whatever other aesthetic virtues they may exhibit, simply didn't "get it right" in the presentation of an accurate depiction of the external world. And to a firmly entrenched establishment, the Cubists themselves were merely exhibitionists of a sort who, if they could lay claim to any valid advancement of painting technique, would have to do so on grounds of novelty or eccentricity, but not accuracy or honesty.

Distortion didn't begin with Cubism: one hopes—for her sake *and* the painter's—that the real Mme Cézanne bore only a faint resemblance to the subject presented in *Mme Cézanne Seated in a Yellow Chair;* the painfully elongated figures in many of El Greco's works may be the result of the master's defective vision, but they are perceived as distorted just the same. In general, although a painter may distort a figure in order to achieve some "higher" artistic purpose—a greater degree of expressiveness or a solider formal arrangement—and be forgiven for it, the distortion will still be perceived for what it is.

Looking back across the twentieth century, it appears that a considerable plurality of systems of representation have come to coexist with one another. In fact, a number of them came to coexist in the artistic consciousness of one remarkable man, Picasso, as he was capable of capturing any scene or object realistically, expressionistically, cubistically, all in the same morning. Yet still it can be expected that people will recognize a certain approach to be the "natural" approach—the one in which the representation actually "looks like" its object—while the others will be seen to deviate from it in varying degrees. This fact concerning representational realism, when juxtaposed with the recent proliferation of systems of representation, deserves some of our attention, for we could well have witnessed in our own century a revolution of a sort unique in the history of painting. Let us pursue this suggestion by considering a few examples.

In a painting by Poussin, say, a realistic mode of representation is employed, and the figures on the canvas interact dynamically with one another (in ways to be examined in greater depth in the next chapter) to bring all our attention into focus, to make us feel the central thrust of the painting. On the other hand, in a painting by the great Russian-Belgian-French artist Nicolas de Staël—*Paysage de Sicile,* for example—with the aid of the title we can recognize something akin to a village, plots of land, sea, sky, and yet we are far removed in it from any naturalistic representation. The sky is black, the land is red and black and orange, the village is white and blue and yellow—only the sea is its "natural" color, and after all, I am inferring it is the sea because it stretches in a blue band through the center of the painting, as the sea might in an ordinary painting: given the other chromatic distortions on this particular canvas, it could well be a sunset! Nor is the "village" itself more than a suggestion of a village effected through an assemblage of rectangular planes. In short, representational content is clearly present in the painting, but it is anything but realistic.

In the de Staël work, as in the Poussin, there is a collaboration among the elements on canvas, pulling and pushing, negotiating a settlement somewhere between the larger yellow rectangle (building) to the lower left of center and the smaller bluish rectangle (building) to its right. But there is, in addition to this formal interplay of visible elements, a dynamic element that is nowhere to be found in the Poussin painting: the interplay between the scene as it is portrayed in the de Staël painting and as it would be portrayed in a more conventional, realistic representation.

In the mature style of the great Portuguese painter Maria Vieira da Silva, planes bend and interlace in manners unbefitting the hard-edged solids—stacks of books, rows of buildings—depicted. Sometimes it is not so much a plane that appears to bend, but an entire dimension! In quite the reverse of traditional painting in which a mobile scene will be captured in a moment, with antecedent and consequent motions implicit in gestures and lines of force, Vieira da Silva takes a static scene and imparts a dizzying mobility to it. The mind "knows" that the represented subject of a work is static, but the eye is forced to follow the clash of planes up, down, across, and around the canvas.

In a word, the very system of representation itself becomes a crucial element in our experience of these paintings, and with it, a new dimension is introduced: the forms, as in any good traditional painting, interact with one another to produce an image—a whole image—but in addition, the image itself interacts with our notion (however we may have come by it) of how such a scene would "really look" if depicted realistically. Much of the interesting painting in the twentieth century derives at least part, and often a major part, of its interest from this further factor, this struggle, waged within the cognitive apparatus of the individual viewer, between a realistic mode of representation and one or another "deviant" modes.

Realistic representation has been toyed and tampered with before. Caricature, for example, thrives on the dissonance between the way individuals "really" look and the way they are made to look in a given sketch: certain satirical renderings of Louis XVIII require us to presuppose naturalistic painting in order for that multichinned dirigible of a monarch to appear amusing. But caricature involves the distortion of one principal feature of an individual—Richard Nixon's nose, Jimmy Carter's teeth, Bill Clinton's jaw—within an otherwise naturalistic framework. What we find in Picasso, de Staël, and Vieira da Silva (and many others) is the distortion of an entire representational scheme.[30]

The additional dynamic feature in the works of these latter artists, then, involves an interaction between that which is seen and something that itself goes unseen but which conditions our way of seeing. What we see are the colored shapes on canvas—these suggest a scene and do so within a certain representational idiom (and to be sure, when done effectively, they organize and reorganize our visual field as strongly as more traditional painting could). What we *don't* see, but without which the painting before us would look very different, is a realistic version of the scene, such as it would have been captured by artists of the past four centuries, or might even be said to be capturable in a simple photograph. In this dialectic, then, between realistic representation, taken as something of a given, and the alternative modes of representation presented to us by various recent artists, lies one special point of fascination in much modern painting. It is a dialectic that plays itself out in our cognitive experience of the world (a phenomenon to be more closely examined in the next chapter, where aesthetic form receives our attention). And it would seem to constitute a development relative to pictorial style at least as significant as the introduction and development some five centuries ago of perspectival representation.

Truthful Representation in the Narrative Arts

For many centuries it was accepted that the truth sought by artists was one that could be captured in their works only by weaving events together in a fashion that suggested their necessary connection, by embedding the message that was to be conveyed in a plot that was perceived as unified. The truth captured by these means was taken to be a higher truth, one with pretensions to universality—all of these themes appear in Aristotle and are passed down through many subsequent generations of philosophers and dramatists.

Aristotle and the Absurd

A number of questions have been raised in modern times as to whether a dramatic work constructed according to Aristotelian specifications is capable of conveying anything that resembles the real, unvarnished truth about the human condition. It is an important fact, many have come to feel, that the necessities that bind together a classical drama simply never operate in the real world; and whereas that fact was surely acknowledged by Aristotle, it seems never to have occurred to him to elevate the contingencies that are liberally sprinkled through our lives to the status of truths worth enunciating. Thus from the Aristotelian perspective it is a sign of a weak plot when a writer is forced to appeal to the occurrence of mere chance events to lead the action to a desired conclusion. If one can't arrange for critical events to emerge from the laws of probability or necessity, then the work should be reconceived and rewritten; otherwise it is condemned to mediocrity.

And yet in a work such as Hardy's *Tess of the D'Urbervilles,* when Tess slides a letter to Angel Clare under his door, and the letter finds its way under a rug, thereby going unperceived, to the most unfortunate of outcomes, this event should not be regarded as an ill-conceived ploy on Hardy's part just to keep the misfortunes piling up. It is instead part of the plan—a plan aiming to illustrate how little control we have over our destinies, how the smallest occurrence can have the most momentous consequences. This sense of planlessness is captured by Clare later in the novel when he muses in his despair (twisting the words of Browning): "God's *not* in his heaven: all's wrong with the world!" Gestures of this sort by Hardy and others led in time to far more sweeping declarations of the absurdity of our treatment of one another, or of our situation in general within the cosmos.

In Erich Maria Remarque's *All Quiet on the Western Front,* Paul Baumer, the principal character, witnesses his regiment being systematically reduced by battle after battle, until he is one of only a few left. Why do the others die while he is spared all this while? No sufficient reason is forthcoming, not through any shortcoming in Remarque's creative abilities, but simply because he is telling us that no matter how deeply we probe the secrets of the universe, we will not succeed in unearthing a sufficient reason. The powers that be who are responsible for pursuing the war surely do not themselves provide any adequate rational ground for the events that transpire. Then at last, on a day declared to be "quiet on the western front," he too dies. Why then?—No reason. The entire war, after all, was unreasonable; our very inhumanity toward one another is unreasonable. These are taken by Remarque to be truths worth telling, and if the telling of them requires stepping outside the traditional (Aristotelian) canons of plot development, then that is what he must do.

In *The Plague,* Albert Camus offers a portrayal of the absurdity of the human situation in a fashion that recalls Remarque's great work. The plague settles upon the city of Oram. Why there? Why then?—No good reason; and for that matter, no bad reason either. It spreads, killing one character after another, sparing no one in its indifference toward any philosophical, religious, or humanitarian commitments. It eventually dies out itself—it is not beaten or outsmarted by human effort or ingenuity. Actually, the first character to contract the malady and survive is a comic character named (ironically?) Grand, a fellow who could never get past the first sentence of his "great novel." Why him?—No good reason.

In short, a considerable number of artists came to believe that plots that proceeded according to the laws of probability or necessity tended to obscure a most important layer of truth, one that truly realistic works brought to the surface. And this new mode of representation exhibited the fragmentariness of life through works that were themselves fragmented; it gave us senseless plots that in their perverse way were congruent with our own senseless existence. It was as if the human condition were being pictured in a manner similar to one of the later self-portraits of Rembrandt—the graceless man with a medium-sized russet potato for a nose.

Viewed in retrospect—for several decades have elapsed since Remarque's novel, while Camus's is similarly the product of a previous generation—such works as these have come almost to take on a classic look in comparison with what was to follow. At least we find well-defined characters in them, and while their actions unfold within a framework that withholds answers to ultimate questions, the actions themselves, at the local level, do follow a certain reasonable order. More recently, it is not at all unusual to find works in which characters remain nameless and seem "characterless," and a sense of pointlessness or incompleteness is everywhere apparent.

Our Splintered Selves

Antonioni's *Blowup,* a film of the mid-sixties, spawned an entire generation of interpretation, simply because there are so many ways to fill in the gaping voids that the filmmaker has created. Two characters are given names; the rest remain nameless. A murder is committed, or seems to have been committed, by a couple frolicking, or who seem to be frolicking, in a park. The police are never summoned; the body disappears. The most eloquent speakers are the mimes, and the only sign of humanness to emerge from the principal character occurs when he tosses an imaginary ball back onto a tennis court so that an imaginary game of tennis can continue. And these are just some of the principal points at which "laws of probability and necessity" falter. Conversations begin but don't end; scenes intrude—the purchase of an airplane propeller, the scramble to retrieve a guitar that is then cast away—without advancing the action in the least. But even that terminology is archaic: there is hardly any action to be advanced, and that fact seems to be a central theme of the work.

In a sense, the specter of Aristotle still looms behind this entire film: only if we *had* been looking for character development, for certain definite modes of continuation, completion and closure, for a plot that could be termed unified, can the actual sequence of nonevents speak to us with their full power. If one aims to shake the foundations, it is essential to know exactly where those foundations lie, and Antonioni does seem to exhibit such knowledge.

But is life as fragmented as all that? Some would claim it is. Listening to the White House tapes from the Watergate era made one aware of how long grown men were capable of carrying on a conversation without any of them uttering a complete sentence, sharing a whole thought. Perhaps if we reflect on our own experience we will find it similarly afflicted with this sense of incompleteness, as bits of conversations swirl around us; a dozen chores are initiated in a day, advanced a little, some never to be returned to; ideas pass through our minds, some repeatedly, some evanescently. Then there is the further influence of that great fragmentation device found in most American homes—the Remote Control. This demonic creation enables us to perform intellectual biopsies on dozens of concurrent events in rapid-fire succession: several basketball games, a hockey game, a few sitcoms, local news, national news (international news appears too rarely to earn mention), a number of mindless talk shows, et cetera, et cetera, without becoming deeply involved in any of them. Perhaps there is more truth to these splintered creations than we might like to admit.

In any case, if absurdity and fragmentariness are the truths we see fit to articulate, it is worth remarking that, if it is done correctly in a work of art, it need only be done once, and all other attempts will prove redundant: there is only one absurd universe, and one collection of unrelated items says no more or no less than any other. The movement toward depicting the unpleasant truth about reality as a whole, therefore, seems to be one that would spend itself in rather short order.

Perhaps the limiting function of the truth-in-representation approach at what I termed above the "local level"—or its *reductio ad absurdum*—was a film credited to Andy Warhol in which a camera was placed in a room, and for four hours it recorded the comings and goings of whoever came and went, their conversations and their silences, capturing them as naturalistically as any people can be captured who are coming and going in a room with a movie camera in it. Here there would appear to be a complete overlap between art and life, as if an unmarked transparency has been superimposed over an image, to the extent that one of them—either art or life; can we be sure which?—seems to have vanished inside the other. If this is the ultimate "truth in representation," then what is involved is either no representation at all—the complete submergence of any representation into the object—or no object at all, a total usurpation of objectivity by the representing medium. How we choose to resolve this either-or will depend on what ax we wish to grind.

This last work cited gives the impression of being extremely far removed from anything art had been doing for the previous few thousand years. If dramatic works constructed in traditional fashion provided the reader or audience with an experience that was somehow fulfilling, the new trend appears willing to sacrifice any such feeling in the interest of portraying the truth, however painful that may be. When Bach, in his *St. John Passion,* depicts Peter's utter anguish upon his realization that he did deny Christ three times before dawn, as was foretold, the music staggers this way, careens that way, never maintaining a solid melodic or rhythmic foothold for long; dissonance is pronounced. And yet it is, in its own way, fulfilling. Cannot the recent artists handle their content with the same skill and purposiveness?

Champions of the absurd are likely to reply that, typically, a tragedy follows the fate of a single individual, the tragic hero, and however much we bring ourselves to identify with such an individual, still it is just one individual, undone by a certain character flaw. We experience the emotions of pity and fear on behalf of the tragic hero, but deep down we know that we have been spared the same fate, or at least that we—wiser for our exposure to the tragic work—could rise above such fatal circumstances if we were to find ourselves in their midst. This is not the case with works whose aim is to depict the absurdity of the human condition, for they place us all within the same scenario: no one among us can ever rise high enough to escape the sting of absurdity.

Just the same, art had been providing us with heightened, enriching experiences, regardless of how painful the content, at least since the time of the crafting of Achilles's shield. There seems reason to wonder at the artistic skill or commitment of those who seek to annul this unspoken covenant with their audience. Is "Truth at any cost," we wonder, really a motto that rightfully belongs within the domain of art?

Perhaps the aesthetically significant element in any representation that makes a claim to truth still lies elsewhere than in the representation itself. Perhaps it lies in the manner in which the representation is formed. Or it may even lie in the experience of sharing a vision of reality with another soul, an experience resulting when an artist successfully expresses this vision to an audience. These two alternatives are examined, respectively, in each of the next two chapters.

— 3 —

Theories of Art: Form

That there is something special about the way an art object is formed, something in the disposition of its elements that sets it apart both from other artifacts and from the objects one finds in nature, is a belief that reaches back into antiquity and extends up to the present with but few challenges. Opinions vary as to just what it is about the form of a work of art that enables it to stand out from among the furnishings of the world and proclaim its difference, but there is general agreement that it has some special quality about it, even if such a quality proves to be capturable only by that charming French hypostatization of analytic exasperation, the *je ne sais quoi*—"I don't know what."

Plato, in his *Philebus,* is clearly focusing on the formal properties of things when he proclaims: "Every man . . . knows that any want of measure and symmetry in any mixture whatever must always of necessity be fatal, both to the elements and to the mixture, which is then not a mixture, but only a confused medley which brings confusion on the possessor of it. . . . [M]easure and symmetry are beauty and virtue all the world over."[1] "Measure" may well be considerably more elusive than "symmetry" when it comes to specifying explicit criteria for these concepts; however, as with most philosophers, Plato undoubtedly saw it as his task only to isolate the more general explanatory features, and to leave it to the following generation to fill in the details.

As it turned out, the following generation proved to be Aristotle, who had contributions of his own to make to our understanding of artistic form, contributions that have proven to be every bit as influential across the centuries as were his observations on representation. It is the dynamic interpretation that he placed on the concept of unity that has resonated so long in aesthetics. A tragedy, he observes is "an imitation of an action which is complete and whole and has some magnitude."[2] And expanding on the notion of "whole," he remarks simply (and tediously, yet ever so profoundly), " 'Whole' is that which has beginning, middle, and end. 'Beginning' is that which does not necessarily follow on something else, but after it something else naturally is or happens; 'end,' the other way round is that which naturally follows on something else, either necessarily or for the most part, but nothing else after it; and 'middle' that which naturally follows on something else and something else on it."[3] In addition to isolating and underscoring the concept of unity in its aesthetic role, Aristotle also called attention to the important relation between a work's magnitude and excellence, by observing that

> beauty depends on size and order; hence neither can a very tiny creature turn out to be beautiful . . . nor an excessively huge one, . . . so, just as in the case of living creatures they must have some size, but one that can be taken in in a single view, so with plots: they should have length, but such that they are easy to remember. As to the limit of the length, . . . [it is] fixed by the very nature of the case: the longer the plot, up to the point of still being perspicuous as a whole, the finer it is so far as size is concerned.[4]

Likening a play to a living organism came to have a profound influence on art criticism, especially during the past two centuries, in establishing a ground for the approach to such criticism known as *organicism*.

Both Plato's emphasis on measure and proportion and Aristotle's on unity and wholeness resounded and rebounded across the centuries that were to follow, from the medieval period through the Renaissance and into modern times. The position suggested above by Aristotle found its way into an account of beauty that became very widespread in modern thinking, namely, in the reciprocal relationship alleged to exist between unity, or uniformity, and variety. Pure unity, the absence of any differentiating features (to the extent that such a notion is even thinkable), is unlikely to provoke any special aesthetic response: a visual field, perhaps, saturated with blue and nothing but blue; a single tone sounding perpetually, excluding all other tones—obviously it is difficult even to fabricate examples of unity-in-itself.

Variety-in-itself, though, is equally challenging, since any perceptual complex we may imagine, no matter how immensely chaotic, will undoubtedly have elements to it that have a certain integrity of their own, enabling us to judge that "this, whatever it is, is not that." The mere recognition of variety in the phenomena of perception involves the consolidation of certain elements in the perceptual field into units. But somehow, somewhere between these barely thinkable extremes of pure unity and pure variety, the thinking goes, lies a realm in which the qualities of objects relate in an aesthetically interesting fashion.

In this chapter, I will examine three of the most prominent and illuminating accounts of aesthetic form that have been offered in the present century. First, I will present and evaluate a theory developed by two thinkers earlier this century—Clive Bell and Roger Fry—known as *formalism*. Responding, apparently, to modern trends and interests in painting, sculpture, and architecture, their views have contributed substantially to our understanding of how art "works."

Second, I will provide a characterization, followed by some critical remarks, of the view known as *organicism*. Grounded in Aristotelianism, the organicist perspective still enjoyed a considerable influence deep into the twentieth century. Third, I will consider the contributions made to our understanding of aesthetic form by the psychological approach known as *Gestalt theory*. This theory, which contains elements of philosophy and philosophy of science as well as a number of significant theses within the psychological domain, suggests answers to questions raised by formalist thinkers and offers a credible account of how some of the age-old formal concepts such as symmetry, measure, and unity-in-variety can be integrated into an intelligible explanation of the power artworks exert upon our emotions.

I will begin this third phase of our analysis (as the Gestalt theorists themselves did) with an application of the theory first to visual phenomena and then to the visual arts, and will follow this with a consideration of how the same psychological approach can be extended into the domain of music.

Formalism

In the early part of this century, the critical and theoretical writings of Clive Bell and Roger Fry placed formalism among the principal theories of art. Associates within the intellectual coterie in London known as the Bloomsbury Group, Fry and Bell developed their views exclusively with respect to the visual arts, which, given the age-old association between painting and representation, is perhaps what brought formalism into special focus. To deny, as they did, that representation was in any way essential to painting as an art form, and to affirm that it could in various ways actually be detrimental to the true aims of painting, made people sit up and listen and *look*.

The Theory

To be sure, Fry and Bell were not theorizing in total isolation, or in antagonism to the entire art world. Bell's major work, *Art,* was first published in

1913, the very year in which Kasimir Malevich had presented to the Moscow public a work consisting of no more than a square penciled onto a white background, which he proclaimed to be emblematic of *suprematism*. This was the name he gave to his "revolutionary" approach to art in which "the visual phenomena of the objective world are, in themselves, meaningless" and "the appropriate means of representation is always the one which gives fullest possible expression to feeling as such and which ignores the familiar appearance of objects."[5] In 1914 Bernard Bosanquet delivered three lectures on aesthetics at University College in which he spoke of a certain a priori pleasurableness that derived from "objects . . . hav[ing] what might be called the simplest formal character," in which "we have no element of representation, or almost none."[6] Likewise, Le Corbusier was distinguishing between primary and secondary plastic elements in works of visual art—primary elements being roughly equivalent to what Fry and Bell termed formal qualities, with secondary elements being more associational in nature—and proclaiming "the great works of the past are those based on primary elements, and this is the only reason why they endure." "A painting," he judges, "is an association of purified, related, and architectural elements, . . . a whole . . . [akin to] a viable organ."[7] And these are but a handful of the more prominent spokesmen for this new approach to understanding art.

In looking at the above citations with a little care, we should note that Malevich seems to be uttering a proclamation of a sort: this is how art *should* proceed. Le Corbusier, on the other hand, while surely affirming that art should proceed in such a fashion, acknowledges as well that when at its best, art has always given close attention to primary plastic ("formal" for Fry and Bell; "nonobjective" for Malevich; "a priori" for Bosanquet) elements. This point is made by the Bloomsbury pair, and acts for them as Ariadne's thread, by which to make their way through the labyrinthine history of art. Let us look with some care at Bell's position, so boldly and succinctly developed in his book *Art*.

Interestingly, Bell begins his analysis in *Art* not by singling out form straightaway as the central aesthetic element, but by focusing on the emotions that we feel in experiencing works of art. This leads him to the observation that a certain type of emotion is engendered by good art, and that it contrasts sharply with those emotions associated with bad art. Such a starting point seems entirely in line with the conclusion reached in the previous section, where our immediate experience of and satisfaction with a work of art was held to be the definitive indication of its unity.

"Descriptive art" is the term he applies to paintings of an inferior sort, paintings whose principal aim is "suggesting emotion or conveying information. Portraits of psychological and historical value, topographical works, pictures that tell stories and suggest situations, illustrations of all sorts belong to this class."[8] Any of the works of "America's favorite artist," Norman Rockwell, would serve as an apt example of bad art, on Bell's terms:* The boy getting his first haircut—he frightened and unruly; his mother at his side, offering him reassurance while showing a bit of embarrassment at his conduct; the barber, having participated in the same ritual countless times, wise and indulgent. Some of us can recall having felt the same terror the boy appears to be feeling; some who have been mothers can think themselves into her situation; few of us can identify directly with the barber, but many a blue-collar worker could well appreciate seeing a man in a "simple" profession such as that of a barber being portrayed as a man of wisdom and dignity. And all of us enjoy the hometown flavor of this and so many of Rockwell's works—after all, when he was creating his weekly covers for the *Saturday Evening Post,* even our big cities divided themselves in neighborhoods that were not unlike small towns.

All of the feelings engendered by a work such as this are normal sentiments, the sort that we encounter in the course of everyday life. As a consequence, art such as this serves merely as an occasion to relive one aspect of life or another; had we stumbled across a commemorative snapshot of our first day at the barbershop, it would have produced much the same emotional effect as the Rockwell illustration. "No new material is added to [our] lives, only the old material is stirred."[9] None of these emotions, according to Bell, resembles the *aesthetic* emotion. The aesthetic emotion is singular in its nature because it alone is produced when we find ourselves face to face with an object whose surface exhibits what Bell terms "significant form." On a surface activated by significant form, the precise manner in which lines, planes, shapes, and colors are arranged is seen to produce an emotional response in a (properly sensitized) viewer, independent of whatever content may be represented there.

Undoubtedly much of the art produced by the Surrealists (and now the Neo-Surrealists) would have fallen victim to Bell's criticism for the same general reason, although with slightly different nuances to it. While Rockwell's art offers a sentimentality that tugs at our heartstrings while bypassing the "legitimate" route of significant form, Surrealism offers visual conundrums that tantalize our intellect but that do so again indifferently to the demands of significant form—Dali will tell us a story, Magritte

---

*In Rockwell's defense, I should mention that he regarded himself as an illustrator, not an artist. And once when asked in an interview if there remained anything he would like to accomplish, he replied "Yes—to do a good painting!"

might speculate on the relationship between words and things and how we go about representing each. Rockwell's audience has little patience for Surrealism; Surrealism's audience has even less patience for Rockwell (intellectuals being impatient types, prone to fancy that intellectual illustration is inherently superior to sentimental illustration); neither enjoys the distinctly aesthetic emotion produced only by significant form.

Such form is found by Bell and Fry to be liberally apportioned among the so-called primitive arts, whereas works that emerge from a "civilized" context run a much greater risk of falling into the decadent rut where representation gains the upper hand on formal construction.*

> In primitive art you will find no accurate representation; you will find only significant form. Yet no other art moves us so profoundly. Whether we consider Sumerian sculpture or pre-dynastic Egyptian art, or ancient Greek, or the We and Tang masterpieces, . . . or whether, coming nearer home, we consider the primitive Byzantine art of the sixth century, . . . or . . . that mysterious and majestic art that flourished in Central and South America before the coming of the white men, in every case we observe three common characteristics—absence of representation, absence of technical swagger, sublimely impressive form.[10]

Fry wonders, quite reasonably, of these pre-Colombian artists "how far one can trust one's aesthetic appreciation to interpret truly the feelings which inspired it." And while offering many reservations, nevertheless he does conclude that "in certain works one cannot doubt that the artist felt just. as we feel in interpreting his work."[11] Though the topic of gauging an artist's intentions will not be dealt with closely until Chapter Five, his remarks underscore the curious, almost miraculous fact that we *do* appreciate such works—that despite enormous differences in cultural orientation and overall belief structures, we still manage to find something deeply rewarding in them. Subtracting the innumerable (and in many cases inscrutable) elements of cultural differentiation, what are we left with to delight in *besides* significant form? And we delight in this form at times much more deeply than we do in the work of a colleague or even an old friend with whom we have shared a sizable portion of our life (much, at times, to the chagrin of the latter). This is not a fact to be taken lightly.

---

*Many cultures in many eras, and not just our own, have gone through similar phases, where increasingly studious care is given to capturing an image "correctly," and formal considerations become secondary. In the domain of oriental rugs, for example, one can find an unfortunate tendency in certain areas at certain times to represent animals in a "lifelike" manner, or even offer portraits in wool or silk of particular individuals.

In the art of the West, Bell finds much to appreciate, and yet between the sixteenth and nineteenth centuries he finds much more to deprecate. The power of architectural form, he judges, began to decline much earlier, in the twelfth century, when the Gothic style began to supplant the Romanesque: "Gothic architecture is juggling in glass. . . . A Gothic cathedral is a *tour de force;* it is also a melodrama. Enter and you will be impressed by the incredible skill of the constructor; perhaps you will be impressed by a sense of dim mystery and might; you will not be moved by pure form. . . . In architecture the new spirit first came to birth; in architecture first it dies."[12] In Giotto, whom Bell finds to be a great artist, he nevertheless detects intimations of a decline similar to that which took place only a bit earlier in architecture. "Giotto heads a movement towards imitation and scientific picture-making. . . . And the spirit of that age . . . moved towards Truth and Nature, away from supernatural ecstasies."[13] Such movement he finds normal in the human spirit, but where art is concerned, it is but the harbinger of an era of decadence.

Throughout this "decadent" era—the next few centuries, as it turns out—Bell finds an occasional artist to laud, but even the greatest of them (Poussin could well be his candidate for this honor) had to labor within strictures imposed by the exigencies of representation and visual narrative. Of the century following Poussin, he remarks, "The painting of the eighteenth century is brilliant illustration still touched with art. For instance, in Watteau, Canaletto, Crome, Cotman, and Guardi there is some art, some brilliance, and a great deal of charming illustration."[14] The real rebirth of art, in Bell's eyes, comes with Cézanne, the first of the moderns to invest his works with the (virtually primordial) sense of formal power that Bell had been looking for in the works of the previous several centuries but having such a difficult time finding. And valued along with Cézanne are certain of the Fauves; numerous Cubist works are found by him to exhibit significant form, though most of them fail to—that is only normal, however, for out of any hundred paintings only a handful will be successful. Still, we need the hundred to guarantee the handful. Such is the manner in which Bell strides across the history of art in the West.

The aesthetic emotion is decidedly not an experience to be taken lightly, according to Bell. He aims not to lead us to some salon and surround us with "aesthetes" who, glass of sparkling wine in hand, enjoy the best that life—for the best of life is art—has to offer. His is a much more austere vision: "A good work of visual art carries a person who is capable of appreciating it out of life into ecstasy."[15] Speaking of music, a matter on which he is heartwarmingly frank in his self-deprecation, Bell observes: "I understand music too ill for music to transport me far into the world of pure aesthetic ecstasy. But at moments I do appreciate music as pure musical form, as sounds according to the laws of a mysterious necessity, as pure art with a tremendous significance of its own and no relation whatever to the significance of life."[16] Ultimately, "the ideas of men go buzz and die like gnats; men change their institutions and their customs as they change their coats; the intellectual triumphs of one age are the follies of another; only great art remains stable and unobscure. Great art remains stable and unobscure because the feelings that it awakens are independent of time and place, because its kingdom is not of this world."[17] Invoking another world brings Bell to the outer limits of aesthetic relevance, since he speaks of the "aesthetic hypothesis" and the "metaphysical hypothesis," the former offering an account for *what* we value in works of art, the latter speculating as to *why* we value it. Up to now, questions of "why?" have been held at a distance. We will have to confront them soon, but not just yet. As we stand before this outer limit, let us pause to survey the terrain behind us and indicate the principal problems faced by formalism.

Problems with the Theory

As theories go, the one forwarded by Bell seems eminently destructible, and many have been quick to indicate that fact. It appears, for one thing, to consist in as tight a circle as could be devised, and for those who find circular reasoning to be invariably vicious, it melts under scrutiny.

1. The principal fault, it is held, is that the two key terms—aesthetic emotion and significant form—maintain an unhealthy dependence on each other. Aesthetic emotion is defined as the emotion that we feel in response to the presence of significant form. But how, we wonder, can we tell whether we are actually in the presence of significant form, or whether some impostor stands before us, beguiling a response from us that we mistakenly identify as the aesthetic emotion? Are we to examine the object more closely to make sure there aren't some formal features we are overlooking? Such a strategy could conceivably be carried out ad infinitum—"I didn't find anything new this year, but maybe next year I'll have better luck." No, the only criterion Bell offers to enable us to identify significant form is that it alone produces the aesthetic emotion. Each of the two principal elements of his theory, in short, testifies for the other.

2. A second problem concerns the aesthetic emotion itself. It seems incontestable that we often do undergo emotional experiences in our confrontations with works of art: we feel chills or a choking sensation, sometimes a mood of great elation overcomes us. Bell seems to believe that the aesthetic emotion somehow lifts us out of our quotidian existence and into

some rarefied realm, but these conative correlates—the chills, choking sensation, and such—are normal accompaniments of normal emotions as well. Is the character of the aesthetic emotion really sufficiently different from other emotions to deserve to be held entirely apart from the rest? Can we really determine that *these* chills are the chills associated with an aesthetic experience, while *those* owe their origin to some more mundane source? Chills are chills. It seems that the only real grounds for differentiating the aesthetic emotion from any other will have to be found not in the quality of the emotion itself, but in the object producing it, and that consideration leads directly back to the problem of circularity discussed in the previous paragraph.

3. The alleged irrelevance of the representational element in painting is the other point that is often strongly contested. John Dewey's remarks directed at Roger Fry best present this line of reasoning, so I will cite them at some length. "Mr. Fry," says Dewey (and obviously he could just as well say "Mr. Bell"),

> is intent upon establishing a radical difference between esthetic values that are intrinsic to things of ordinary experience and the esthetic value with which the artist is concerned. His implication is that the former is directly connected with subject matter, the latter with form that is separated from any subject matter, save what is, esthetically, an accident. Were it possible for an artist to approach a scene with no interests and attitudes, no background of values, drawn from his prior experience, he might, theoretically, see lines and colors exclusively in terms of their relationships as lines and colors. But this is a condition impossible to fulfill. . . . No matter how ardently the artist might desire it, he cannot divest himself, in his new perception, of meanings funded from his past intercourse with his surroundings, nor can he free himself from the influence they exert upon the substance and manner of his present seeing. If he could and did, there would be nothing left in the way of an object for him to see.[18]

A portrait of a woman, even where the subject is chopped up and reassembled in the Cubist manner, remains a portrait of a woman. Rembrandt's self-portraits, however formally powerful as they might be, still owe no small measure of their significance to the quality of the face depicted: the Rembrandt who looks back at us from one of those canvases, his gaze stretching across the centuries, is far more than a blob of whiteness against a predominantly dark background. Bell and Fry, in elevating formal construction to a position of total preeminence, have taken a necessary condition for artistic success and attempted to convert it into a sufficient condition. And yet there is merit in overstating a case—lawyers do it all the time, and it does succeed in catching the jury's attention. Sensitized to the crucial role played by form in our appreciation of art, our experience can never again return to the (formerly) comfortable and reassuring plane where worldly sentiment stood dominant.

There is an almost mystic side to Bell's theorizing, and as with all varieties of mysticism, gaining access to the desired state of mind when one has any doubts as to what exactly constitutes the desired state of mind is a serious problem. And yet we should pay him heed, I think: not all circles are necessarily vicious, and the one he has drawn encloses many keen insights.

More needs to be said, however, about the precise manner in which works of art interact with our consciousness to produce this affective response that Bell (as well as so many others) holds so dear. We questioned whether there could properly be said to be an aesthetic emotion that somehow differed qualitatively from any other emotion. But we never questioned that there is emotion involved in our experience of a work of art, nor did we question that certain peculiarities of the form of an object that interests us aesthetically were responsible in part—and perhaps in large part—for producing this emotional response. The question that demands to be asked, therefore, is "How does aesthetic form succeed in engaging us emotionally?" Before venturing a psychologically grounded answer to this question, however, let us look closely at another theory of artistic form that reaches well beyond the parameters of visual art—the view known as organicism. Perhaps after seeing what the organicists have to offer, the final stages of our journey will be more clearly marked out.

Organicism

As we have seen, Aristotle likened the work of art to a living organism, in observing that "neither can a very tiny creature turn out to be beautiful . . . nor an excessively huge one." In the eighteenth century, the great German philosopher Immanuel Kant (whose views will be dealt with more closely in Chapter Six) noted important correlations between our judgments concerning the beautiful, on the one hand, and the peculiar, purposive structure that a living organism possesses, on the other. These are but two of the many instances in which art is alleged to possess something akin to an organic structure.

In modern times, much of the appeal of organicism derives from the applications made across the spectrum of the arts by the immensely influential nineteenth-century philosopher G.W.F. Hegel, with a succinct statement of the Hegelian position having come from Bernard Bosanquet in his *Three Lectures on Aesthetic*. And surely John Dewey's landmark work in aesthetics, *Art as Experience,* is thoroughly imbued with the organicist spirit. Let us begin this section with a general characterization of the position, then see how the theory looks in the hands of a critic, selecting for that purpose the great English music critic Donald F. Tovey.

The Organic Whole

In specifying that a work, to be regarded as a whole, should possess a beginning, middle, and end, Aristotle was declaring much more than that any such work should start, continue on for a while, then at some point terminate. One could say as much regarding any finite process. What is important about a true beginning is that it contains implications as to how events could well proceed, and these implications, while being sufficiently determinate to set us thinking and anticipating along certain definite lines, will be sufficiently open-ended to permit of various modes of continuation.

In *Hamlet,* for example, the early appearance and disappearance of the ghost of the former king, Hamlet's father—an appearance real enough to be noted by several individuals presumably of sound mind—forewarns us of some malaise in the castle. This is clarified a bit by the current king's reference to "our dear brother's death," the memory of which is still "green," while hints of the source of the malaise emerge in Hamlet's open-ing line—a barbed aside uttered in response to the king's calling him "my cousin Hamlet, and my son": "A little more than kin and less than kind." We are led step by step to see that a murder has been committed prior to the initiation of the action in the play, and that the theme of revenge will be central to the development of the plot. But will such revenge be effected, or will Hamlet forever waver, perhaps taking his own life out of dismay, perhaps going insane from the stress? Perhaps the king (no fool, after all) will discern Hamlet's intentions and take steps to ensure that no revenge is forthcoming. None of these modes of continuation is to be ruled out at the outset, though some are less likely than others—the others that we fear could eventuate.

The middle of this work carries the plot forward, all and only through presenting scenes that either take us closer to the act of revenge (in Hamlet's case, at times seemingly asymptotically), illustrate and enrich our sense of the character of the individuals involved, or offer reflections of the gravity of the matter at hand. Jesting, which serves to punctuate the tension, ought to have some relevant philosophical content somehow embedded in it (as of course it does in this work); otherwise it would be felt to be irrele-vant, and would detract from the impact of the whole.

The end must be in some respect a fulfillment of the implications set forward in the beginning and focused and concentrated during the unfolding of the middle. Only the imminence of Hamlet's death, it appears, is sufficient to provide the spur necessary to provoke him into taking the revenge he has contemplated all through the play. (Did he really believe, after all, that it was the king hiding behind the curtain—that the king was the sort of man who would hide behind a curtain rather than face him squarely—when he killed Polonius "by mistake"?) Thus the play is brought to a satisfactory conclusion—the deed at last is done, though in its doing, the doer has, of necessity, been done in.

Essential to the organicist interpretation of wholeness or unity is the elimination of all events or elements that do not contribute directly to the completion of an action. And this wholesale integration of the components of a drama, or of any work of art, bears a strong analogy to the integration found among the tissues, members, and organs of a living being. Indeed, it is common procedure in the study of any animal to ask the question, "What does this do—how does it contribute to the survival of the individual creature or its species?" when perplexed, say, by some seemingly abnormal appendage, such as the "bait" dangled by the angler fish, or some eccentricity in coloration, such as the peculiar stripes of the zebra, which, as it turns out, enable it to fade into the background at dusk, when the lions become restless. A creature saddled with useless appendages is not long for this world. A work of art riddled with elements irrelevant to a single, unified thrust will similarly be devoured by critics.

We become acutely aware of this need for wholeness in a work of art precisely at those times when some element is allowed to intrude into it that distracts our attention from the direction in which the work seemed to be tending. Certainly plots do take unforeseen twists and turns—they would be boring if they didn't (*Hamlet* is enriched when Hamlet stabs Polonius)—but every such twist must be integrated into the flow of the action, perhaps taking it to a new level of intensity or exposing a heretofore unacknowledged dimension. A twist that leads nowhere adds nothing and in fact detracts from a work: "an element whose addition or subtraction makes no perceptible extra difference is not really a part of the whole."[19]

Another concept central to the organicist approach, in addition to that of unity, is uniqueness. Just as every person can in some respect lay claim to being a unique individual, so too, it is held, can a work of art, at least a work of art worthy of the name, be regarded as a unique entity. If it is thought that artistic forms consist in general patterns—the sonnet, the five-act drama, sonata form—that can be instantiated in various ways by different artists, the organicist replies that these forms supply but the barest specifications for how a work should be constructed. The more closely we look into any genuine work of art, the more we will come to realize that it possesses individual themes or embodies particular ideas that are developed in ways unique to that particular work.

To see how this approach can be brought to bear on individual works, and how the individuality of such works comes to occupy a position of great importance, let us consider some of the evaluative writings of the renowned music critic Donald F. Tovey.

Organicism in D.F. Tovey's Criticism

Tovey, let us note at the outset, speaks not of organic form but of "artistic form," and he opposes this notion to "living form," when, for example, he judges that "Beethoven's forms become more and more precise in his later works, and if thereby they become less and less like each other, this is what anyone who understands the nature of artistic forms as opposed to living forms ought to expect."[20] And yet the concept of "living form," in this context, seems to suggest something along the lines of a species of plant or animal, whereby an individual is seen as an exemplar of a certain type. "Artistic form," on the other hand, points toward treating each composition as itself a unique entity; indeed, his criticism aims to highlight such uniqueness and show how each work works as no other work works.

He refers contemptuously to "people who talk *a priori* nonsense about the sonata forms, as if these forms were stereotyped moulds into which you shovel your music in the hope that it may set there like a jelly."[21] Instead, he insists that "every individual work must be judged on its own merits," and endeavors, in his own criticism, to demonstrate how this is possible.[22] Clearly, judging on its own merits each work one confronts is in effect treating each work as a unique, self-sufficient organism.

"Beethoven's work," Tovey claims, "developed so rapidly that he seems to be driven to invent a new technique for almost each composition."[23] Of the latter's Ninth Symphony, he urges that "we shall never make head or tail of [it] until we treat it as a law unto itself,"[24] and of Mozart's C-major Piano Concerto (K. 503) he says, "[A]ll that we can be sure of is that nothing will be without its function, and that everything will be unexpected and inevitable."[25] His judging that everything will be unexpected should be taken to imply that in light of prescribed procedures (those "jelly moulds" he speaks of), the listener is in for many a surprise; saying that the unexpected should, or even could, be inevitable is meant to suggest that once we become attuned to the "inner law" of the work, we will realize that whatever does occur must occur as it does.

As captivating as is Tovey's elaboration of organicism, there are never-

theless a few observations that deserve to be made about it. Let us consider
the principal objections that can be raised.

Critical Reflections

1. It must be noted that criticism of this sort has a definite retrospective
character about it: a judgment is made as to the inevitability or necessity of
certain elements of a work, but this judgment comes after hearing them and
only them in the context of that work. What is the case, however, is that
each phrase, each gesture within any work is alive with alternative possibilities of continuation and completion. A composition can be viewed as a
series of choices: a good composer makes interesting choices, a mediocre
one is content to live within the confines set by "standard procedure." But
in neither case is it all that helpful to regard the choices made as in any way
having been necessitated. We can at the present time only wonder how
many of Bach's "inevitable" choices were later penned over in versions that
have been lost to us.

It appears that Tovey has lived with certain works long enough for
them to tell him where they were going, then he has turned around and
declared that that is precisely where they *must* go. We are glad, of
course, that certain works—those felt to be of exceptional merit—follow
the patterns they do, but we must not fancy that the composer's range of
choices is settled once the first few decisions regarding formal structure
have been made.

Talk of necessity and inevitability in the artistic realm really boils
down to asserting that (a) one approves of X the way it is, and (b) one
lacks the creativity to conceive of any more effective alternative. This is
perhaps the reason a view such as Tovey's attaches itself so readily to
great music, for it is in the great music that the techniques employed and
the results produced quite outdistance the creative capacities of even the
most imaginative of critics.

2. In addition to the danger involved in fancying that any of us, regardless of how skilled we may be in the art of listening, is in touch with
aesthetic necessities, there is a further risk that accompanies the use of such
concepts as uniqueness, unity, and the very notion of an organic whole. I
speak of the risk that is taken when these concepts are treated as if they
somehow constitute objective standards by which we measure the adequacy
or inadequacy of such works—standards capable of being dispassionately
applied by anyone to any work of art in the same manner that a laboratory
technician might test for the presence of a certain enzyme in a blood sample. Recall Tovey's claim that Beethoven's forms become more singular

and precise in his late works—a claim about which he boasts, "[I]f proof is required I am ready for it with any work and any part of a work in Beethoven's third period."[26]

The truth of the matter, however, is that the unity of a work is something that can only be apprehended—*felt*. A work is whole only when we feel it to be whole, and when we feel it to be whole, it is so, regardless of whether it meets or fails to meet any of the "objective" criteria of unity that may be offered. Bach's B-minor Mass is sometimes assailed as lacking unity because (a) different sections were composed at different periods in his life, (b) portions have been lifted from other of his works, (c) the final choral section is lifted from the "Gloria" of the mass itself, and (d) it is set more in D-major than B-minor, for all that is worth. But all these irregularities fade away when we listen to the work; our ears and whatever else is involved in our apprehension and appreciation of the work assure us of the oneness of the whole.

On the other hand, all the analyses Tovey could provide as to the unity of any work will not convince us a bit if the work itself, when heard, fails to settle into our consciousness as a whole. If any such analysis does help us hear things that might have been escaping us, so much the better—this is the service critics are supposed to provide—but it is the hearing that is important: formal analysis should never purport to be more than a tool for the enhancement of our experience.

Consider the third movement of Mozart's Violin Concerto in A (K. 219) to see how this contention plays itself out in an individual work. This particular movement adheres politely to the rondo form, a common form for a third movement to take. Its initial theme suggests a minuet, which alternates with other graceful, delicate themes—up to a point. Then suddenly, from nowhere, a most incongruous section intrudes, one based on a Turkish march borrowed from an earlier work of Mozart's (*Lucia Scylla,* K. 135). This newcomer bursts in and swaggers along for a time in bull-in-the-china-shop fashion, utterly in conflict with the pace and mood of the rest of the movement and the entire piece. Ultimately, though, it spends itself and winds down; the original theme returns, order is restored, the movement ends: we are satisfied.

By organicist standards, or for that matter just about any other standards of artistic unity, this piece would appear to suffer from some fatal discontinuity—one has the impression that the pages from two separate compositions might have fallen with a swoosh off Mozart's desk, and that when he reassembled them, a couple of sheets from one were inadvertently tucked in among those of the other.

But is it in spite of or—what is more likely—*because* of these seeming incongruities that this work can lay claim to being the most played of Mozart's violin concertos, and audiences can regularly be heard to express their wholehearted approval of this very movement? Tovey himself refers to this intruder theme as being "scored with the grotesque effects character-istic of the real dance-music of the Viennese public ball-rooms in 1778," and yet in the end he judges that it "triumphantly . . . enlarges the range of the finale."[27] That is to say, even he finds some grounds to declare the piece to be a satisfying whole. And I suggest that the primary grounds, whether he realized it or not, are that in the end he is wholly satisfied by it.

In short, I believe our sense of the wholeness of a work not only is integral to our direct experience of it, but emerges as a consequence of our appreciation of it. To discover that any work is "one" or "whole" we must consult our emotional experience; to proclaim it to be "one" or "whole" is to express our approval of it. That any work does or does not embody a successful integration of diverse elements (the "unity in variety" extolled by so many theoreticians) is not a conclusion that can be reached merely by studying a score or a script and discerning whether some single principle has been adhered to throughout. Tools of formal analysis are powerless—drill bits and hammers of Styrofoam—when disengaged from the profound experience that first prompted us (rational creatures that we are) to seek to understand the power of art.

Surely Tovey and the organicists were intent upon explaining aesthetic value. However, they appear to have reversed the proper order in which such value is to be sought. We do not go looking for the inner principle that governs the generation of any work of art and, upon finding it, pronounce the work to be excellent and perhaps allow ourselves to enjoy it. What we do is interact with a work, respond to it, allow ourselves to be led this way and that by it. And then, only after it has wrung whatever it can wring from us, and we have reached some sense of fulfillment through this encounter, will we be in any position to reflect upon its unity or its uniqueness.

How can we best account for this mysterious power that artistic form is capable of exerting upon our emotions? Here again, different artistic media undoubtedly work in different ways, and to seek for or claim to have found the one principle that applies or explains universally is to engage in self-deception. One psychological theory in particular, however, shows some promise of yield-ing positive results, and that is the Gestalt theory, to which we now turn.

The Gestalt Approach: General Theory

Gestalt psychology appears to link in intriguing ways our perception of visual and auditory patterns with our capacity for emotional response. Consequently, the arts of painting, sculpture, architecture, music, and dance would thus be touched by this theory. Two figures in particular spring to mind and deserve our attention: Rudolf Arnheim and Leonard Meyer. In works such as *Art and Visual Perception* and *The Dynamics of Architectural Form,* Arnheim explores the effects that visual phenomena can exert on our emotions; Meyer engages in a similar inquiry with respect to the auditory domain in *Emotion and Meaning in Music* and *Music, the Arts, and Ideas.* Both lean heavily on the theoretical framework provided by Gestalt psychology. To appreciate best their contributions to aesthetics, then, we must acquaint ourselves a bit with the Gestalt approach.

Gestalt theory in general stresses the active involvement of mind in the constituting of experience. The word *"Gestalt"* in German means "form" or "shape," hence it is no surprise to find the theory focusing on the formation of objects—"the general dynamics of the formation of form"—and aiming to reveal something of the *forces* at work in the act of perception.[28] As a recognizable school of thought, Gestalt theory made its appearance in the 1920s, championed by Wolfgang Köhler, Kurt Koffka, and Max Wertheimer.

It is foundational to the Gestalt approach that in perceptual experience the whole is greater than the sum of its parts. This contention has both a negative and a positive dimension. Negatively, the theory aims to deny that an exhaustive account of our experience of the world can be supplied by what might generally be termed "learning theory," the view that holds perception—thinking here primarily of *visual* perception—to be a product of the passive reception and transmission of sensations through the eyes to the mind. On this view, our visual experience of the world is judged to be built up of simpler elements; these elements are themselves responsible for their own arrangement, and the mind is hardly more than the container in which the external world is perceptually reassembled. Receptivity would seem to be the principal power possessed by the mind. Such a view was captured a few centuries earlier in John Locke's famous characterization of the mind as a *tabula rasa*—a blank slate upon which experience writes.

A simple example should suffice to show that this *tabula rasa* notion is inadequate. Consider a diagram in which two straight lines of equal length are juxtaposed one above the other: they are of equal length and they appear to be of equal length. However, enclose one between wedges that point inward and the other between wedges pointing outward and all of a sudden one of them—the one with the outward-pointing wedges—appears to be longer than the other, and it now takes an overwhelming effort on our part to see them as equal. Nothing has changed in the length of the lines, but the intrusion of the brackets has disrupted the dynamics of the visual field and troubled our perception of equality.

Such an effect would not occur if our visual field were simply built up from the elements transmitted to the mind through the senses. If this were the correct account, we would describe this complex as we saw it: "two lines of equal length flanked in one instance by wedges aimed inward and in the other by wedges aimed outward," and that would be the end of it. The parts would have told their story, but it is not enough; the whole, consisting of this assemblage of lines, urges a different interpretation upon us.

Different theoreticians came to focus on different areas of pattern perception in their research, leading to the articulation of a number of different "laws" governing our visual experience. It is worthwhile to mention some of the more widespread and fundamental of them, especially those that have direct bearing on aesthetic experience.

> *Naturalness of form.* A field tends to become organized and to take on form. Groups tend to form structures, and disconnected units to become connected.[29]

A collection of dots on a page will not remain a collection of discrete dots, but will take on a shape as one looks at it, perhaps a simple geometric shape (the simplest and solidest the mind can manage, given the material presented to it) or a resemblance to some known object. It was in this latter fashion that the constellations among the stars were discerned; the Rorschach inkblot test, popular at one time among psychoanalysts (still popular among television screenwriters), in which one is asked to describe what one sees when in fact all one "sees" is an inkblot shaped at random, also gives evidence of this tendency.

> *Figure and ground.* A form tends to be a figure set upon a ground, and the figure-ground dichotomy is fundamental to all perception.

Our visual sensations consist of a welter of colored shapes, but the mind rapidly moves beyond that, brings certain shapes together to form a whole, and sets that whole against a recessive backdrop of colored shapes. Quite likely this tendency rests on grounds of brute survival: if the mind didn't distinguish and bring into special focus that welter of colored shapes that comprised a saber-toothed tiger, that particular mind wouldn't have been around to do any further cognizing.

> *Good and poor forms.* A good form is well articulated and as such tends to impress itself upon the observer, to persist and recur. A circle is a good form.

> *Strong and weak forms.* A strong form coheres and resists disintegration by analysis into parts or by fusion with another form.

Open and closed forms. An open form tends to change toward a certain good form. When a form has assumed stable equilibrium, it has achieved closure. Thus a nearly circular series of dots may achieve closure by being perceived as a circle.

It should not be thought that some external sense of "goodness" has been imported into the theoretical framework: "goodness" as it is used here simply indicates a certain fundamental habit of mind and should be taken to mark out precisely and only that kind of form that sets the mind's cognitive energies at rest. It is definitely not to be thought of as equivalent to "beautiful," though, as will be developed shortly, there could well be an important dynamic relationship existing between these two concepts.

Proper form. A form tends to preserve its proper shape, size and color.

"Proper" means not the shape or color that the form actually possesses, but the one that is "assigned to it" or "impressed upon it." That is, a form is "proper" when the shaping powers of the mind have worked upon it—squared it up, rounded it off, smoothed it out—brought it into line, to whatever extent possible, with the demands of cognition.

Symmetry of form. A form tends toward symmetry, balance, and proportion.

Symmetry, balance, and proportion are all concepts, as we have seen, that have been employed in the aesthetic domain for a few millennia now. What is crucial is to see that the Gestalt approach speaks of our tendency toward such states and not our direct perception of them. Symmetry and balance are what put the mind at rest. And yet the aesthetic state of mind is not a restful one. As Arnheim puts it in *Art and Visual Perception,* "[J]ust as the emphasis of living is on directed activity, not on empty repose, so the emphasis of the work of art is not on balance, harmony, unity, but on a pattern of directed forces that are being balanced, ordered, unified."[30]

Gestalt Theory and the Visual Arts

Rudolf Arnheim puts axioms of the above sort to work in proposing an explanation of the power a work of art can exert over our emotions. The concept of balance has an immediate relevance to our lives, inasmuch as we are beings with goals and purposes, who strive toward the fulfillment of these goals and suffer frequent disruptions on the way to their realization. Psychologically, it is a state of repose we arrive at when one goal is realized and another has not yet been initiated. Pictorial balance, similarly, is a state realized when all such factors as shape, direction, and location are mutually determined by each other in such a way that no change seems possible, and the whole assumes the character of "necessity" in all its parts. An unbalanced composition looks accidental, transitory, and therefore invalid. Its elements show a tendency to change place or shape in order to bring about a state better fitted to the total structure. Under such conditions the artistic statement becomes incomprehensible.[31]

It is understood here, though, that the forces and stresses at work in negotiating a balanced composition are those that can be attributed to the being—the person—who is engaged in perceiving an (art) object. The balance is predicated of the object, but it is through the activity of our perceptual faculties that a sense of repose is achieved. *We* feel our cognitive powers negotiating a mutual resolution in the face of the balanced object; and likewise, where balance has not been attained, we feel a sense of dissatisfaction, an uneasiness, as the elements of a painting, say, threaten to topple over from having been injudiciously aligned.

A variety of factors collaborate in producing these feelings: different "weight" is assigned to objects depending on whether they appear on the left or the right of a painting, or toward the top as opposed to the bottom; different colors have different weights; the shape of an element in a composition can likewise be assigned a weight, and the direction it appears to be tending can carry various other elements along with it, or can be deflected by the intrusion of yet other visual factors. And in an assemblage of elements all interacting with one another, we ourselves are "pulling" in favor of some propitious resolution of the various forces.

Representational factors also contribute (contrary to the contentions of Bell and Fry) to the interplay of forces in a painting: a pair of eyes in a face, in strictest formal terms, are just two dark dots in a white expanse—or, if the face is that of a black person, two white dots in a dark expanse—yet when they suggest contemplation or introspection they can act to hold our attention in focus, while when they appear to be gazing at something with intensity, they can force us to follow with our own eyes the direction they suggest. An elephant at some remove in the background will still weigh more than a mouse in the foreground, even though the two creatures are colored the same and the area occupied on the canvas by the mouse may actually be greater. The old joke "Which weighs more, a pound of feathers or a pound of lead?" is amusing because we tend to think first, "Feathers, light; lead, heavy," before we realize that a pound is a pound, whatever it might be a pound of. But a mass of lead, depicted in a painting, will definitely "weigh" more than a mass of feathers of similar (visual) size.

In putting such forces as these to work on a canvas, an artist will likely arrange to have them come to focus on one point, a point near the center of the work. What is interesting, however, is that this point is itself often devoid of interest—a dead space on the canvas. That point toward which all forces conspire need not and probably should not be active in itself. Vincent van Gogh's celebrated *Starry Night,* for example, is a turbulent work: the moon doesn't just sit in the sky (in the upper right corner of the canvas), it shimmers and vibrates there; the stars don't sparkle, they swirl and careen, as if swept along by the clouds; a cypress twists and writhes from the lower left foreground toward the sky. Only the little church in the valley (at the lower right center) seems at rest, at peace—all else is in a maddening flux. None of these elements stands anywhere near the actual *or* the visual center of the painting, but each pulls our attention this way, then that, again and again across the center. We feel where the forces lead, but our consciousness can never come to rest just there.

A genuine emotional response is provoked by this interplay of visual forces. "Emotion or affect is aroused when a tendency to respond is arrested or inhibited."[32] In slightly different terms, we may say that emotions are aroused when events deviate from expected patterns and we *lose control* over our surroundings. Meyer suggests that when a habitual smoker "wants a cigarette and, reaching into his pocket, finds one, there will be no affective response. . . . If, however, the man finds no cigarette in his pocket, discovers that there are none in the house, and then remembers that the stores are closed and he cannot purchase any, he will very likely begin to respond in an emotional way. He will feel restless, excited, then irritated, and finally angry."[33] Where our apprehension of artworks is concerned, this control over our responses is embodied in our nativistic tendency to order, regularize, round off, *simplify* the visual field. But a work such as *Starry Night* plays upon—preys upon—these tendencies. Its formal arrangement initiates a visual struggle and yet inhibits any ultimate, satisfactory resolution to this struggle. All the while, it offers (to whoever gazes upon it, for a moment, forever) the promise of such resolution; and it makes this offer with a strength that is sufficient to sustain indefinitely our interest in the painting and reward our efforts at rendering it (cognitively) intelligible.

The "aesthetic emotion" lauded by Bell and Fry, on this account, turns out to differ from other emotions only with regard to the nature of the stimulus—a work of art, as opposed to a football game or a ride on the expressway. But unlike the football game or the expressway ride, the work of art is capable of both stimulating and controlling our response—holding it in state, so to speak, while leading us to place a certain interpretation upon the feelings thus provoked. And so one viewer may feel that van Gogh's little village (with its focal point, the church) positively shrivels in importance when placed alongside nature in all its dynamism, while another is led to feel that the village (through its focal point, the church) offers the only hope of stability in an otherwise wild and untamable world. But neither of these emotionally tinged interpretations would have been possible if the form of the painting had not agitated our emotions.

Alongside the aesthetically intelligible "jumble" of visual elements offered by *Starry Night,* we might, for the sake of contrast, envision an object possessing a readily recognizable symmetry. Symmetrical paintings, though, as a trip through any museum should convince us, are quite rare; perhaps it is necessary to retreat several centuries in order to find works of stature that even approximate symmetry. But this is not because symmetry is difficult to attain—quite the contrary, symmetry is one of the easiest accomplishments, something that someone with a little talent and a nice new set of drafting tools could manage in short order. Indeed, this would seem to be precisely the shortcoming of symmetry: the ease with which it can be produced is matched by the ease with which it can be grasped, comprehended. Seeming exceptions to this suggestion, however, come from architecture and certain crafts, so they deserve to be looked at briefly in order to dispel this air of exceptionality.

Architectural constructions, even (perhaps especially) those that are regarded as being artistically successful, are often symmetrical in shape. The Louvre, for example, is biaxially symmetrical, and only recently a new element has been introduced into its courtyard astride its axis—a glass pyramid, which happens to possess a symmetry of its own. Does this imply that the Louvre is a boring structure architecturally? I would say not, and the principal reason for saying this is that the Louvre's symmetry is perceived only by airborne tourists and the pigeons of Paris. Even when standing precisely on the line constituting the central axis of the structure one does not see enough of it to judge effectively that it is truly symmetrical, especially with that pyramid of glass impeding or deflecting one's view.

A building is something we walk around, through; once inside we might go upstairs and down, pass through this chamber and that, get a glimpse of the outside from this window, then that: its overall symmetry is evident on the architect's drawings, but our experience of it is ever varying. And if by chance we do find ourselves in a position where a symmetrical vista suddenly opens up before us, we may indeed take delight in this moment of visual repose, but that does not imply that it is such symmetry alone that we value—rather, it is valued either for the way it effectively interrupts an otherwise syncopated visual texture, or for the manner in which it imparts intelligibility to the myriad of perspectives from which a single structure can be viewed.

An oriental rug will often be found to exhibit considerable symmetry, yet such creations are valued the world over for their beauty. Here again, though, several qualifications come to mind. First, we often find ourselves seeking out asymmetries within the patterns, and taking pleasure in finding them, for they indicate to us that human hands have fashioned the product (though even machine-made rugs can be found to have "built-in" irregularities—a sinister response to this very inclination). Thus in a sense we shrink away from symmetries, even when they seem to present themselves quite unabashedly. Secondly, the colors or the subsidiary patterning may well be factors that capture our attention, and we take delight in such features in spite of or without paying heed to the large-scale symmetry that is present. Finally, irregularities have often been introduced by the fabricants themselves because "God alone can create true symmetry," hence it would constitute a species of impiety to create rugs that were "too perfect."

In short, instances of a pure symmetry are rare in the art world, and even where they do occur, and are largely felt to be successful, either the manner in which they are to be apprehended or the broader set of circumstances in which they have been placed will tend to leave us with an experience much richer than if we had simply been gazing at an object whose two sides exactly balanced each other.

Gestalt Theory and Music

In music, tones can occur simultaneously, but they must occur in sequence. That is to say, there is a temporality that is essential to music, which requires a reinterpretation of the laws of pattern perception if any successful application of Gestalt theory is to be made within the musical domain. Since notes are sounded and then give way immediately to other notes, our memory must play a significant role in enabling us to interact with the structure of a musical work. And along with memory, which sustains the past through the ever-advancing present, goes our capacity to anticipate future occurrences, make inferences, and form expectations as to how a composition is likely to proceed. It is only by reaching both backward and forward that our cognitive powers engage in the interplay with a musical composition that will lead us to respond affectively to it.

The distinctions between strong and weak forms, good and poor forms, open and closed forms, and the like must here be drawn so as to address forms that reveal themselves over a certain expanse of time. Nevertheless, let us keep in mind that the normative terminology employed here—"good," "poor," "weak," and so on—does not directly qualify the musical work any more than it did the visual object. Strong or good forms do not necessarily make for strong or good compositions; in fact, weakness and poverty of form are just as vital to producing effective, affective music. "[S]ome of the greatest music is great precisely because the composer has not feared to let his music tremble on the brink of chaos, thus inspiring the listener's awe, apprehension, and anxiety and, at the same time, exciting his emotions and his intellect."[34]

Let us also note this further peculiarity, namely, that the cognitive dispositions that ground our response to music must also be processed by any listener in terms of certain scale systems, harmonic probabilities, rhythmic patterns—in short, our confrontation with a work of music is never brute, but is always shaped by the determinants of a certain style system. It may well be that visual arts appeal more directly to our simple native dispositions; otherwise how are we to explain the attraction we feel to many paintings or sculptures of cultures far removed from our own in either time or place or both? But the attraction we will feel for music of styles that differ radically from any we are familiar with is more likely to be historic or scholarly rather than aesthetic.

In a process that unfolds temporally, continuation becomes a key element. Good continuation implies that "a shape or pattern will, other things being equal, tend to be continued in its initial mode of operation."[35] But as we have seen, the objectified language Gestalt theory employs tends to conceal the fact that continuation is a mental process initiated by a certain stimulus, "and it is this mental process which, following the mental line of least resistance, tends to be perpetuated and continued."[36] And as we have just noted, good continuation does not immediately qualify the musical work, but instead points to the set of mental dispositions with which the musical work interacts, here gratifying our urge for simplicity, there sharpening this urge by refusing to comply with our cognitive demands.

Disturbing the continuation of a musical process, either by interposing gaps of one sort or another or by initiating unimplied processes, is thus essential to keeping the music alive. Clearly, however, we can discern important limits to tendencies both to disruption and fulfillment. Music that *never* went where we expected it to go would not sustain our interest for long—we would become first irritated, then bored, as we came to discover that no amount of attention on our part was to be rewarded. Persistent disruption would quickly cease to be disruptive. On the other hand, as with perfectly symmetrical visible shapes, music that slavishly adhered to good continuation would also become boring rather quickly, not for posing insurmountable challenges, but for failing to challenge our cognitive dispositions sufficiently, leading to a slackening in attentiveness.

The dissatisfaction with atonal music, registered over the past several decades by all but the most specialized audiences, is evidence in favor of the former contention: inasmuch as atonal music by design avoids all the traditional routes of melodic construction and aims to discourage the formation of expectations, it is only natural to find people "tuning out" upon realizing that none of their tendencies, no matter how deeply ingrained, is going to be fulfilled.

The very growth of musical styles is evidence of the other limiting function at work, for when certain patterns constitutive of a style are repeated ad indefinitum, all but the most unskilled listener will begin to crave some variation, and such cravings are gratified by presupposing the old patterns as basic and building upon them until they can sustain no further development. Then stylistic revolution occurs. This tendency can be observed in the growth of the Baroque style, its culmination in Bach, and its abandonment in favor of novel (though simpler) approaches by the next generation of composers (which even included some of Bach's sons). One can see the same progression through the Romantic period; through the development of jazz from, say, the 1920s into the 1960s and beyond; in rock 'n' roll from its beginnings in the 1950s to the point where it dropped the " 'n' roll" a couple of decades later, and so on.

A dynamic interplay, therefore, between our listening dispositions, attuned to forming a certain set of expectations, and the musical work that, when interestingly constructed, deviates from these expectations (though never so much as to discourage the formation of further expectations) is how our experience of music might best be characterized.

Our expectations, or tendencies to respond, can be effectively impeded in a variety of ways. Perception of a sequence of tones (a melody), similar to the perception of visual forms, also inclines us to favor "closed" shapes, and to listen for melodic gaps or skips to be filled in straightaway. Thus if a melody leaps a minor sixth (from C to A-flat), as, for example, at the beginning of the "Lacrimosa" in Mozart's *Requiem,* something in us tends to want this considerable gap to be filled in by a series of notes heading in the opposite direction. But Mozart does not do so: he feigns an effort in that direction, but stops short and then repeats the original leap, doubling our uneasiness. He then has the melody rise by a long series of steps as the bass line continually pulls away in the opposite direction, emphasizing another gap between voices that longs to be filled in. It is only after quite some time that this longing is fulfilled.

Beethoven, in his later years, experimented with increasingly wide gaps between voices, often to dramatic effect. In his Piano Sonata, Op. 111, the climactic moment is reached at precisely the point where the upper melody and the bass line (the right hand and the left) are fully five and a half octaves apart! This is extremely disquieting to the listener, and, as if in acknowledgment that such a drastic separation was the point all along, Beethoven quickly fills in this yawning gap and leaves the left hand reassuringly stressing the midpoint between these extremes for some time thereafter.

Rhythms are often tampered with, to good effect. Pounding with mechanical regularity on a drum can become irritating, unless there is enough variety among the other musical parameters to sustain our interest. But rhythm itself can be varied, and when, for example, a melody that had been articulated in double meter (two or four beats per measure) is all of a sudden divided into threes, a disruption of this sort can be most effective. Chopin observed "the singing hand [the hand carrying the melody in a piano piece] may deviate from strict time, but the accompanying hand must keep time."[37] This very phenomenon can be observed over and over in rap music, the best of which involves the layering of rhythms, the upper layer of which consists in the rhythm of language, here following the fundamental rhythmic impulse, and there offering its own delectable syncopations (though few rap artists would likely be pleased with my choice of adjectives here).

Harmonic relationships also create certain expectations in us; indeed, the study of harmony is grounded in a certain set of probabilities declaring what chords follow what chords frequently, occasionally, and rarely. Here again it bears remembering that these probabilities are stylistically grounded, and that many a relationship that occurred frequently in the late nineteenth century would have occurred rarely in the sixteenth century: the expansion of harmonic resources was a primary element in stylistic development during this period and well beyond. Where there are probabilities, naturally there are ample opportunities for deviating from anticipated paths through irregular patterns of development and resolution, and composers have been taking advantage of such possibilities for centuries. And it bears remarking that where a harmonic framework is relatively fixed, such as in the classical sixteen-bar blues progression, the music is kept alive by other factors, most notably rhythmic play, melodic improvisation, and the rhythmic counterplay that a set of lyrics can provide.

For beings such as ourselves, constituted so as to "keep the world centered in front of us," and to keep it simple enough to permit of ready comprehension, the disruptions a talented composer is capable of inflicting on our urge for order and completeness are capable of eliciting strong emotional responses from us. It is important, of course, that order ultimately triumph, otherwise the emotions aroused would terminate negatively; but it shouldn't be a victory easily won. And it is important that at all times we trust that a composer has sufficient competence to be able to lead us through occasional thickets, and sufficient integrity to be willing to do so. Without such confidence, the listening experience could easily be as harrowing for us as when we are forced to hear a moderately talented child stagger through a more-than-moderately difficult piece.

Final Thoughts

This purely cognitive play and the pleasure or emotional satisfaction it produces are not, on either Arnheim's or Meyer's account, the ultimate aim of art—at least of art at its best. Though some such account of our response to a work of art is essential to a complete theory of art, it is not the whole story. While, in Arnheim's words, "the primary effect of visual expression is ... derived from, and controlled by, formal properties of the visual shapes themselves,"[38] the primary effect is not the only effect. Artistic symbolism and expression likewise owe their being to the dynamic interplay between our cognitive apparatus and a tantalizingly resistant object: "To be seen as expressive, the shape of an object must be seen as dynamic. There is nothing expressive, and therefore nothing symbolic, in a set of stairs or a staircase as long as it is seen as a mere geometrical configuration. Only when one perceives the gradual rising of the steps from the ground as a dynamic crescendo does the configuration exhibit an expressive quality, which carries a self-evident symbolism."[39]

The manner in which an art object induces us to interact with it thus lends that distinctive quality to aesthetic experience that other modes of experience lack: "The dynamic quality of perceptual experiences accounts ... for the difference between mere intellectual information received indirectly through the eyes and the direct reverberation within us of the forces we experience in the objects we see."[40]

Thus Arnheim arrives, through an analysis of the formal properties of art objects and their effects on our cognitive faculties, at the matter of expression. His painfully dry, geometrical analysis of Cézanne's *Mme Cézanne in a Yellow Chair* leads ultimately to less abstract considerations: "Only because shapes are recognized as head, body, hands, chair, do they play their particular compositional role. The fact that the head harbors the mind is at least as important as its shape, color, or location. ... And the observer's knowledge of what a seated, middle-aged woman signifies contributes strongly to the deeper meaning of the work."[41]

In this work, then, the formal elements collaborate to draw and focus our attention, to stir feelings of a deep sort within us, while the represented image offers to clothe and domesticate these feelings and ensure that we grasp the expressive intent of the work.

As it turns out, expressiveness is precisely the point at which Clive Bell saw theory departing from the aesthetic realm and entering the metaphysical. Recall there were two questions to be dealt with on Bell's account—"What is it that is central to art?" and "Why is it central?" The answer to the "what?" question was "significant form"; the answer to the "why?" question has been held in abeyance here until we could explore in greater depth the dynamics of significant form. Bell himself regarded any answer to this second question as dangerously speculative, and yet he had no qualms about offering his own speculations, and they turn on the notion of expression.

"It seems to me possible, though by no means certain," Bell suggests, "that created form moves us so profoundly because it expresses the emotion of its creator."[42] The experience that an artist has in which objects in the world are somehow viewed as pure forms is an experience, he believes, in which such objects are seen as ends in themselves, and this produces a more powerful emotion than we ever receive from perceiving them as means to some end or other. Indeed, he wonders, "[S]hall I be altogether fantastic in suggesting, what some of the profoundest thinkers have believed, that the significance of the thing in itself is the significance of Reality?"[43] When we ask, then, "Why are we so profoundly moved by certain combinations of lines and colours?" may we not answer "Because artists can express in combinations of lines and colours an emotion felt for reality which reveals itself through line and colour?"[44] Thus the artist might—just might—be offering us a glimpse of Ultimate Reality. But this, Bell has assured us, is only a hypothesis.

It is time, in any case, that we attended closely to this notion of expression, for it has been practically ubiquitous in aesthetic discussions for the past couple of centuries, and hinted at by quite enough theorists (including myself) to this point in the present study.

— 4 —

Theories of Art: Expression

In the middle of the eighteenth century, a theory emerged that was to dominate aesthetic thinking for the next two hundred years. This theory is expressionism. Although closely allied with Romanticism, which flourished through the nineteenth and into the twentieth century, expressionism quite outlived that movement: even now expressionist theories of art are put forward, although as we shall see, some of them have very little in common with their eighteenth- and nineteenth-century ancestors.

All through the period when representation was being taken as central to the artistic process (as was discussed in Chapter Two), the term "expression" was used liberally, especially in characterizing how gestures and looks were to be captured. Normally, such gestures and looks would be taken to be indicative of a certain state of feeling or emotion displayed by the subject of the work. Consequently, a representation of the Crucifixion would be said to be expressive of suffering, meaning that the figure of Christ would be cast in a fashion that would convey to a viewer a sense of His suffering.

Sometimes this sense of expression is referred to as *objective* expression, indicating that the expressive properties are borne exclusively by the art object itself, and that no inferences whatever are to be made concerning the personal convictions or the emotional state of the artist. A representation would be (objectively) expressive, then, when and only when it adequately captured some (actual, historical, or mythical) individual in the act of expressing a certain emotion.

Subjective expression only became a salient concept in aesthetics when artistic creation took on a more personal significance, and works of art came to be taken as expressive of the spiritual state of the *artist*. In this chapter we shall focus on expression understood in this subjective sense; thus those thinkers who are concerned to allege some vital connection between an artist and an audience (mediated, of course, by the work of art) will receive our principal attention. Inasmuch as extensive criticism has been leveled at this position across the decades and has led to many a reappraisal of the significance of expression in art, some of the more recent versions of the theory—versions that have been purified of any subjective element—must also receive some of our attention.

It could well be the case—indeed I think it is the case—that works created before the time when an artist's subjectivity was taken to be on display nevertheless do reveal something of this inner state. This is only to say, however, that the range of a theory's applicability at times reaches beyond the period of its advocacy, which is neither surprising nor unusual. What it may imply is that at one time certain considerations are treated as significant that at another time pass relatively unnoticed. Thus once we become attuned to looking for some personal statement in art, we cannot but seek for such testimony in anything we regard as art.

It is easy, for example, to imagine that the Medicis and the Pope were utterly unconcerned with Michelangelo's spiritual state, and were interested only in whether he produced works that were flattering or otherwise appealing. In our time, the film depicting his life is intent on showing the considerable suffering he underwent and the deep satisfaction he felt in realizing his Sistine Chapel ceiling; were a film to have been made in 1550 that featured the Sistine Chapel ceiling, it might well have made only passing reference to Michelangelo. Times change, and with the times come changes in attitudes: a theory captures an attitude.

The longevity of expressionism derives from its resiliency—it is a theory that has shown itself capable of adjusting to a variety of different intellectual climates, from the deeply theistic to the atheistic, from the sentimental to the scientific, from the artistically traditional to the avant-garde. And although it hardly sounds flattering to say so, this resiliency seems to derive from a certain ambiguity that pervades its central themes.

Many questions can be raised concerning one aspect or another of these central themes. One may wonder, for example, "Just what is it that gets expressed?" or "Who (or what) does the expressing?" or "By what means is this act of expression accomplished?" or "Is anything transmitted—communicated—in the act of expression, or does the expressive act constitute its own fulfillment?" The many answers that can be (and have been) provided to these questions have in some instances provided grounding for expressionist theories of greatly contrasting natures, and in other instances been taken to supply reasons for rejecting the expressionist project entirely. Let us look a bit more closely at these questions, sketching some of the principal answers that have been offered to them before launching into a more detailed consideration of particular theories.

1. What gets expressed: a thought, an idea, an attitude, or an emotion? We can be said to express our *views* on world peace, democracy, the value of a sound education, voter fraud, lawn care, or cheese soufflés, and we can also express how we *feel* toward any such notions, institutions, phenomena, or entities. In addition, much that we are said to express does not find its way into words: a smile expresses warmth or approval, a sneer contempt, a wave of the hand dismissal, and so forth. And of course a painting can express religious exaltation, lust, or despair. In most versions of the expression theory, though, it is some feeling or emotion that is said to be expressed, and in those cases where we still may want to say that something along the lines of an idea or opinion gains expression, this would still be accomplished through expressing the emotions that normally accompany one's contemplation of the idea or holding of the opinion. The notion that art expresses emotion is perhaps the least disputable claim we will make about expression theories.

2. But who (or what) does the expressing? Here the schools of thought divide into two principal camps. One holds that it is the *artist* who is said to express emotion *through* the work of art. The work of art is here viewed as something of a linguistic device, or at least a significance-bearing entity, which embodies and conveys to us some interesting feature of the artist's emotional life: Chopin expressed a feeling of unfulfilled longing in his B minor prelude (Opus 28, No. 6). The other principal approach contends that it is the *work of art itself* that should be said to express this or that feeling. To be sure, a work of art is fabricated by an artist, yet there are too many hazardous inferential leaps to make if we are to determine the emotional makeup of the artist, and we should let the work speak for itself: for example, Chopin's B minor prelude expresses a sense of unfulfilled longing. Chopin himself, after all, might have been feeling somewhat giddy the day he composed that prelude, but went ahead with it just the same, perhaps in an effort to talk himself out of his giddiness. Who knows whether he succeeded?

3. By what means is the act of expression accomplished? The easy answer to this is "through signs or symbols," but we must then ask what signs and symbols *are,* and how they function in an aesthetic context. A stop sign is a sign, but its message is not an emotional one, and almost no one would claim it was a work of art. The bald eagle was adopted as a symbol of America, but certainly the bird itself is no work of art, and only certain representations of it can claim to be artistic. (At present, the most symbolic aspect of the eagle may lie in the fact that we have driven it to the edge of extinction.) Is the symbolic content of a work of art, as some claim, merely read off the surface of the work—discerned, as it were—or does a symbol make its content known by making it felt, in the manner suggested by

Beethoven on the title page of his *Missa Solemnis:* "From the heart, may it go to the heart?"

4. Is anything transmitted (communicated) in the act of expression? This last quotation from Beethoven suggests an act of communication, from him to us, and that indeed is a widespread view of artistic expression, wherein an artist and an audience coexist in some necessary, symbiotic relationship. But it is sometimes claimed, even by artists themselves, that the urge to create and the satisfaction that derives from the fulfillment of this urge are purely personal concerns, that it is a matter of indifference to them whether anyone else views or reads their work, and even less so whether it is appreciated or understood "as intended." The act of expression from this perspective is one of clarification and unencumberment, in which some gnawing emotion is brought to light and its pernicious hold on the artist is thereby dissipated. "Ex-pression," after all, merely makes mention of the squeezing out of something; it tells nothing of the fate of that something once it has been externalized.

As we consider these questions one by one, and examine the variety of responses that can be and have been given to them over the years, we will come to see what a rich and diverse history expressionism has enjoyed.

The etymology of the term "expression" was just mentioned above, where its two principal components—"ex" and "press"—were set off from one another. To express is to squeeze out, a simple description that carries heavy implications. For whatever gets squeezed *out* must theretofore have been, in some sense, *in;* thus embedded in the term itself there exists a distinction between the inner and the outer, a distinction that, especially in the early flowering of expressionism, was laden with metaphysical implications. This inner something was taken to be inner not in any physical sense (as one's alimentary functions, for example, take place inside one's body), but in a metaphysical sense: it was nothing short of the state of one's mind or soul that received expression. A work of art, therefore, or any object that may be deemed expressive (and many proponents of the theory have contended that *all* objects are in some respect expressive), would constitute the outward and perceivable realization of an inward and spiritual state.

In and by itself, the reasoning goes, the content of a person's mind or soul is utterly inaccessible to anyone other than that very person. It is claimed that we are all aware of our own inner states immediately, through the testimony of our consciousness; and we have the impression that we have a degree of control over the content and the direction of the flow of our ideas, thus enabling us to lead something of an "inner life," out of the reach of the minds, however prying, of others. But it mustn't be inferred from this that we are somehow hopelessly introverted—off-limits to others, who in their turn are off-limits to us—for there are means by which we can make our consciousness or our emotional states known to others, and by which others can make their own such states known to us. This externalization of our inner life is accomplished through the employment of *signs or symbols.*

Expressionism at its fullest can thus be found to contain reference to the following four elements: (a) an individual who possesses a consciousness and who is moved by an urge to express certain states (emotions, ideas) of this consciousness (the artist); (b) some set of physical manifestations of such states capable of being grasped through one or more of our senses (the work of art); (c) a second individual consciousness or mind that is witness to such physical manifestations (the reader, viewer, listener); (d) an interpretive framework that would elevate these physical manifestations to a level where they become signs or symbols, thereby providing the second individual with a glimpse into the consciousness of the first. At the core of expression, therefore, we find an act of communication taking place.

Let us now sample some of the variety of expression theories that have come down to us across the centuries. We will consider first an eighteenth-century version, then one from the nineteenth century, then a twentieth-century one. I will withhold most criticisms until after the third of these has been presented. Once we see where the critical issues lie, we can consider a few approaches to expressionism that have attempted to circumvent its major problem areas. Finally, I will offer a brief evaluation of these latter (which also happen to be latter-day) versions.

Thomas Reid

Though many expressionist theories emerged in the eighteenth century, Reid's is important both for the clarity of its formulation and the breadth of its influence. A Scot, and a Presbyterian minister beyond his academic calling, he exerted a profound influence not only on numerous Scottish thinkers contemporary with himself (the most important of whom was Dugald Stewart), but also on French thought during the nineteenth century (through Victor Cousin, a disciple, also known for promulgating the "art for art's sake" doctrine), and in nineteenth-century America, where his views attained the status of orthodoxy in a great many universities across the land.

In truth, Reid's version of expressionism pays less attention to the artist than it does simply to the person, viewed as a morally responsible agent (though of course any artist, by virtue simply of being a person, *is* a moral agent). Furthermore, even nature is treated as expressive, a sentiment that derives simply from Reid's conviction that nature is the handiwork of the greatest Artist—and Moral Authority—of all.

Whenever we find something to be beautiful, Reid contends, we believe two things of it: that it possesses some perfection or excellence, and that these qualities are found "originally and properly, in qualities of mind."[1] The object that receives the label "beautiful" is thus said to derive its beauty from an original mental or spiritual source.

Whether it is the beauty of nature, of a fellow human being, or of a work of art that is in question, that which deserves truly to be called beautiful, on Reid's account, is the spiritual interior—of the artist, of the person, of God—and this spiritual interior thus expresses itself through material means, in the form of a statue, a face, a forest, or the like. Even a machine can be judged beautiful for this reason. Reid invites us to "[s]uppose that an expert mechanic views a well constructed machine. He sees all its parts to be made of the fittest materials, and of the most proper form; nothing superfluous, nothing deficient; every part adapted to its use, and the whole fitted in the most perfect manner to the end for which it is intended. He pronounces it to be a beautiful machine."[2] This machine could be said to possess a rational structure; but we know that such a structure must have been imparted to it by an organizing mind—the machine didn't make itself. While we do admire the machine, Reid contends that at the core of our appreciation for its efficiency and economy lies an admiration for the mind that designed it.

Given Reid's calling in the ministry, it is understandable that he should interpret the concepts of perfection or excellence—those that provoke in us the sense of beauty—principally in moral terms (principally, but not entirely, for that beautiful machine seems more a product of intellect than rectitude). That we find nature beautiful, therefore, derives from the fact that we see in it a mirror of God's goodness; that we find a fellow human to be beautiful (or ugly) similarly follows from the moral disposition of the inner state of the person and the manner in which this inner state outwardly manifests itself.

Reid believed that there exists a system of natural signs, universal in its scope, which provides people of all cultures with some insight into each other's character and attitudes, even where the precise content of their utterances may lay buried beneath the foreignness of their language. Laughter, cries of pain, the stiffness induced by fear—these are examples he cites. He notes, interestingly, that while one might have to study and practice long hours in order to master the techniques of the art of mime, a child is capable, with no training whatsoever, of immediately seizing the gist of what a (competent) mime is intending to express. If this is not the definitive argument in favor of natural signs, it is at least a very provocative one.

The anthropological and intercultural research conducted in the centuries between Reid's time and our own have cast considerable doubt on the idea that there exists any such universal vocabulary of natural signs. Even what would seem to be the most obvious and pure instances of significatory behavior—cries of pain, shrieks of joy, or the like—turn out to manifest subtle differences from one culture to the next. The catalogue of mistaken inferences drawn from seemingly "natural" behavior is immense: "He was laughing all night! I could have *sworn* he was having a good time!"; "How could anyone so polite and shy *do* such a thing?"; and so on.

Despite the insights that have accompanied the increased interaction among cultures, one of Reid's arguments in favor of accepting certain signs as part of our natural cognitive endowment is highly tantalizing. He suggests, quite simply, that "if mankind had not a natural language, they could never have invented an artificial one by their reason and ingenuity."[3] His contention here seems to be that while by far the greater part of our communication takes place through the medium of artificial, arbitrary signs, we could never even reach an agreement about what was to stand arbitrarily for what unless we had some natural means of giving and registering assent.

To prove that this is the case, suppose we employ a phrase such as "We are all in agreement, then?" as something of a signature of such mutual assent. For this phrase to accomplish a purpose of this sort, it must be the case that somewhere, sometime in the history of our language, an antecedent accord was arrived at that would have determined what this particular phrase signified. And if this accord was itself framed in some verbally arbitrary manner, then such a prior convention must in turn have been assented to at some earlier point in linguistic history, and so on. Thus we are left either with an infinite regress of linguistic conventions or with some primordial, natural (preconventional) gesture capable of signifying assent.

What is more, this system of natural signs was seen by Reid to be an essential component of the expressiveness that lies at the heart of our aesthetic experience. Arbitrary signs and symbols, he saw, are bloodless, lifeless; they enable us to articulate our thoughts, but not to express our feelings. And as these arbitrary symbols come to play a larger and larger role in our life, we find ourselves increasingly distanced from the expressive side of our nature: "[I]t were easy to show that the fine arts of the musician, the painter, the actor, and the orator, so far as they are expressive . . . yet they are nothing else but the language of nature, which we brought into the world with us, but have unlearned by disuse, and so find the greatest difficulty in recovering it. Abolish the use of articulate sounds and writing among mankind for a century, and every man would be a painter, an actor, and an orator."[4]

Reid himself, though, seems to have been more concerned to explain beauty as it manifested itself in human beings and in nature than in art. As mentioned earlier, where human beauty is concerned, he found it to reside principally in our moral nature, and as the above considerations would suggest, he thought that a virtuous character would "appear on the surface" of the virtuous person so as to be "readable" by the rest of us. And this readability would derive not from the deeds done by that person (though surely one's actions, once known in their entirety, would have to tell the same story as one's appearance), but from a variety of signs given off by the tone of one's voice, the disposition of one's physiognomy, and even one's carriage and bearing.

Dated as such an outlook may seem, it is not to be cast aside without some serious consideration. What is it that enables us to warm right up to certain individuals or prompts us to stand coolly apart from others when we first meet them? Is it not a quick read of the disposition of their features, or of the attitude their entire body projects? That phenomenon known as love at first sight is anything but a simpleminded attraction to a certain shade of hair and color of eyes; it involves, rather, an inference to the effect that this surface upon which one's eyes have just fallen expresses depths of a sort with which one will find sympathy. A pair of eyes, after all, can be deep and welcoming or steely and menacing; a strong, muscular physique can invite a feeling of security or pose a mortal threat. The shallowest among us sees beyond and beneath surfaces.

The image peddlers in Hollywood relentlessly cast handsome individuals in winsome roles, while inflicting the less attractive parts on the less attractive actors: James Bond versus Goldfinger. Undeniably this practice is sustained in a most unsubtle manner, to the point of constituting an abuse of the tendency in question—even a dangerous abuse, since it can easily create or reinforce prejudices that we carry out of the theater and back into the world—but the abuse of a tendency nevertheless stands as confirmation of the reality of that tendency. Often we err in our initial judgments: closer attention reveals an insincerity we at first overlooked—a slight catch in the laugh, a smile that collapses too quickly—but where it is possible to be wrong it is also possible to be right. And this is all the theory is asking for.

If we stir in Reid's theistic beliefs, we can see how nature comes to be seen by us as beautiful. Just as a work of art or a cleverly constructed artifact opens a window for us into the able mind of its creator, and in so doing provides us with a certain pleasure, so too, Reid contends, perhaps even more so, does that greatest of all contrivances—nature as a whole—provide us with pleasurable glimpses into the infinite wisdom of our Creator. Everywhere we turn, our gaze falls upon some aspect or other of nature that discloses a distinct sense of purposiveness, and purposiveness implies a consciousness (or in this case, a Consciousness) acting with a certain goal in mind. In the case of nature, the goal is one we cannot fathom, but faith assures us that it is a noble one.

Clearly an outlook such as this will have some difficulty accounting for ugliness in nature, since the divine mind harbors no evil thoughts, hence nature will everywhere be expressive only of beauty. Barrenness and putrefaction, or any other unsavory element within the scheme of things, would have to be seen as somehow contributory to the Grand Design, though in ways that may well be inscrutable to us. But after all, the whole system is fundamentally inscrutable to us. Stumbling by accident across the rotting corpse of a deer while strolling through the woods might be seen as analogous to walking into an organ recital in the midst of a prolonged dissonance.

It would be interesting to speculate for a moment about what we find beautiful about nature if we subtract Reid's theistic outlook; I suspect nature's surface still has ways to invite us to look behind and beyond itself, and to find pleasure in so doing. Perhaps natural selection itself could constitute a sufficient cause for wonderment, by virtue of the balance that is struck among innumerable species to share nature's provender in a manner suited to sustaining each of them: the lion helps the zebra by eliminating the weaker members of the herd, the zebra helps the lion by serving as dinner for the pride, the vultures and jackals clean the table, and so forth. Natural selection also introduces a temporal factor capable of inducing reverie: that the characteristics of individual species and the balance negotiated among species is something achievable only over unthinkably long periods of time. The interplay of creatures upon the globe thus leads our thought well beyond the plane on which this interplay transpires.

Indeed, the element of time seems to play a considerable role even in our appreciation of nonorganic wonders of nature such as the Grand Canyon or the stone "monuments" of southern Utah. To be sure, the shapes and colors are striking, and yet these shapes and colors are immeasurably enriched by the thought that all this carving was done over countless millennia, by wind, water, and sand, through climatic alterations and amidst the coming and going and coming and going of all manner of creatures, the last and most fleeting of which is ourselves. Thoughts of this sort involve the contemplation of factors that lie entirely beyond the compass of our immediate experience. Yet not to allow such factors to creep into our perception-induced reverie would seriously impoverish the delight or awe we feel.

To verify the reality of this temporal inference, imagine that Bryce Canyon was simply and entirely the creation of the Disney Corporation. It was they who bought the land—as gray and uninteresting when they bought it as the Nevada desert—colored the sand, pieced together the pinnacles and taluses in workshops in southern California, then hauled them to Utah (taxes being lower there than in southern California; otherwise Bryce Canyon would be situated just east of Loma Linda), set them in place, and commenced phase two of the operation: the Media Blitz.

Have I not just drawn up a scenario that is every bit as revolting as Bryce Canyon is magnificent, simply by replacing time and the elements with commercialism and technology? But the important point is this: the *surfaces* are the same in both cases. Hence, it appears that the aesthetically crucial factors are far from exhausted by the surface features of the spectacle. Of course both natural selection (in the Darwinian model) and erosion are purely mechanistic accounts of physical processes, hence if we are to speak properly there can be no question of expression—no conscious interior making itself seen or felt. But this fact, if it is one, does not in the least prevent us from imagining or hypothesizing such an interior, and allowing this imaginary "world soul" to suffuse our experience.

These latter peregrinations, however much they may have been occasioned by Reid's expressionist doctrine, have led us somewhat afield from his central contentions. Let us briefly summarize his position by indicating what his answers are to the four questions with which we began this chapter. (a) What gets expressed? Inner states—states of mind or soul—are the content of any expressive vehicle. (b) Who (or what) does the expressing? Persons are properly regarded as the source of any expression, and in the ultimate instance, nature is regarded as an expression of the Person God is. (c) By what means is expression accomplished? A system of natural signs lies at the heart of Reid's account, a system which we may have to learn to employ, but which we seem to be able to comprehend without any special training. (d) Is anything transmitted or communicated in the act of expression? It could be said that the state of one's soul is transmitted, but that this transmission should involve an *act* of communication seems not to be a necessary component of Reid's theory. Indeed in the central case, where the virtue of a morally upright person shows through in that person's appearance and demeanor, any *intent* on the part of a person to effect such communication could well be self-defeating, since it would constitute a show of vanity antagonistic to the virtue of humility—effecting would give way to affecting.

When the expressiveness of *art* assumes the central position in a theory, however, communication is more likely to become "of the essence." Let us now look at one such theory.

Leo Tolstoy

Certainly communication is central to the expression theory put forward a century ago by the great Russian novelist Leo Tolstoy; emotion appears at every juncture as well. Let us briefly consider Tolstoy's main theses.

Tolstoy, as should be imagined, took his art seriously. Scornful of the notion that art exists to provide us with pleasure, or, worse yet, that it constitutes some form of play or amusement, he saw it as forging a bond of a certain sort between artist and audience—a bond of feeling. He exemplifies the artistic process, interestingly, not by citing any experiences of his own or of his fellow novelists, but by imagining a boy who has been frightened by a wolf, and who proceeds to relate the incident.

> In order to evoke in others the feeling he has experienced, [the boy] describes himself, his condition before the encounter, the surroundings, the wood, his own lightheartedness, and then the wolf's appearance, its movements, the distance between himself and the wolf, and so forth. All this, if only the boy when telling the story again experiences the feelings he had lived through, and infects the hearers and compels them to feel what he had experienced—is art. Even if the boy had not seen a wolf but had frequently been afraid of one, and if wishing to evoke in others the fear he had felt, he invented an encounter with a wolf and recounted it so as to make his hearers share the feelings he experienced when he feared the wolf, that also would be art. . . .
>
> The feelings with which the artist infects others may be most various—very strong or very weak, very important or very insignificant, very bad or very good. . . . If only the spectators or auditors are infected by the feelings which the author has felt, it is art.[5]

And more generally yet, art is characterized by Tolstoy as a human activity in which one person "consciously by means of certain external signs, hands on to others feelings he has lived through, and that others are infected by these feelings and also experience them."[6]

Notice the occurrence and recurrence of emotion in and through this process. First, some feeling is asserted to preexist in the artist's consciousness. It does not develop as the expressive act unfolds, but it is already present, and the artist feels compelled to express it. Second, this feeling is re-created in the artist through the telling of the story, or through whatever medium a particular artist works in. Third, the same feeling is then engendered in the listeners, or in the audience in general; they are said to be "infected" with it, and this infection is produced by the signs the artist is adept at manipulating. Thus for Tolstoy, communication is the ultimate aim of art, with the end of communication itself being something akin to universal brotherhood, in which art is "a means of union among men joining them together in the same feelings."[7]

This infectiousness is of primary importance in Tolstoy's theory—the "one indubitable sign distinguishing real art from its counterfeit."[8] And it brings with it yet another feeling, though one "quite distinct from all other feelings," namely, "that feeling . . . of joy and of spiritual union with another (the author) and with others (those who are also infected by it)."[9] However varied may be the emotions expressed by this or that artist in this or that work, the feeling of joy accompanying our experience of a genuine and significant work of art will always be of the same character. And indeed there does seem to arise in us some feeling of this sort in the presence of great art: be it Michelangelo's *Pietà,* Bach's "Es ist Vollbracht" aria, Picasso's *Guernica,* we do find some distinctively positive emotional experience emerging from our confrontation with these works, however somber may be the thoughts and associations they bring with their painful subject matter. And it is just possible that this sense of a "communion of spirits" lies at the heart of such an experience.

The degree of infectiousness of art, Tolstoy judges, depends on three conditions:

> (1) On the greater or lesser individuality of the feeling transmitted; (2) on the greater or lesser clearness with which the feeling is transmitted; (3) on the sincerity of the artist, that is, on the greater or lesser force with which the artist himself feels the emotions he transmits.[10]

Of these three, it is sincerity that Tolstoy ranks in the highest position; in fact, the other two follow from it, in a sense, since the sincere artist will transmit the most individual of feelings, and will inevitably do so with the greatest clarity. And he feels that a knowledgeable audience will detect such sincerity, or will in many cases detect its absence; where this latter circumstance occurs, "resistance immediately springs up, and the most individual and the newest feelings and the cleverest technique not only fail to produce any infection but actually repel."[11] In other words, when we feel we are being manipulated by a would-be artist for some purpose other than the earnest communication of an emotion deeply felt—be it for profit or glory or just the perverse satisfaction that some individuals derive from exercising control over others—we cease to resonate sympathetically with the artist, and the joyousness of the experience evaporates. We will have occasion to return to this notion of sincerity when we take up in full detail the question of intention in art. Surely no aesthetician ever leaned more heavily on it than Tolstoy.

Tolstoy's responses to our four questions thus differ somewhat from Reid's: (a) that which receives expression are feelings or emotions; (b) it is vital that we see this act of expression as emanating from one of our fellow human beings—in this, Tolstoy and Reid are largely in agreement: both regard it as insufficient merely to see a certain object as expressive, but Tolstoy is concerned to show that it is the *artist* who expresses certain feelings *through* the work of art; (c) the work itself consists in an arrangement of signs (though Tolstoy is not wedded to a theory of natural signs) that succeeds in recreating a certain feeling within the artist, and infecting an audience with that same feeling—the realization of the work causes artist and audience to resonate as one, emotionally; (d) this sympathetic resonation constitutes an act of *communication,* for no real artist creates in a vacuum; all artists project their works toward an audience (whether actual or hypothetical). And yet it is central to artists' purpose to recreate a particular feeling in themselves; merely manipulating an audience into undergoing certain feelings on their own is an activity antipathetic to the artistic process. Genuine communication requires sincerity; artistic sincerity demands that the emotions expressed be shared.

There are certain expression theories that regard this sharing as only a contingent aspect of the artistic process, and not of the essence of art. Let us now look at one such theory.

R. G. Collingwood

An interesting set of variations on these themes emerged several decades later, during the period between the two world wars, in the writings of the English philosopher-historian R.G. Collingwood. While not the artist Tolstoy was (though a clever stylist in his own right), Collingwood nevertheless articulated a theory of art that emphasized the process of *creation* as strongly as did Tolstoy's. Indeed, it could be claimed that creation occupies an even more central position in Collingwood, since Tolstoy's view shows a clear artist-audience separation (to be bridged, of course, by the work of art), while for Collingwood appreciating a work of art turns out itself to be a creative act.

Collingwood shared with Tolstoy the conviction that the emotion expressed in a work of art traces directly back to the artist; the work, that is to say, is not to be taken to be expressive in and of itself, apart from its connection to the mind that created it. Expression is a personal achievement, not a mere objective fact. But from this point onward, their theories diverge sharply, and even where they share similar intuitions, as they often do, about what is valuable in and what is antipathetic to the artistic process, they differ as to *why* this is the case.

The singular nature of Collingwood's approach first appears in the sharp distinction he draws between art and craft (though as should soon become apparent, much that we think of as art turns out, on Collingwood's analysis, to be craft, and many an object that we may regard as a product of craft has, on his account, a distinctly artistic component). He judges that "craft always involves a distinction between means and end, each clearly conceived as something distinct from the other but related to it," and that craft likewise "involves a distinction between planning and execution. The result to be obtained is preconceived or thought out before being arrived at."[12]

An end constitutes an interest—we are interested in achieving this or that goal—hence Collingwood strives to convince us that artistic creation is in no way end-oriented. He refers to those theories that ascribe to art this purpose or that as instances of the *technical* theory of art, and criticizes them with vehemence. His arguments have a distinctly intuitive character about them, in which an object we all can agree to be a product of craft is placed alongside one that we similarly will have no difficulty in calling a genuine work of art, and the critical characteristics of each are then elucidated. What have we to go on when we seek to divide up a certain conceptual terrain, after all, besides our intuition as to what lies where?

Among the theories that (mistakenly) attribute some goal or other to art would be included the one that Tolstoy developed, inasmuch as Tolstoy saw art ultimately as a form of communication and judged that this communication was effected through the evocation of emotions similar to those felt and expressed by the artist. Both of these elements, the evocation of particular emotions and the act of communication itself, constitute ends or purposes— interests, if you like—and Collingwood is intent on dismissing them from the realm of art proper. Interestingly, he shares Tolstoy's distaste for the "manipulation" of an audience; but *any* attempt at wringing emotional reactions from an audience is viewed by him as manipulative: even, therefore, the attempt made by the boy who had been frightened by the wolf.

The purest, most tawdry instance of a craft, as Collingwood conceives this notion, would be something like the fabrication of those small brass statuettes of the Eiffel Tower that are sold throughout Paris as souvenirs. The manufacturer begins with a crude likeness of the tower, makes a casting of it, then churns out thousands upon thousands of the statuettes—as many as the market will support. The idea precedes the fabrication; the raw material is agreed upon, and may be varied to suit different price levels (it may be tried in crystal, or in oak); the production follows mechanically; the items produced are qualitatively indistinguishable; the ultimate goal is to turn a profit. It is easy to see that this paradigm readily accommodates itself to much if not most of what is churned out for mass consumption by the television, cinema, and popular music industries these days, regardless how much they may seek to justify their more horrific and offensive productions by making appeal to "artistic" freedom. And in truth, a great many works that have found their way into museums or onto bookshelves or concert programs display that cast-from-the-same-mold appearance.

The paradigm instance of a work of art may be something akin to a lyric poem, in which the only goal is the realization of the poem itself. The ultimate shape it takes, however—the structure it adopts, the point it makes—all develop in the writing process itself, while the effect it produces on the reading public (if it ever gets that far) is purely a contingent matter.

In between these two paradigms stretches a nearly limitless expanse of objects that share to varying degrees properties of both art and craft. But, Collingwood believes, that great stretch of indeterminacy should not inhibit us from specifying the fundamental characteristics of the polar extremes, nor from seeking to fathom the extent to which each is embodied in any particular work. To close our eyes or ears to anything but those (few) works that unqualifiedly merit the description "pure art" would be to miss out on almost all of the great creations of the human spirit. All architecture would have to be dismissed, for all buildings serve some purpose; all religious art would have to be dismissed, as well as all works with a political or social message, for messages in general seek to alter the conduct of others; all painting that has as part of its aim to represent a scene would be disqualified, and so on. In drawing our attention to the art-craft distinction, therefore, Collingwood is merely attempting to (a) encourage us to focus on the artistic quality embedded in certain creations, and (b) avoid confusing this artistic quality with certain other features of artifacts that frequently cohabit with the artistic.

Expressiveness is at the heart of this artistic quality. The very characteristics that Tolstoy found to constitute the hallmarks of expressiveness—intensity, clarity, sincerity—enjoy an equally important status in Collingwood's account, only they can in no way be seen to contribute to any purpose, even the purpose of communication. They are, rather, hallmarks of a very individualized act, one in which, on finding an intense feeling welling up within us, we strive through the manipulation of some medium—words, colors, tones—to clarify to ourselves the content of this feeling. If we pursue this urge toward clarification sincerely, to a state of completion, we will have succeeded in expressing the heretofore elusive feeling; and we will be, for a precious moment, artists. Tolstoy's paradigmatic artist, the boy who had taken fright, still deserves, on Collingwood's view, to be considered an artist, but not for his having evoked certain feelings in his audience, not for his having communicated to them anything of his situation, and certainly not for his having previously undergone an experience of an intense sort; he would be an artist purely for having clarified to his own satisfaction the nature or essence of an emotion that had been squirming about inside him. Tolstoy did demand this, but he demanded so much more; Collingwood's judgment is that the largest part of this "so much more" falls within the domain of craft, not art.

Anyone who derives satisfaction from the work of others, as we may say of the average (or especially the *above*-average) member of an audience, turns out, on Collingwood's account, to be active and creative, much as the artist was, though perhaps to a lesser degree. What we get out of a concert, for example, "is something which we have to reconstruct in our own minds, and by our own efforts; something which remains forever inaccessible to a person who cannot or will not make efforts of the right kind."[13] And though a certain susceptibility to the pleasure of sound may lead some people *to* music, nevertheless "they must, in proportion as they are more susceptible, take the more pains to prevent that susceptibility from interfering with their power of listening."[14] That is to say, if we listen to music seriously—by which I mean that we actually *listen* to it, rather than let it wash over us or serve as a background for some other more "important" activity—we find ourselves, under the guidance of the work in question, focusing and channeling the flow of our own emotions as we (a) form expectations, (b) revise these expectations when the music takes an unforeseen turn and opens up new auditory vistas before us, (c) struggle to grasp the sequence of discrete sounds as a whole, and so forth. It may take years of training to develop one's skill at composition, but it takes as much effort, though of a somewhat different sort, to become a skilled listener. The urge toward clarity, the intensity of feeling, the sincerity of purpose, Collingwood contends, are as much present in the activity of a serious listener as they are in that of a serious composer.

It should not be inferred from the emphasis that Collingwood places on the personal nature of artistic expression that he sees the artist as working, and being content to work, in a sort of vacuum, distanced from the reactions of any audience, whether actual or hypothetical. Just as we often learn more about ourselves through dialogues we have with others than we would if we remained in isolation, so too can an audience lead an artist to ever greater depths of self-realization. Flaubert once declared that he directed his writings toward *les amis inconnus;* a painter of my acquaintance, in a description of his method, included as one of the necessary steps the "imagined laughter of family and friends."[15] Reference to an absent or even a hypothetical public is a frequent companion to the more general urge to create; here it may open up a path worth pursuing, there it may impose a vital constraint on an otherwise unbridled imagination. "Whatever airs they may give themselves," Collingwood asserts, "artists have always been in the habit of treating the public as collaborators."[16] When any artist undertakes a certain task,

> it is a labour in which he invites the community to participate; for their function as audience is not passively to accept his work, but to do it over again for themselves. . . . The audience is perpetually present to him as a

factor in his artistic labour; not as an anti-aesthetic factor, corrupting the sincerity of his work by considerations of reputation and reward, but as an aesthetic factor, defining what the problem is which as an artist he is trying to solve . . . and what constitutes a solution to it.[17]

Collaboration between artist and audience, on Collingwood's view, thus turns out to be something of a practical expedient—perhaps even a practical necessity—if any genuinely expressive act is to take place. And yet it is not "of the essence" of art, properly considered, inasmuch as expression is regarded by him to be an ultimately personal gesture.

Art, for Collingwood, constitutes something of a language; in fact, it includes many languages—as many as there are media. This is a common theme among aestheticians, but what makes Collingwood's version of it special is his construal of language in general as expressive *in essence*. His basic thesis involves the striking claim that "the expression of *any* given thought is effected through the emotion accompanying it."[18] Responding to those who see the essence of language as consisting in a system of arbitrary symbols agreed upon by convention, he reasons (in an argument very similar to the one we saw Reid employing to establish the reality of natural signs) that we could not even reach any such agreement if we were not already in possession of a language by which to register our agreement: "intellectualized language thus presupposes imaginative language or language proper."[19]

Reversing a common misapprehension—that conventional discourse allows us to express ourselves clearly (for we can agree on precise meanings of our terms), while art muddies thought by allowing feeling to intrude—Collingwood believes that in fact it is the artist who can speak most clearly of all, being in closer touch with original modes of expression than those who depend on mere arbitrary symbols: "the dance is the mother of all languages."[20] Still, it is not to be forgotten that the language of art is self-originative and self-expressive at base, and while communication is a natural, useful, and perhaps inevitable product of language, it is not, on his view, an essential component.

There is much that is insightful in Collingwood's aesthetics, much that is interesting and provocative, and much that borders on the absurd. In some respects his theory could be deemed to constitute a laudable effort at toning down some of the excessive demands of a theory such as Tolstoy's. The first phase of Tolstoy's account is done away with entirely in Collingwood's: an artist, for Collingwood, doesn't begin with an experience clearly felt and understood, but with an impulse, an urgency to exteriorize a feeling that, at its onset, is obscure even to the artist. Expression thus *becomes* clarification. Second, an audience will not, for Collingwood, be "infected" with anything (infection implies an undesirable intrusion from outside); instead, they will use the "entity" fabricated by the artist in order to bring their own experience to a point of heightened clarity. Artistic expression is thus seen to be rather liberally distributed among the population, and not necessarily concentrated in those select few who carry the noble rank of "artist."

Negatively, an excessively rigorous commitment away from any kinds of artistic purposes or interests leads Collingwood to personalize expression in a most unnatural fashion, thereby relegating communication to a subordinate position, at least within his conceptual hierarchy, and generating a philosophy of the origin and nature of language that is difficult to believe, to say nothing of defend.

Thus, briefly: (a) what, for Collingwood, gets expressed?—emotions; (b) who does the expressing?—the artist, though it must be understood that *each of us* is an artist to the extent that we succeed in clarifying our own emotions to ourselves through the interaction we undertake with a "work of art"; (c) by what means is this expression accomplished?—by the manipulation of language, given the understanding that "language" reaches far beyond mere words and into all manner of expressive domains, such as colors, shapes, movements, or sounds; (d) is anything communicated in the act of expression?—not necessarily, though communication is a frequent expedient to expression.

A Pause for Reflection

Numerous objections can be and have been raised against expressionism over the years. Let us arrange these objections into two broad categories, one encompassing considerations pertinent to the "inner-outer" distinction and the other raising questions about emotions and how well we can know and describe them.

Inner-Outer

If an inference to some inner state is a critical element in our overall appreciation of a work of art, then it would seem that an enormous number of artworks immediately place themselves beyond all possibility of our aesthetic enrichment or enjoyment. What can we possibly know of the inner, spiritual state of a pre-Columbian sculptor, an ancient Greek potter, a medieval stained-glass master, a court composer under the reign of Henry IV? We may at least know the name of the last of these, and two facts about his life, but that is precious little to go on. Was the pre-Columbian sculptor expressing personal sentiments in stone or producing carvings under mortal threat from a peevish tyrant? All the anonymous and virtually anonymous artists leave behind works that can have only the most speculative connection to the consciousness from which they emerged: is not our appreciation of them destined to be as limited as our knowledge of the true character of the elderly woman whose portrait photo caught our eye at a flea market? And yet we do appreciate these works. Often they appear in museums; private individuals clamber over one another to purchase them; books are written about them. The obvious inference would seem to be that we are looking for or finding in them something other than the record of an individual consciousness.

To complicate matters, there has been a tendency in recent philosophy to look askance at the very notion of "inner" or "spiritual" states, to regard them as fictions of outmoded philosophical systems that fail to align themselves with current psychological findings, and to search for ways to explain them away. Thus the identity theorist with materialist leanings will regard these so-called inner states as reducible in their entirety to some set of bodily determinants;* the behaviorist will focus only on the perceivable aspects of behavior, dismissing any alleged "hidden" source of such behavior as scientifically irrelevant; the epiphenomenalist will treat our mental life as something of a byproduct of our physical life, as smoke is the byproduct of the phenomenon of combustion. And although "mind" constitutes a byproduct that is sufficiently different from its source and sufficiently interesting in its effects to merit a name of its own, the causal or productive relationship is strictly one-directional, that is, body always generates mind; mind never generates anything on its own.

It stands to reason that this attitude toward mental phenomena should make itself felt in the aesthetic domain as well, and, as may be expected, one of the first casualties was the expression theory. On any of the approaches that we have considered to this point, the inner-outer relationship is critical: for Reid, one's character makes itself apparent through external, behavioral signs; for Tolstoy, one's emotional life is captured and transmitted through one artistic medium or another; for Collingwood, indistinct feelings work their way to clarity through a process of exteriorization. But if it should prove to be the case that there *is* nothing beyond observable behavior—the signs or the artistic forms—then either the expression theory

---

*An identity theorist with idealist leanings, on the other hand, will reduce so-called bodily phenomena to various states of mind. Despite their being in the right, identity theorists of this persuasion are in short supply these days.

should be abandoned, or it should receive some radical revision, in which any allusion to anything inner is written out.

Emotion

Even with artists whom we fancy we know quite well, the notion that some form of communication is effected through their works at the emotional level—"from the heart, may it go to the heart"—appears to involve some precarious leaps. Van Gogh, for example, said of his painting of the bridge at Trinquetaille ("in which sky and river are the color of absinthe, the quais a shade of lilac, . . . the iron bridge an intense blue," and so on), "*I am trying to get something utterly heartbroken.*"[21] Now, must it be the case that *my* heart must absolutely break in order for me to appreciate this work?—to appreciate it *properly?* Will anyone's heart break at the sight of this painting, as van Gogh's did, for some mysterious reason, at the sight of the bridge, or at least in a manner that somehow found perfect expression in this representation of the bridge? His mental instability is well documented; must one, in effect, be similarly unbalanced to get on the same wavelength as this work? This would indeed place bizarre restrictions on the concept of a "qualified viewer."

J.W.N. Sullivan, in his book *Beethoven,* cites some program notes for Schubert's unfinished symphony:

> We begin with deep earnestness, out of which springs perturbation; after which almost painful anxieties are conjured up till the dissolution draws the veil from an unexpected solace, which is soon infused with cheerfulness, to be however abruptly checked. After an instant of apprehension, we are startled by a threat destructive to the very capability of rest, which in its turn subsides. From the terrible we pass to the joyful, and soon to playfulness and tenderness.[22]

And on and on it goes. Even though such descriptive terms may be applicable to portions of the music, it seems unreasonable to expect any listener to experience such a sequence of states in rapid-fire succession, and unlikely that Schubert himself underwent any corresponding emotional odyssey. The likelihood of any significant coincidence between the response of a listener and the experience of the creator would itself be the product reached by multiplying these two improbabilities together; and yet that is what the "heart to heart" approach to expression seems to demand.

Speaking more generally, must religious art provoke in us religious sentiments? Must nihilistic art make nihilists of us? Can we place such strictures on the types of response that are appropriate to works of art? And how do we police these restrictions? Surely some reactions do seem decidedly inappropriate. For example, in the thoroughly mediocre film *Never on Sunday*, the character played by Melina Mercouri takes leave from her usual profession on Sundays and goes instead to the amphitheater, where she avidly watches performances of ancient Greek tragedies. Regardless of the work being performed, whether *Oedipus* or *Antigone*, she invariably provides a synopsis of the plot that ends with her saying "and they all go to the seashore." Now clearly her response to these works is eccentric. Is she not overlooking some major features of the action (the ripping out of one's eyeballs seems hardly to be an act that would be followed by a playful romp in the sand)?

But there are many less extreme cases, where people of considerable artistic sensitivity find seemingly conflicting messages in one and the same work: any two analyses, say, of Eliot's *Four Quartets* should convince us of this. Is only one of them right, or is "right" not a concept to be employed in such circumstances?

How well, for that matter, do we even know our own emotional states? We are treated by legions of unimaginative journalists to interviews in which the question "How do you feel about . . .?" is invariably asked, and the answers are invariably unilluminating. Certain versions of the expression theory, however, such as Tolstoy's, require some awareness on our part of how we are feeling, and some awareness by artists as to how they are feeling—indeed, the artists are called upon to match feelings once felt with feelings now rekindled. Demands of this nature are not easily met.

"Wiser" (?) Approaches

Actually, although criticisms of the above sort have become almost commonplace in the past few decades, versions of expressionism sensitive to such considerations have been "in the public domain" for quite some time. Let us look briefly at one older theory and two more recent ones.

Sully-Prudhomme

The French poet-philosopher René F.-A. Sully-Prudhomme wrestles with the problem of the inner-outer relationship in his *L'Expression dans les beaux-arts*, which was published in 1883—thirteen years earlier than Tolstoy's *What is Art?* In this work, he observes that we quite systematically distinguish in the language between mental phenomena and material phenomena. And while significant inroads may have been made by materialists and physiologists in explaining human behavior in nonspiritualistic terms, there nevertheless exists no vocabulary that effectively "material-izes" mind and its activities. Hence, speaking in terms of some exterior-interior relationship is not only understandable by anyone, independent of philosophical commitments, it is in fact the only effective means at hand for dealing with a huge class of highly significant phenomena. In his own words:

> When we thus speak of soul and body, of the faculties of the soul, of mind and matter, it is to avoid an offensive neologism, . . . and we mean only to distinguish within the human domain between two empirically distinct classes of phenomena, one of which, generally referred to as "physical," affects the senses of the observer and can be directly observed by him mani-fested on the exterior of certain kindred beings, the other of which, called in general moral *(moraux)*, is only directly observable in himself. We leave completely in reserve the question of what the substratum of these two classes of phenomena consists in, how these substances differ if they really are distinct, or if there really are substances involved at all.[23]

Sully-Prudhomme then proceeds to develop an account of expression that traces out a certain identity of character between the vehicle of expres-sion—the sensible component in any gesture seen as expressive—and the state expressed. Thus the weeping willow whose branches droop limply and are tossed about at the whim of the wind shares something in its languid character with an individual in the grip of sadness; a melody we term "sprightly" tends to bounce about playfully, much as we ourselves do when we are in a sprightly mood.

Suzanne Langer

Several decades later, Suzanne Langer, in *Philosophy in a New Key,* reached the conclusion that "music is not the cause or cure of feeling but its logical expression."[24] The negative portion of this thesis is established by arguments similar to those sketched above; the positive component—that music is the logical expression of feeling—is grounded in her claim (one similar to that suggested by Sully-Prudhomme) that there can be observed a variety of congruences between musical phenomena and emotional states.

Actually, the philosopher Wittgenstein (whom we met in Chapter One) developed a theory of linguistic meaning early in his career that proved to have a profound influence on Langer's aesthetics. Known as the picture theory of meaning, Wittgenstein suggested that while a photograph might offer a picture of the visible form of a state of affairs, a verbal description of that state of affairs succeeded in designating it by providing a picture of its logical form.[25] Some mysterious, isomorphic relationship was thus asserted to exist between the world and statements about the world. The philosophical community was not overwhelmed by this theory; few even claimed to understand what it meant to talk about the "logical form" of reality (though Suzanne Langer was among those few); and Wittgenstein himself repudiated the whole enterprise in his later writings.

But while the picture theory, as a theory of linguistic meaning in general, deserved the icy reception it received, it contains elements that sit very well in an account of *artistic* meaning. While no isomorphic relationship can reasonably by detected between the statement "The broom is in the closet" and an actual broom actually standing in an actual closet, there is something to be said for the notion that works of art and human beings are both describable by terms that make references to states of feeling. People and paintings alike are readily referred to as "somber" or "sprightly," and these parallel ascriptions could well be based on the existence of certain congruences between human behavior and the appearance given off by the figures on a canvas. Such congruences, then, would allow certain artworks to function as symbols of our emotional life.

In her major work *Feeling and Form,* Langer developed this theme with respect to all the arts, not just music, declaring there that "art is the creation of forms symbolic of human feeling."[26] The term "expression" has been replaced with the concept of the symbolic, but the spirit remains the same: we are not to focus on how the artist felt or how the artwork makes us feel, but on what we can learn of our own emotional life from a close consideration of the arts.

The notion of significant form, which we met with first in our consideration of Clive Bell's formalist aesthetic, is adopted by Langer but remade in a most critical respect. Whereas for Bell "significant" carried principally the connotation of "highly important," for Langer it assumes more of the sense that is packed into it etymologically: sign-ificant. Art presents us with forms that signify, in their own peculiar manner, feeling states common to human life. Surely these forms still deserve to be thought of as "highly important," but their importance, on her account, derives not from provoking that peculiar "aesthetic emotion" that Bell speaks of, but from symbolically embodying emotions, as only art can do:

> The tonal structures we call "music" bear a close logical similarity to the forms of human feeling—forms of growth and attenuation, flowing and stowing, conflict and resolution, speed, arrest, terrific excitement, calm, or subtle activation and dreamy lapses—not joy and sorrow, perhaps, but the poignancy of either and both—the greatness and brevity and eternal passing of

everything vitally felt. Such is the pattern, or logical form, of sentience; and the pattern of music is that same form worked out in pure, measured sound and silence. Music is a tonal analogue of emotive life.[27]

And so is it with all the other arts, each offering an analogue of our emotive life in terms dictated by its own medium—painting presenting colored shapes in two-dimensional space, sculpture introducing solid substances and a third dimension, literature playing within the domain of verbal depictions of life.

Langer continues to speak in terms of a "logical expression" of feeling, but clearly this expression needn't go *from* the heart (as so many expressionists have claimed) nor *to* the heart: rather, it is *about* the heart. Our everyday language, she believes, is drastically deficient when it comes to describing or characterizing our emotional states; we can offer only the most wooden accounts of our feelings when called upon to do so. Art picks up where language leaves off, however, and through means unique to its province (for language, as normally employed, rarely operates analogically—it offers analogies, it doesn't embody them), it provides enlightenment concerning this rich and complex area of human experience.

Alan Tormey

The language of aesthetic discourse becomes of paramount importance in Tormey's critical revision of expressionism. He argues against any and all versions of the theory that stress a connection between an artist and a work of art, claiming: "Common to all theories of this type are two assumptions: (1) that an artist, in creating a work of art, is invariably engaged in expressing something; and (2) that the expressive qualities of the art work are the direct consequence of this act of expression. I shall argue that there is no reason to accept these assumptions."[28]

If artworks are not to be taken as expressive of an artist's inner state, then it might be inferred that art is not expressive at all; but this is not the inference Tormey makes. We speak so readily of works of art as being expressive that it is important not to dismiss such attributions summarily, but to know what we are doing when we make them. And in his estimate, statements attributing expressive properties to works of art "should be construed as statements *about the works themselves;* and the presence of expressive properties does not entail the occurrence of a prior *act* of expression."[29]

Tormey declares the term "expressive" to be "systematically ambiguous," at times leading us to infer some state behind the expressive phenomenon—sadness behind the face that expresses sadness—and at times carrying no such inferential overtones—the "cruel" face unhappily possessed by the nicest of individuals. The latter face possesses what Tormey calls the "expressive property" cruelty, rather than simply the property of cruelty. The property of cruelty, when perceived, provokes hatred, fear or anger; the *expressive* property cruelty is an occasion for none of these, and it may even arouse pity—"How unfortunate, that such a nice man should have a face like that!"[30]

Artworks commonly possess expressive properties, and such properties are those "whose names also designate intentional states of persons."[31] Furthermore, their expressive properties owe their being in some imprecise way to nonexpressive properties. Thus the tender, nostalgic nature of Ravel's *Pavane pour une infante défunte* depends upon "the contour of the melodic line, the quasi-modal harmonic structure, the moderate tempo, and the limited dynamic range."[32]

Tormey thus asserts that a certain analogy exists between artworks and persons, but it is radically different from the one alleged to exist by Langer and Sully-Prudhomme. For these latter two, some congruence could be observed between human conative behavior and the qualities discerned in certain art objects, which leads us to judge the one—the art objects—to be expressive of the other. For Tormey, just as certain modes of (externally observable) behavior correlate with certain emotional states in the expressive actions of a person, so too do certain nonexpressive properties of artworks correlate with their expressive properties. But—and this is the critical difference between the two analogies—Tormey does not force us to infer across from the artistic realm to the human, as do Langer and Sully-Prudhomme. On Tormey's view, a simple parallel exists between the behavior-expression relation in the person and the nonexpressive-expressive relation in an artwork; for the other two, the parallel between certain qualities in artworks and certain patterns discernible in human behavior enable the former to express or symbolize the latter. (And let us remember that even they discourage us from inferring from the qualities of an art object to the inner state of the artist.)

Nonexpressive properties are said by Tormey to "constitute" expressive properties, but only loosely or ambiguously—no set of nonexpressive properties will ever be agreed upon as constituting necessary and sufficient conditions for a given expressive property. And unlike the behavior-expression relation in persons, we cannot question artworks as we question people to determine just what their gestures express: the nonexpressive properties are all we have to go on.

What we have from Tormey, therefore, is, first, a dismissal of traditional expressionist theories, such as the three we examined at the beginning of this chapter. Furthermore, he even recommends an abandonment of any symbolist interpretation of art, inasmuch as a symbol points beyond itself, while the expressive properties of art objects, on his view, inhere in these objects and exercise no designative function. Finally, we are offered a description of certain of the linguistic conventions embedded in our aesthetic discourse, principal among these being the conventions that govern our use of the term "expressive," and an account of why they function as they do. It would thus seem more appropriate to term this approach, not an expression theory, but an "expression" theory.

Wisdom Renounced

Emotion

There are plausible answers that can be offered to a number of the objections raised against the expression theory in certain of its versions. The variety of descriptions of emotional states allegedly expressed in a single artwork, for example, needn't be taken to indicate a degree of ambiguity that would be fatal to the overall theory. The fact that different people happen to settle on different terms by which to characterize the emotional tone of a work can be explained in any of several ways.

First, it seems undeniable that our language is rather stiff and unsubtle when it comes to describing emotions. As J.W.N. Sullivan observes, "Language . . . is poor in names for subjective states, and consequently in names for the imputed properties of objects that produce those states. Even such words as love and hate, dealing with emotions to which mankind has always paid great attention, are merely portmanteau words. Within their meanings are not only differences of degree, but differences of kind."[33] Actually, we do stumble around noticeably when trying to capture in words what it is that we feel, or what we think someone or something is expressing. Indeed, of all our uses of language this could well be the one about which we are tempted to say, as Wittgenstein once said of philosophizing, "One gets to the point where one would like just to emit an inarticulate sound."[34]

It may be possible to make an analogy between emotion-descriptions and color-descriptions in the following fashion: Display a particular color sample to a group of people, a sample that contains an unusual or unfamiliar blend of pigments, and we can expect a variety of different descriptions of the color to be offered. We are not tempted by this diversity, however, to say that each person actually saw the color differently. This being the case, it stands to reason that our characterizations of the emotional content of particular works of art will vary as well.

Sullivan cites a remark of Mendelssohn in support of the above line of thinking. According to Mendelssohn, "What any music *I* like expresses for me is not *thoughts too indefinite* to clothe in words, but *too definite.*—If you asked me what I thought on the occasion in question, I say, the song itself precisely as it stands."[35] Hence it could well be that those who contend that the variance among people's descriptions of the content expressed by a certain work of art reflects unfavorably on the expression theory seem to have an excessively high regard either for the precision of our language, or for our ability to use it precisely.

Second, it could well be the case that what appears as variance at one level is in some sense uniformity at a deeper level. If several people were asked to describe something deliciously sweet, person A might mention a piece of chocolate, person B a ripe peach, and person C a dish of ice cream. Now it so happens that person B gets headaches from chocolate, person A gets toothaches from ice cream, and person C breaks out in hives at the mere mention of peaches; yet for all that, there is a certain underlying compatibility among their responses—it is not as if they didn't understand what was being requested of them, or supplied answers that were somehow contradictory. In the same way, our descriptions of artworks may *seem* at times to be at variance, but may in reality circumscribe an area of conformity.

Third, though admittedly it is difficult, if not impossible, to establish acceptable canons of adjudication, it seems undeniable that some people are better at describing emotions than others. It would be astonishing, in fact, if this were *not* the case—if each of us showed an equal aptitude for capturing emotions in words. We might just as soon assert that we all possess equal gymnastic abilities! However stubborn some people may be when it comes to relinquishing their own emotional characterizations, it nevertheless seems perfectly reasonable to prefer certain descriptions over others. And this may go a long way toward resolving apparent ambiguities.

There is the further question of what we are to do with the emotion felt both in producing and in appreciating works of art. To be sure, the terrain here is filled with tangles and brambles; but simply to renounce all attempts at making headway in this area—to declare, as Langer does, that art is neither the cause nor the cure of feeling, or focus, as Tormey does, on expressive properties to the complete exclusion of the dynamics of aesthetic experience—is to be guilty, in the theoretical domain, of a certain "bad faith."

The fact is, we choke and tremble, or to speak more accurately, *I* choked and trembled on entering the Eglise St. Philibert in Tournus, unsure whether the edifice that suddenly enclosed me was constructed of stone dappled with light, or of light punctuated by stone; the fact is that I was obliged to leave a concert after Beethoven's Opus 111 piano sonata because I was so thoroughly shaken and so lovingly assuaged by it that the remainder of the program (Liszt and Debussy, I think) would have constituted an unthinkable affront to my emotions. Each of us can supply instances of our own in which we have been profoundly moved and indelibly marked by one work of art or another. These are facts that must be dealt with.

Nor are artists mere machines that create. Of course many works have been mechanically produced over the centuries, just as many meals have been thrown together simply out of the need to put food into our stomachs; but some meals, and some works of art, are assembled with a care that bespeaks love. Collingwood recognized this and constructed his distinction between art and craft to do justice to it. If we find his theory of art-as-language and language-as-expression to be excessive and implausible, we must still give him credit for facing the facts—the *emotional* facts of aesthetic experience—head on, and not shunting them to the side in favor of a theoretical approach which, finding such facts to be erratic and unstable, chooses to ignore them.

Surely Tolstoy's theory suffers from excesses similar in degree, if not in kind, to Collingwood's. It is just not the case that the members of an audience—even the most intense and sympathetic ones—undergo the same emotional experience as that of the artist, and highly unlikely that the artist undergoes the kind of experience in the process of creation that Tolstoy demands. No matter how gripping an account may be of the terror felt in a particular circumstance, when read in the comfort of one's home or viewed in the relative comfort provided by a theater, the work will not terrify us. We will feel something, and the better the account, the stronger the feeling; but it will not be terror. No one, in the entire history of humankind, ever read *anything* while terrified. The people who sit next to me on the plane and read all the while that I am in a state of terror are not themselves terrified. If the turbulence mounts to a level at which they are a bit agitated, they may force themselves to continue reading to attempt to drown out any anxieties; but when terror really strikes, the book slams shut.

The artist, too, is not likely to undergo the same emotional experience, even while striving to re-create it in description. The wolf is gone, and the hostile, unsympathetic forest has been replaced by a familiar and welcoming room; a feeling of some urgency compels the artist to keep writing, but that feeling is not one of terror. And in those circumstances where, under some delusional influence, we may actually feel something akin to terror, it is practically unthinkable that we will have the composure and presence of mind to craft a convincing account of it. Still, even if Tolstoy and others have misdescribed the nature of the emotional experience, it doesn't follow that it is not worth taking the trouble to capture it in theory, and it surely doesn't follow that there is no such experience to capture.

Communication

In addition to the emotional element in aesthetic experience, the expression theory, in most of its versions, acknowledges some form of communication between artist and audience. In this, as in any instance of communication, something is emitted and something received, and the family of problems normally attributed to expression theory focuses on (a) the indeterminacy of the message sent, (b) the uncertainty surrounding what we take ourselves to have received, and (c) the matter of whether we received what the artist intended us to receive. Some possible means of dealing with (a) and (b) have been suggested above, in our discussion of the alleged ambiguity of emotional experience and our descriptions of it. It could well be that at some level of experience we resonate sympathetically with works of art and with one another, and it is perfectly easy to imagine that such resonance is indeed difficult to capture in words.

Furthermore, it would be a strange sort of coincidence if, when we do find ourselves in sympathy with a work of art, it should be for reasons utterly dissimilar to those that led the artist to instill the work with precisely those qualities that we value. Surely this happens sometimes, but it would be bizarre if it happened as a rule. I, the listener, am touched by what I can only characterize as the sweet melancholy of a Chopin nocturne; Chopin, the composer, imparted that sweet melancholy to his work and meant for me to receive it. Perhaps I cannot say in any precise terms how the work makes me feel; surely I cannot dictate how Chopin must have felt in composing it; and yet he wove something into the nocturne that I unravel as I listen to it. What more do we need in order to claim that an act of communication has taken place? And this communication is realized through the expressive object that is the work of art.

Point c above—whether we received what the artist intended us to receive—is not a matter to be dealt with in any summary fashion. The question of the role of an artist's intentions in aesthetic discernment is an enormously important one, and has accordingly received an enormous amount of attention in critical and philosophical writings during the past half century. The type of answer one gives to this question tells a great deal about the nature of one's overall commitment to art and its objects. Our next chapter, therefore, is devoted to examining the matter of artistic intention in some detail.

— 5 —

Intentions, Intentionality, and Artistic Communication

For the past several decades, philosophers, critics, and artists themselves have carried on an earnest debate as to whether, in order to arrive at a proper understanding and appreciation of a work of art, it is necessary to have some knowledge of what the artist intended to express or accomplish in it.

The belief that such knowledge is vital has been held by various individuals at various times, reaching back well before just "the past several decades": we saw the importance of the intentional component in Tolstoy's theory of art (written over a century ago), inasmuch as the notion of sincerity is central to his analysis, and sincerity can only be understood in terms of intentionality. Through the Romantic period the aims and the emotional states of artists were commonly cited in critical analyses (smudges on the title page of Beethoven's *Missa Solemnis,* for example, were taken to be teardrops, providing a specially intimate glimpse into the consciousness of the composer). Even as early as the first century A.D., we find the rhetorician Longinus showing an inclination to peek behind a work into the mind of its creator when he observes that "sublimity is the echo of a great soul," and suggests that "Homer enters into the sublime actions of his heroes" and "shares the full inspiration of the combat."[1]

While it is thus difficult to affix a date to the origin of the intentional hypothesis, it was in 1946 that this hypothesis was proclaimed to be fallacious, in a celebrated article by William Wimsatt and Monroe Beardsley entitled "The Intentional Fallacy." This one article touched off a debate that burned for decades, and while it would seem that all facets of the issue must by now have been explored, it is still doubtful that we have heard the last

109

word on the matter. Indeed, it is hoped that if no new words are uttered here, at least some new light might be shed, for I hold this to be not a tangential issue of passing concern, but a pivotal question of abiding importance.

The Intentional Fallacy

The very title of Wimsatt and Beardsley's article imparted to their denial of the intentional thesis a certain air of importance. It is one thing to be wrong on an issue—everybody is wrong some of the time, and most people are wrong most of the time. But to be guilty of having committed a fallacy is most egregious. A fallacy is a mental error of a peculiar, systematic sort, in which anyone or everyone who pursues a certain line of thinking does so wrongheadedly. Once apprised of this wrongheadedness, however, it is expected that they will recognize their error for what it is and thenceforth "think straight." Some years earlier, the philosopher G.E. Moore had deemed a certain position in ethics to be guilty of the "naturalistic fallacy," and the formidable tremors produced by this declaration may have encouraged Wimsatt and Beardsley to patent a fallacy of their own. Whether or not this was the motivation, the effect was similarly momentous within the field of aesthetics.

Focusing almost exclusively on poetry, Wimsatt and Beardsley isolated as their principal point of concern a certain tendency on the part of critics and teachers to retreat into questions of biography, socio- or psychobiography, history, cultural studies, or the like the moment a poem might cease speaking clearly and directly to a reader. Their recommendation is that instead of turning away from the poem and toward these peripheral studies, we should immerse ourselves more deeply in the poem itself: "the poem . . . is detached from the author at birth and goes about the world beyond his power to intend about it or control it."[2] Whatever was intended by it, whatever control was exercised over it should be seen as packed into the poem itself at the moment of its issue, not as looming behind it as some diaphanous "declaration of intent." In short, "the poet's aim must be judged . . . by the art of the poem itself."[3]

At first glance this outlook has much to recommend it. For one thing, it can never do any harm for us to pay closer attention to the details, the ins and outs of any work of art, poem or otherwise. To be sure, such scrutiny is not always rewarded. We may look or listen in vain for depths that are nowhere to be found, but this too is important to know. If it is a poem we are considering, there is a genuine sense in which the language is given, and it is up to us to work to make the images cohere and to discern where they are pointing. Occasionally we may have to look up a word: "poly-philoprogenitive" is not part of anyone's *basic* vocabulary, though a select few may know its meaning even before running afoul of it in T.S. Eliot's poem "Mr. Eliot's Sunday Morning Service" (and those few probably wouldn't have to look up "sutlers," in the next line, nor "superfetation," a bit further on, either). Still, knowledge of that sort falls far short of some sort of biographical minutia—the circumstances under which Eliot first came across this word, what personal significance it held for him—that allegedly would help place the word in the poem and pull the whole work together.

In fact, the position Wimsatt and Beardsley take underscores the respon-sibility of the poet to craft a work in a way that doesn't require a reader to probe into the details of the poet's private life. Though they stress the critical aspect of the experience of a poem, it is a clear corollary of their view that poets ought not appeal to arcane details of their private lives that may be difficult for a reader to gain access to. What strike us are the images that conjure up experiences we are in a position—by virtue of our common humanness and our common linguistic heritage—to *share* with the poet. Those that are of a singularly private significance are employed at the poet's own risk.

To give an example, suppose I were to include, in a poem of my own, the following line: "I have waded in the ripe waters of Mystic Islands." It would be reasonable for a reader, coming across this utterance, to think that I am suggesting I have been nibbling at the edges of the transcendent, probing the transnormal, or perhaps engaging in some sort of reverie. This is what the words would suggest to anyone conversant with the English language, and who perhaps knows a thing or two about religion; this is the kind of knowledge and information it is reasonable for me to expect from any reader. It would be absolutely unreasonable on my part to demand that any reader, in order to qualify as sufficiently informed to do justice to my poem, be apprised of the fact that one summer I worked (for $1.50 an hour) at an incredibly tacky housing development on the southern New Jersey shore which bears, to this day, the stunningly pompous and incongruous name "Mystic Islands"; that my particular assignment there was with the water and sewer company; and that consequently I did spend many an hour wading in waters that from time to time could justly be termed "ripe"! The introduction of this set of biographical facts can hardly overwhelm the natural implications of the language and impose a different slant on the poem. The oddity here is, if I were enough of a poet to generate sufficient interest in myself that certain of my admirers would go careening off on an attempt to piece together a picture of my life, I would not have been using arcane and misleading imagery such as this to begin with. And if I had made a career out of appeals to arcana, it would have been a most solitary and unheralded career.

In short, just as, on Wimsatt and Beardsley's account, the reader ought to stay "within the confines" of the poem in endeavoring to understand it, so too should the poet leave a sufficiency of scraps of meaning within those confines in order to encourage the reader to tarry there. And those who don't should be prepared to pay the price of noncomprehension.

Furthermore, Wimsatt and Beardsley are well aware that artists are seldom the best persons to turn to in search of a deeper understanding of their works. To begin with, among the practitioners of the principal art forms, only those whose special competence involves use of language—poets, novelists, playwrights—can reasonably be expected to provide acceptable verbal accounts of what they are intending. And yet—a curious irony—in the artists' own eyes, with respect to any given work, they must feel that they have already done just that. There it all is, in the poem or the play— isn't it plain as day?

Consequently, it is not at all uncommon for poets and playwrights, when questioned about their intentions, to give answers ranging from the curt and cryptic to the sportive and evasive: "It means what you want it to mean," "It means just what it says." After a while, we may find ourselves wondering, "Did he mean what he said when we asked him about what he meant?" or "What *did* he mean by replying in that way to our question?" We seem to be setting out on a hopelessly regressive path here.

The great Swiss sculptor Giacometti once remarked in an interview, with a look of deep earnestness on his face, that as a sculptor he saw himself as an utter failure. He could do no more, he went on to say, than capture in a work—say, a bust of his brother Diego, one of his most frequent subjects— what he *saw,* in some sense of the word; but try as he might, he could not produce a bust that even he, when he stood back and looked at it objectively, could think for a moment actually *resembled* Diego (in the manner that Sherlock Holmes's bust, we might suppose, looked sufficiently like Holmes to induce one Colonel Sebastian Moran to take a shot at it). Giacometti's remarks are intriguing; they provoke us to wonder just what kind of a cognitive struggle sculpting involved for him. But are we to take it at its face value? Quite likely not. The best we can do is to place it alongside the statues themselves and allow it to provide, as each individual work provides, just one more sidelong glance into a deep and obscure artistic consciousness.

Composers, painters, sculptors, architects are first and foremost masters of nonverbal media. They may or may not be able to come up with some appropriate elucidatory commentary on what they are up to, but we have no particularly strong grounds for expecting it. This is by no means a universal rule, but it is surely the case that we are generally on safer grounds, in our quest for the meaning of a work, if we try to squeeze that meaning out of the work itself, rather than look to the artist to draw it out for us.

Inside and Outside a Poem

Obviously the question must be raised as to just how we are to determine the "bounds" of a poem: What can properly be taken to lie "within" it and what ought to be declared "outside" it? Many of the critiques of Wimsatt and Beardsley have focused on this very issue, but it is not as if these two weren't aware that it was potentially an area of considerable difficulty. In distinguishing internal from external evidence for poetic meaning, Wimsatt and Beardsley note a certain oddity attaching itself to these terms, namely, that "what is internal is also public . . . what is external is private and idiosyncratic."[4] Typically, in philosophy, that which is internal is taken to be private, available only through introspection, while the external is out in the open, there for everyone, not just the introspecting subject, to see. In this case, though, whatever is deemed internal to a poem is carried about by that poem, so whenever you have the poem you also have, along with it, everything that is internal to it. On this view, the so-called external considerations are not connected in any essential way to the poem, hence it will not be the case that being in possession of the poem immediately puts you in possession of them: they are available only to a certain few—perhaps even to no one but the poet.

To give an example of this external-internal distinction at work, it is not uncommon to seek elucidation for a text by examining earlier drafts of it and noting what has been replaced by what, what has been eliminated in its entirety, what comments might have been scrawled in the margins, what works of other authors are mentioned there, and so forth. From Wimsatt and Beardsley's viewpoint, however, all these considerations should be deemed external to the final product. The author may have stumbled about for a time, undergone a series of opinion changes as the definitive statement worked its way toward expression, entertained and then rejected certain thoughts, jotted down personal reminders as to other works or other lines of thought worth pursuing elsewhere. What speaks loudest and most unambiguously is the final draft—the one offered to the public. All these other items of information may be interesting in their own right, but as far as reaching a critical understanding of the text is concerned, they distract rather than illuminate; and whoever dwells on them and not on the text at hand is guilty of the intentional fallacy.

The realm internal to the poem is said to include "our habitual knowl-edge of the language" and is knowable "through grammars, dictionaries, and all the literature which is the source of dictionaries, in general through all that makes a language and culture."[5] Thus our confrontation with an individual poem is not blunt, one-on-one, devoid of any mediating factors; rather, it is mediated by our own familiarity with the language in which the poem is written, with the culture that expresses itself through that language, and with the literary works themselves that dot, like monuments and vil-lages, the literary landscape of that culture.

The Inside-Outside Distinction Evaluated

The interpretation Wimsatt and Beardsley provide for internal evidence seems perilously broad and inclusive; after all, a language system and all its attendant social and cultural implications sprawls rather ungracefully across centuries and continents. And yet it appears that their view can hardly sustain itself with a more restrictive one. For a fleeting moment we might have thought that somehow when we looked at a sonnet on a page, our gaze, in some sense, took it all in. But we quickly come to see that there is much more dwelling within the poem than just the fourteen lines printed on the page—so much more, in fact, that those fourteen lines come to appear like a mote upon some broad Siberian lake. What vast, indeterminate fields are language, literature, culture; yet all are said to be *in* the poem! Actually the mote-on-a-lake simile inverts the true character of the poem (the *poem,* that is, and not the mere fourteen lines on a page): we might better view it not as a tiny, neatly circumscribed entity, but as an absurdly distended, amorphous mass—a jellyfish of nightmar-ish proportions. For the poem supposedly contains the rules of syntax, gram-mar, vocabulary, all of which exist in a symbiotic relationship with a culture; this culture has a past, a present, and a future; its past consists of deeds done, deeds left undone, and deeds not even contemplated; its present is characterized as much by its aspirations as by its accomplishments, and so on. One is prompted to wonder, if a single poem contains so much within its allowable boundaries, why trouble to exclude a handful of desiderata that happen to have some relevance to the life of the poet.

More to the point, there are two critical questions that must be asked regarding this manner of construing a poem, namely, how much knowledge of the linguistic-historic-cultural underpinnings of the poem do *I,* the reader, possess, and how much of it has been packed into the poem itself, that is, how much in the way of such knowledge did the author possess? As it turns out, answering either of these questions leads us into the allegedly pro-scribed domain of intentions.

What the Reader Knows

When a poet's linguistic-cultural environment and our own overlap considerably and we are comfortable believing that we are equal to the interpretive task posed by an individual work, communication is effected smoothly and we are inclined to say, with Wimsatt and Beardsley, that the poem's meaning resides in the poem itself, for in coming to understand it we looked nowhere else than to the page on which it was written. However, let us suppose that we misunderstand a poetic utterance, or at least fail to grasp its full significance, and that this failure comes about through no fault of the poet's, but through our own ignorance or lack of critical acumen. Under this circumstance, meaning can clearly be seen to spill over into "external" regions.

To take a simple example of critical shortsightedness, in Randy Newman's song "Sail Away" the refrain says "Sail away . . . we will cross the mighty ocean into Charleston Bay." Now Charleston is a rather charming resort city anymore, with a quaint old-town section and many chic bed-and-breakfasts. If this were all we knew of Charleston, the rest of the lyrics would be obscure, even bizarre: "In America you'll get food to eat/ Won't have to run through the jungle and scuff up your feet" or "Ain't no lions or tigers—Ain't no mamba snake/ Just the sweet watermelon and the buckwheat cake." These are odd claims to make if one is trying to sell someone on a vacation sojourn in South Carolina. But *of course* Charleston Bay just happened to be the slave trading center of America for many decades. I emphasize the "of course" because surely both Wimsatt and Beardsley would have known that fact right away; and yet not everyone does, and those who are ignorant of it may find the gist of this song perplexing. Once informed, however, things fall into place, and our puzzled listener now hears it as a sardonic yet tongue-in-cheek parody of the bill of goods some slave trader might have used to lure his victims on board. (If only they had been this civil!)

Leading someone from confusion to comprehension here involved inquiring into and clarifying the songwriter's *intentions:* "What does he mean, that is, *intend* by this?—*This* is what he's getting at, dummy!" And it appears that it is no fault at all of the writer's: it is purely our hypothetical listener's ignorance of American history that led to our failure to understand. Wimsatt and Beardsley would say the meaning inhered in the song itself, but they are only half right: Randy Newman put it there, but we failed to find it there. Consequently, we needed someone to step in and help us sort out the intentions that had been embedded in the work. Wimsatt and Beardsley, being unarguably first-rate critics, are accordingly somewhat

myopic when it comes to the interpretive problems that others face—problems
that can only be resolved by making intentions clear to an individual reader
through whatever means are necessary.

To give another example, suppose we happen to enter a cathedral and,
faced straightaway with a jumble of arches and alcoves, pronounce the
structure to be ill-conceived, to "make no sense." Someone overhearing our
expression of discontent, though, comes up to us and says, "I'm sorry, but
you have just come in through the side door; here, come this way and see
how it looks from the point where it was *intended* that you enter." In this, as
in the previous example, through a fault entirely our own, we missed out on
what was to have been the central thrust of the edifice and we are set
straight by an appeal to the intentions of the creator—intentions which were
clear enough, if only we had the sense to recognize them for what they are.

In short, the reader (viewer, listener) is responsible for being properly
informed and oriented, just as the artist is responsible for making the intent
of the work as clear as possible. Failure to appreciate the artist's efforts is
not always the artist's fault, and when it does occur, an appeal to the artist's
intentions is a thoroughly legitimate means of setting a disoriented audience
straight. Where communication is effected smoothly, we tend to overlook
the intentional component and fancy we are interacting "with the work
itself"; when communication breaks down, the question of intent surges to
the forefront, and we must not always lay the burden of responsibility for
this breakdown on the artist's doorstep.

Clarity must not be treated as a property that inheres exclusively in any
expression taken by itself: it arises and dwells in the relation between a
transmitter (speaker, poet) and a receiver (listener, reader). "Go to bed" may
be a perfectly clear order to all of us; but how clear is it to a six-month-old
child, or a speaker of Balinese, or a cat?

What the Poet Knew

It seems entirely legitimate, in drawing meaning out of a work of art, to
wonder just what the artist could have been *in a position* to put into it. And
here too it appears we could well find ourselves making inquiries into areas
that may be deemed external to the work itself. Wimsatt and Beardsley
discuss the lines in John Donne's "A Valediction Forbidding Mourning"
that make reference to "moving of th'earth" and "trepidation of the spheres"
and wonder whether, as some critics have thought, they play on a certain
opposition between the old geocentric astronomy and the new heliocentric
astronomy. To establish that they did, these latter critics have proceeded to
give evidence from a variety of sources indicating that Donne was indeed

conversant with and interested in the science of his time. Such appeals, Wimsatt and Beardsley claim, "disregard the English language" and "prefer private evidence to public, external to internal."[6] But wouldn't it settle the matter decisively and entirely if it could be shown that the poem had been written at a time well prior to the date when the heliocentric theory had even been dreamed about? It wasn't, but just suppose it was. In this case, we could safely rule out a given interpretation strictly on historical, chronological grounds and trouble ourselves no more about it. The significance internal to the poem would have been delimited in important respects through clearly external considerations.

Internalizing the External

Perhaps the ultimate collapse of the internal-external distinction is to be found in John Dewey's well-known book *Art as Experience,* published a decade earlier than Wimsatt and Beardsley's article. Dewey, in effect, treats a supposedly external notion such as sincerity as a property genuinely internal to any work of art when he judges "insincerity in art has an aesthetic not just a moral source; it is found wherever substance and form fall apart."[7]

Just how are we to go about detecting this dissolution of form and substance? Perhaps it is to be found in a production that purports to possess momentous scope—swallowing up years in chapters, leading us into and out of battles that altered the course of human destiny, following the lives of "significant" people through their ascendancy and downfall—but in the end presents us with mere hollow stereotypes rather than characters, and simply rehashes history without breathing any new life into it. What I have just described is the formula for the average television miniseries—invariably an exercise in insincerity. But I made no mention of commercial success or failure, or of the interpersonal or impersonal machinations that stand behind such productions. I merely indicated that the form purports to epic proportions, but the content rattles around inside it.

In spite of the awards heaped upon *Forrest Gump* (Hollywood congratulating Hollywood!), and the commercial success the film enjoyed, it too wears its insincerity on its sleeve. From the beginning of the story, when Gump the boy runs out of his braces, to near the end, when Gump the man runs back and forth across the country, the central character is presented as a comic figure of the most absurd sort, one for whom the laws of probability and nature are regularly bent and occasionally broken. Such a character can lay no proper claim to our sympathy, for such sympathy is reserved only for those with whom we can conceivably identify, and Forrest Gump benefits from too many miracles to qualify as being "like us." The tears we are supposed to shed on his behalf at the end of the film are nothing more than the tears required by a typically formulaic Hollywood ending. Perhaps the writer of the screenplay simply couldn't figure out what to do with this character he had created (and if I don't know who the writer was, I can't be engaging in biographical speculation or personal denigration here); perhaps he opted for a "proven" mode of pseudo-resolution (laughter combined with tears often makes for a box office bonanza). But whatever the motivation, the crucial phase of climax and closure is imposed on the film artificially, and not by the internal flow of events. Forrest Gump was simply allowed infinitely more comic license than any real tragedy or even any successful melodrama can support. And herein lies the reason Dewey would (rightly) accuse it of insincerity.

On Dewey's view, the development of an artistic idea from inspiration to completion will be dictated as much by the character of the inspiration as by the technique of the artist. Once the urge to create is provoked into activity, the artist will, in a curious way, be as much at the mercy of this creation as in control of it:

> If one examines into the reason why certain works of art offend us, one is likely to find that the cause is that there is no personally felt emotion guiding the selecting and assembling of the materials presented. We derive the impression that the artist, say the author of a novel, is trying to regulate by conscious intent the nature of the emotion aroused. We are irritated by a feeling that he is manipulating materials to secure an effect decided upon in advance. The facets of the work, the variety so indispensable to it, are held together by some external force. The movement of the parts and the conclusion disclose no logical necessity. The author, not the subject matter, is the arbiter.[8]

The correct spirit is captured (ever more simply and artistically) by Frank O'Connor, who once observed, "After a while, my characters begin to talk back to me." Actions he may have originally wished to impose on certain characters or traits he may initially have wished to instill in them must be surrendered once the momentum of the story takes charge and the characters become more than abstract sketches. And the sensitive reader cannot help but notice. Sincerity, in brief, is eminently detectable by means that Wimsatt and Beardsley themselves would have to regard as internal in scope.

Originality

The question of artistic originality brings to light a number of issues of further importance to the intentionalist debate. Of course, if the whole of a language and culture is to be considered internal to a poem, as Wimsatt and Beardsley insist, then matters of priority, succession and dependence should be inside the poem as well. Indeed, the *Oxford English Dictionary* not only gives the meanings of terms, but also charts their histories—when a particular meaning first came to be affixed to a word, by whom, in what context, and the like. And yet their insistence that the words in a poem should speak for themselves makes it appear that it would be of little importance whether the words in question emerged from one writer's consciousness, or were expropriated from the inspiration of another.

I am referring here not to the borrowing and sharing that has long gone on among artists of all sorts, but to the actual representation of someone else's ideas as one's own—artistic plagiarism. All ideas come from somewhere, and it stands to reason that one of the principal sources for artistic ideas would be . . . other artists. It is a waste of time to attempt to establish whether it was Picasso who fueled Braque's imagination during the early flight of Cubism, or Braque who gave inspiration to Picasso: the two consciousnesses seemed to feed off each other, giving and taking and giving back. Probably neither, in complete isolation from the other, would have come close to developing the Cubist style in the manner they did while working alongside one another; both share the credit equally for the originality of the movement itself.

Indeed, movements generally transcend the creative powers of any one individual participant, and in so doing actually lead individual artists to heights they might not otherwise have attained. The Abstract Expressionist movement in France during the 1950s and 1960s shows such an interchange of inspiration, as Manessier, Bissière, Singier, Bazaine, Le Moal, and others coalesced in a joyous spiral of achievement. Was Bissière, the elder of the group, something of its godfather, as the others often assert? Not according to Bissière himself, who claims to have profited immeasurably in his role as "teacher." And even the techniques developed across the Atlantic by Pollock, while providing the French artists with yet another source of inspiration, were transformed in their hands, brought under control and made subservient to their individual, expressive aims.

It is one thing, however, to enrich one's own artistic capabilities through exposure to the works of others, but quite another thing merely to ape another's style, or to present the ideas of another as if they were one's own. In the former instance, Wimsatt and Beardsley would be correct in focusing our attention on the individual work itself and consigning any questions of influence to the realm of art history, not art criticism. But in cases of the latter sort, it is definitely important to know who preceded whom, and that question seems to take us outside the work—unless, as mentioned before, we trivialize the notion of "inside" by bringing the whole history of art and culture within the work.

Some Facts

Debussy felt that Ravel, in composing his string quartet, had drawn his inspiration a bit too deeply from Debussy's own string quartet, and the relations between the two men were strained from that point onward. While there is room to suspect that Debussy's emotions here were colored by a shade of jealousy, as he might have perceived not only that there were certain telling similarities between the works, but that Ravel actually might have "outdone him at his own game," the example does show that originality is something artists themselves take very seriously.

Audiences take the matter of originality seriously, too. I laughed less hard than I might have when Tony Banta, in *Taxi,* spoke of a particular burden as weighing on him "like an albacore around his neck," simply because I had heard that particular malaprop uttered some years earlier by Archie Bunker. (And there may be yet other precedents of which I am ignorant—Gracie Allen? the Kingfish?—knowledge of which would lead me to further reappraisals.) It is true that the image itself is an amusing one, but our response to it can and will fluctuate according to how original we perceive it to be. The ostentatious opening measures to Richard Strauss's *Also sprach Zarathustra* were interestingly employed in *2001: A Space Odyssey,* wittily iterated (accompanying the entrance of General Dreedle's private secretary) in *Catch-22,* and annoyingly repeated in movie after movie through the 1970s and 1980s, rapidly achieving the status of pure cliché—"Oh, no!" we would mutter, "not *that* again!" Surely Kubrick's use of that particular musical morsel should be spared the label of cliché, as well, perhaps, as its use in *Catch-22.* Clichés, however, are real, and are really annoying. And the recognition that something is a cliché requires knowledge that reaches outside the bounds of the gesture itself, and into the chronology of occurrences of similar gestures.

What to Do with These Facts

Facts of the above sort bring to the forefront a methodological point of considerable importance to aesthetic analysis, one that deserves to be brought out clearly but often isn't. The point in question has to do with where theorizing properly begins, and where it *must* begin, a matter of vital concern not only within aesthetics but within all domains of philosophy. If we are to make sense of any area of human endeavor—art, morality, science, language—we must first discern and agree upon what phenomena are to be taken as basic to that area. This is an activity that must be carried out with the utmost care, for it is devilishly easy to allow our theoretical predilections to guide our selection of the relevant facts of the matter. Theoreticians often call upon facts the way evangelists summon forth biblical quotations: there's one out there (or in there) somewhere that perfectly substantiates the point they are making, *whatever* that point may be.

What is more, phenomena themselves are "rich" in properties, perhaps even to an indefinite degree, hence close attention is required to bring the relevant ones to the surface. For example, it is important, aesthetically, to know that *Wheatfield with Crows* (a) was painted by van Gogh, (b) was the last painting he completed, and (c) consists principally of blue, gold, green, and reddish brown colors. Different aspects of aesthetic analysis will select different attributes to focus upon. In the same vein, it is quite unimportant to know that (a) the canvas along with its current frame weighs eleven pounds, (b) it hangs in a spot 1,145 kilometers from the Arc de Triomphe, (c) Bret Favre has never laid eyes on it.*

Now if we examine carefully our responses to various works of art, and note how these responses vary depending on whether we take these works to be genuinely original or cliché-ridden, it should be apparent that originality makes a difference. We delight in its occurrence and grumble—"Same old wine in new bottles!"—about its absence. It is not always obvious to each and every member of an audience whether a line, a gesture, a scene is original or not, since their degrees of exposure to the recent and distant history of a given work will vary. But it is obvious that to the extent that any work is perceived as trite or unoriginal, its value will be seen to diminish accordingly. No critic is going to praise any playwright for exhibiting a "marvelous predilection for clichés" or for "deftly inserting many a hackneyed turn of phrase"!

That originality makes a difference in our appraisal of a work of art I therefore take to be a basic fact—one upon which theory can then build, and one to which theory must defer. One could well object here that whatever our inclinations may be, we ought to disregard questions of temporal succession, derivation, and dependence, and allow the individual work to speak for itself. But it is clear that to do so would be to bypass this basic fact concerning originality and approach the unexplained phenomena with an explanation already in hand, whether we are aware of this or not. If we allow ourselves to be led by the phenomena in question toward an appropri-

---

*I don't certify any of these "facts," but you get the picture.

ate explanation, then we will concede the importance of originality, and we will allow this concession to lead us to the recognition that intentionality is relevant to aesthetic analysis, inasmuch as originality and intentionality go hand in hand.

Is it not possible to treat originality as a property exclusively of a work itself, no different from its length or its subject matter, and thereby dispense with any pesky intentional elements? Disengage it from any intentional elements, I would say, and we lose any means of explaining why it makes the emotional difference to us that it does. It seems to be the case, for example, that a joke or play or sonata that we appreciate at least in part for its originality will continue to amuse or please or gratify us on subsequent hearings (though perhaps to a lesser degree), whereas once we get the idea that a work is merely imitative, the spark of appreciation goes out and cannot be rekindled. Let us schematize these claims to bring out this point more clearly.

If A is known to be the original work and B the derivative one, then the experience of A followed by the experience of A followed by the experience of A (allowing sufficient "recovery time") will quite likely meet with our approval from start to finish. Although repeated exposure to anything that at the outset was perceived as novel, or that carried a surprise with it, will blunt the effect of the surprise or the novelty, these are merely alterations in the intensity of the experience, not in its quality: we show no reluctance to rehear the music we love, to watch again (and again) our favorite films. However, let our experience of A be followed by a couple of repetitions of B, and in all likelihood we will find ourselves in the end feeling disappointed with B, or even irritated by it. The famous barroom scene from *Star Wars* was (and still is) genuinely delightful, but the grade-B imitations, each presenting its own panoply of peculiar life forms, rather quickly became tedious.

Once again, let our exposure to these works follow a more eccentric sequence, in which we first confront the derivative work B, perhaps a couple of times, and only later come to experience A—the paradigm—and our feelings themselves will undoubtedly succeed one another in a complicated manner, since retrospection and reevaluation have entered the arena. We will probably feel a certain discouragement when we discover that something we had taken to be original isn't. Some denial, even, might take place, in our efforts to preserve a sense of the legitimacy of our earlier experience, such as occurs when someone we had trusted turns out to have been lying to us. At the same time, a certain respect for the true original comes over us and warms our experience of it, though this warmth will likely be tempered somewhat, to the extent that any surprise or novelty the work might have offered has been removed by our antecedent exposure to its imitations.

Mere temporal situation—occupying this position rather than that in the eternal flow of events—seems hardly to be a factor capable of exercising any great sway over our emotions. Indeed, it seems to be precisely the kind of fact about any work of art that might properly be declared to stand outside the realm of critical relevance. And yet whether or not a work is perceived as original or derivative does have a direct and often powerful influence upon the attitude we adopt toward it. Hence there is something more to these concepts than mere temporal situation. This something more, I suggest, involves, if not the apprehension of a certain state of mind transferred by a creator to a work of art, then at least the earnest conviction that some such state of mind exists and is worth the trouble to comprehend. Originality is an *intentional* concept.

Art's "Tragic Demise"

When Wimsatt and Beardsley contend that the work, once completed and offered to that public, is thereby set free to live a life of its own, it is clear that they envision such a work deriving the nourishment to sustain itself from a certain linguistic-cultural environment in which it participates. It is the presence of this given that enables us to do away with references to artists' intentions yet continue to seek the meaning of the work. But while a work may be said to be on its own, it is certainly not free, on their account, to do and say anything that it likes. They do allow that "the history of words *after* a poem is written may contribute meanings which . . . should not be ruled out by a scruple about intention," but by the same token, neither should such meanings be ruled *in* without any scruples, for even these, they tell us, must at least be "relevant to the original pattern."[9]

Not all critics or interpreters have deferred to this latter scruple, however, and often works of an earlier time do get "rewritten" in later times. To cite a small example of this, the word "weird" has come, in current English, to bear connotations of "bizarre" or "highly eccentric," whereas in Shakespeare's time it suggested primarily a certain communion with fate or destiny. The "weird sisters" in *Macbeth* were thus simply fortune-tellers, but in deference to the more modern use of the term they are often portrayed as grotesquely strange creatures. (Actually, "weird" seems to be a corruption of "wayward," the term preferred in the Folios: if this latter version were to be rendered on the contemporary stage, given the semantic migration in yet a different direction of "wayward," we might find the sisters in question being represented as punky, blue-haired, black-lipped witches!)

Oddly enough, a significant movement in critical theory subsequent to Wimsatt and Beardsley did take this very turn toward loosening the bond between a given work and the linguistic-cultural context drawn upon by its author and (to some extent) shared by its audience. Within this movement, not only do the author's intentions cease to be of importance, but the language and culture within which the author created is deemed to have no stronger claim to priority than any other linguistic-cultural context into which an errant work may stumble while wandering about "on its own." In the words of Roland Barthes, "*We now know* that a text is not a line of words releasing a single 'theological' meaning (the 'message' of an Author-God) but a multi-dimensional space in which a variety of writings, none of them original, blend and clash. The text is a tissue of quotations drawn from the innumerable centers of culture."[10] Context, in a word, determines text, and not vice versa.

A view such as this seems to annihilate the integrity of the work of art and the aesthetic experience, setting a text adrift in a frail dinghy upon a literary-cultural sea of unknown breadth and tempestuousness. Instead of allowing for the complete dissolution of the art object, however, Barthes urges a certain refocusing of the welter of forces formerly taken to hold the work of art together: "there is one place where this multiplicity is focused and that place is the reader, not, as was hitherto said, the author."[11]

Barthes has made a stunning move: by beginning with a consideration of the kinds of factors that can obscure the meaning attributable to certain works of art, he endeavors to lead us to see these factors, ultimately, as constitutive of an entirely novel conception of artistic meaning, indeed of the art object itself. The reader brings to any work a set of beliefs, habits, and predispositions, as well as a fund of experience consisting of works read and works unread, thoughts thought and thoughts unthought, life lived and life unlived. Each of us occupies a unique point in the intersection of innumerable cultural determinants, and we can only approach and grasp a work of art from the perspective we embody.

There is some truth to this view, and yet it appears dangerously misleading. To be sure, we cannot look upon a painting and see it as paintings were seen when perspectival techniques were first being developed; nor can we see it with eyes of the sort that were aghast at the license taken by the Impressionists. We cannot hear Beethoven as he was heard by contemporary audiences: for better or for worse, Wagner and Stravinsky and Schoenberg and Ellington and Elvis and Snoop Doggy Dogg have intervened and indelibly colored our listening consciousness, and there is no way we can "uneducate" ourselves and strain away these influences. We are who we are: *"sumus quid sumus"*—the motto of Lake Wobegonians—applies universally.

And yet there are many traits, attitudes, beliefs, and experiences shared by all of us, across time, across cultures, which do allow us to communicate with one another, and which allow artists of other times and other places to touch us. The American in me deplores kings, but the human in me finds Lear to be a fellow worthy of my sympathy; likewise one regrets to observe that the face of hypocrisy, worn by Regan and Goneril, shows little signs of age over the past four hundred (and probably over the past four thousand or forty thousand) years. If *King Lear* were only about questions of royal succession, I could well find myself entirely out of sympathy with it and would read it only as one reads any historical document. But royal succession is only the pretext for engaging issues such as trust and betrayal, honesty and treachery, ignorance and knowledge. And these are all elements in our everyday life, as they were in Shakespeare's time, as they will continue to be.

Roger Fry, in *Vision and Design,* muses:

> In looking at the artistic remains of so remote and strange a civilisation [the Mayas of Central America] one sometimes wonders how far one can trust one's aesthetic appreciation to interpret truly the feelings which inspired it. *In certain works one cannot doubt that the artist felt just as we feel in appreciating his work.* This must, I think, hold on the one hand of the rich ornamental arabesques of Maya buildings or the marvelous inlaid feather and jewel work of either culture [Maya and Aztec]; and on the other hand, when we look at the caricatural realistic figures of Truxillo pottery *we need scarcely doubt that the artist's intention agrees with our appreciation,* for such a use of the figure is more or less common to all civilisations. But when we look at the stylistic sculpture of Maya and Aztec art, are we, one wonders, reading in an intention which was not really present?[12]

Fry's reflections invoke the notion, examined in the chapter on artistic form, that certain aspects of our visual perception appear to be common to a rather broad segment of humankind, inasmuch as they are grounded in cognitive dispositions embedded deep in our nature. It could well be the case that these dispositions facilitate artistic communication among individuals of otherwise radically different cultures, and render us far more open to sharing one another's experiences than Barthes suggests.

Similarly, if we hypothesize, as we did above, that subsequent generations of musical composition and performance may render us unfit to hear Beethoven as his contemporaries did, we should at least acknowledge the possibility that these later adventures leave us *more* fit to appreciate Beethoven than his contemporaries were. Rimsky-Korsakov "combed out" numerous harmonic irregularities in his orchestral transcription of Mussorgsky's *Pictures at an Exhibition* that later transcriptions readily left in. It appears that after being exposed to works by Debussy, Stravinsky, and others, these "irregularities" were no longer as shocking to the general musical sensibility as they were, apparently, to Rimsky-Korsakov's.

In short, to allow a text to be "reconstituted" with each separate reading of it seems both a radical and a groundless reaction to the problems that naturally accompany textual interpretation. All readers of any text do bring something individual, something unique, to their experience of that text; and yet they often also bring a capacity for sharing the experiences even of writers from drastically different cultural milieus. And far from it being the case that all of the impediments that could arise between an author and a reader are a priori insurmountable, a great many of them can be overcome through more careful attention, a little scholarship, or just a dose of sympathy.

What is at stake in the present dispute is simply a question of communication. Is a work of art to be dealt with as arbitrarily as a stone we find in the road, a stone that could serve as a doorstop, a paperweight, a curiosity, or whatever else we make of it? Or are we to regard an artwork as an attempt on the part of one human being to communicate something of importance to another human being? Is mere self-indulgence our ultimate calling, or may we not aspire to some "communion of souls"? Clearly, the tendentious way in which I have formulated these questions suggests how I should like to hear them answered. In the words of John Dewey again:

> Those who are moved feel, as Tolstoi says, that what the work expresses is as if it were something one had oneself been longing to express. Meantime, the artist works to create an audience to which he does communicate. In the end, works of art are the only media of complete and unhindered communication between man and man that can occur in a world full of gulfs and walls that limit community of experience.[13]

Art at its best is capable of providing us with insight into what the systematic pursuit of intentions is or can be like. If intentions in everyday life tend to be cloudy, ambiguous, at times even contradictory, instead of transferring these problems to the domain of art, we should instead recognize and appreciate the quantitative difference between our ordinary experience and our experience of a work of art, and should endeavor to bring the former up to the standard set by the latter.

If art can be seen as one of the principal bonds among human beings— perhaps, as Dewey maintains, the most clear-cut instance of such a bond— then there is no avoiding the conclusion that art is terribly serious business. No such conclusion, however, falls out of the anti-intentionalists' position. Once "the meaning of X" can no longer be taken to assert "what A meant by X," meaning itself is cut adrift from its proper moorings and is free to fluctuate unchecked from epoch to epoch, culture to culture, individual to individual. It may be that what a poet means by a term constitutes part of the word's history and meaning, but then so does what I mean by it. When the umbilical link between artist and work is severed and the work is set free to live a life of its own, questions of meaning become meaningless. Art ceases to be a serious matter.

The Human Factor in Art

The seriousness of art, it is being suggested here, derives from its capacity to facilitate communication between an artist and an audience in a manner quite unlike and at a depth more profound than our ordinary channels of communication. When intentions are straightforwardly emitted and received, as was so often the case with critics as discerning as Wimsatt and Beardsley, there is no need to inquire after them; we are able to concentrate exclusively on the message. But that in no way implies that the intentional input is of no importance; it merely means that we are taking it for granted. Let there be a trace of obscurity in the message, as we have seen, and we are immediately prompted to ask "What was meant (that is, intended) by that?" And even if we frame the question in a seemingly objective manner—"What does that expression mean in the context of this poem?"—and even if we resolve to arrive at a satisfactory answer solely by weighing the words themselves, we are still treating the poem as reflective of the intentions of another human being. This point is sufficiently important to merit a few examples.

Recently an art gallery in Vienna offered an exhibit of paintings that stirred but mild interest until it was brought to light that the paintings had been produced by an orangutan. Working in the medium of vegetable dyes—since she alternated between applying the paint to the canvas and licking it off her brush (an unhealthy habit with oils and acrylics)—the orangutan generated works that might have been described as in the Abstract Expressionist vein, but I say "might have been" to indicate that they would only be described in that fashion up to the point when one learned the true identity of the "artist."

One man, when asked to describe what he saw in a work—a swirling, bluish piece—characterized it as a sort of seascape; then when told who did it, he burst out laughing. What else was he to do? The joke was on him—and it was only a joke, because the consciousness, the web of intentions that he had seen embedded in the work, evaporated before his eyes on the telling. The good faith that is normally accorded an artist had to be withdrawn, but at least it was replaced with mirth, not hostility or indignation, as would have been the case if he were a noted critic whose reputation had just taken a direct hit, or a collector who had just bought one of the works under false pretenses.

This example underscores the fact, one that we all take for granted in normal circumstances, that behind a work lies a mind like our own, struggling to illuminate some aspect of experience that in some measure we hope and strive to share. But who could possibly hope to plug into the mind of an orangutan? It bears mention that there was at least *some* human intentionality involved in these paintings, for it would be a *person* who determined that a certain work had been "completed," that no further paint should be applied, that a satisfactory finished product had been achieved—the artist herself was content to go on smearing paint and licking brushes, if not indefinitely, at least not within the framework of any knowable *aesthetic* parameters.

To consider another example, Wimsatt and Beardsley grant, with Stoll, that "the words of a poem . . . come out of a head, not out of a hat."[14] But let us suppose that some words did in some circumstance come out of a hat, and imagine how different our reaction would be. Say I put some adjectives in one hat, nouns in another, verbs in another, adverbs in another, and so on. Then I pull out one from each and I get a couplet that reads:

Blue dawn despises houses;
Hideous time invites lovely seashells.

I can see a reader coming across these "images" and pondering their significance at length, trying to put "blue" and "dawn" together—"blue" the color, or "blue" the metaphor for a certain emotional state, or to some extent both—trying to imagine how dawn could despise anything, how time could invite anything, and on and on at great length. But if I then tell my patient reader, "I just picked them out of a hat—really," the struggle will end abruptly, perhaps with laughter, perhaps in anger. There would be no purpose in attempting further to unpack the sense of the images, because to begin with they were simply not arranged by an intellect trying to impart one sense rather than another to them. I may find one of them appealing, and attempt to construct something interesting around it, but obviously my own mind has now taken charge of it and is imparting this as opposed to that shape to it.

Or again, an object that is taken to be a statue found in a cave may well be hauled out and placed in an art museum; let it be discovered, however, that the "statue" was really a large rock whose shape had resulted from limestone deposits coupled with the effects of erosion, and in all likelihood it will straightaway be hauled out of the art museum and carted instead over to a museum of natural history. There it will be viewed by an entirely different set of people, with interests and reactions entirely different from those who viewed it in the art museum. Clearly, the principal difference between the two perspectives is that in one it is seen to have the shape it was *intended* to have, while in the other it is seen as merely having the shape imposed upon it by random forces.

New Hampshire's "Old Man of the Mountain" is a natural curiosity; Rapid City's four presidents in a mountain is a monstrosity. Aside from the latter's bearing a closer resemblance to the presidents than the "old man" does to any actual old man, the critical factor that distinguishes these two tourist attractions is that only the one in Rapid City embodies a fellow human's intentions. But this one factor from the very outset guides and controls the attitude we adopt toward each phenomenon.

Considerations of the above sort introduce a dimension into the discussion of intentions that reaches beyond, or beneath, the mere question of what a particular poet intended by a certain turn of phrase: they make us attend more closely to the importance of a certain human factor in art. And humans are bundles of intentions.

Treating Works of Art as Persons

We adopt a great variety of attitudes toward other people and enjoy a rich variety of relationships with them. I suggest that there is a worthwhile analogy to be drawn between our experiences with other people, on the one hand, and the experiences we often do and perhaps more often should enjoy with works of art, on the other hand. Let us pursue this analogy a bit.

There are some works that we find ourselves deeply and (to all appearances) permanently attached to, as we are to our family and inner circle of friends. These works seem to speak directly to us, as do most of those people in our inner circle, people who often have to say little or nothing in order to communicate successfully with us. On the other hand, there are works that have the appearance of being hopelessly inaccessible—as if a lifetime of exposure to them would not increase one iota our appreciation of them (an attitude we might have, say, toward someone who worked on the floor of the stock exchange on Wall Street, screaming bids this way and that all day—the mentality of a contract killer seems more readily fathomable!).

The great range of people who to some measure participate in our world dwell somewhere near its periphery: we have occasional dealings with them, we find ourselves superficially attracted to certain of them and repulsed by others, intrigued by some while bored by others, and so forth. And yet we cannot or should not say that we truly *know* any of them to an extent similar to that in which we know our most intimate acquaintances. We figure that often enough we can discern what their conduct implies, and quite regularly, for better or for worse, they fulfill our expectations: the salesman who insists rather precipitously on establishing a first-name relationship with us, who tells us of his children and who asks after ours, will soon have his life insurance portfolio spread out before us; we would faint from astonishment if he were at some moment to declare, "Life insurance is all a crock! Let's go somewhere for a beer!" and it would be some time before we allowed ourselves to abandon the belief that at any moment the mutual fund portfolio would be drawn out of its special hiding place.

The same can happen in the aesthetic realm. The facile but disingenuous character of any number of Steven Spielberg's films may lead us to turn a cold shoulder toward one that actually dealt seriously with an issue *(Schindler's List)*, while our enthusiasm for Mozart's music may prompt our indulgence toward a mediocre, hastily constructed piece that Mozart himself, if truth be told, would have willingly disavowed.

Can we ever hope to come to an understanding of all the intricacies woven into a rich and complex work, something along the order of Eliot's *Quartets*—a work about which many volumes have been written, not all of which entirely agree with one another? The simple answer is probably not. For every loose end that we fancy we've accounted for, a couple more will unravel elsewhere; perhaps we will not even be able to account fully for the significance of all the titles. But such insufficiencies need not dampen our overall appreciation for the work, nor discourage us from returning to it again and again. Similarly, our most cherished acquaintance may at any moment display a wrinkle, express an opinion, betray an emotion that catches us entirely off guard: there is no person, however close to us, whom we can presume to know inside and out—indeed, the individuals who fascinate us most seem always to have one more surprise in store for us. We don't abandon people because we are unable to comprehend them fully; nor do we cease trying, come what may, to deepen our understanding of them. So too, when a particular work by an artist in whom we have developed great confidence rebuffs our efforts to "bring it under control," the better advice is to try a different tack on it, rather than conclude that the search for intentions is a fundamentally hopeless one.

Might we not be systematically wrong about the intent and purport of a given work of art, miss an author's tongue-in-cheek approach, or fail to detect the particular tone of a scene (a description by Tolstoy of a gala social affair, for example, may be taken as idolatrous—something that

Robin Leach might have produced—rather than harshly cynical)? Of course, but real-life experience shows that we are susceptible (just as King Lear was) to similar misapprehensions concerning the intentions of others. Lear, however, had (tragically) allowed himself to get out of touch with the reality closest to him, and had lost track of whom, in his own family, he should and should not trust. In our own lives, there are a couple of people in whom we place all our trust; similarly, there are some works of art that strike us as so genuine that we might sooner forget our own name than "lose faith" in them.

As an example of such a work, I find it astonishing that some scholars question whether the "Lacrimosa" from Mozart's *Requiem* is truly his own, or whether it was his student Süssmayr who deserves the credit (as he was helping Mozart—who was drawing near death at the time—with the actual inscribing of the music, and the score for it is in his hand). Let them but *listen*, and they will hear that it is one of the most profound musical utterances of all time, an incredible blend of power and simplicity—indeed, the power that emerges from a deftly handled simplicity—then let them ask, of the two people in the room at the time, which one was really capable of such majestic composition? What is Süssmayr's musical legacy? The work proclaims its authorship, regardless in whose hand the final draft appears.

The position taken by Wimsatt and Beardsley seems in fact to be in agreement with the above approach to art appreciation, at least in the cases where works under consideration stand near one polar extreme or the other on the greatness scale. For in the case of those works that we are inclined to regard as masterpieces, their genuine character is so clearly inscribed on them that no amount of (decadent, cynical) scholarship could convince us that any dissemblance could be involved. On the other hand, works that are patently inept and disingenuous tend not to stay around long enough for questions to be raised and sustained—they slip ingloriously into the realm of the forgotten. Wimsatt and Beardslay's position weakens, we have seen, when questions arise concerning a work from the broad middle range between the poles. There, as with people or businesses we have to deal with but of whom we know not a great deal, it may be wise to do a bit of background checking. And just as we ask around, call the Better Business Bureau or the like, we may, for the work of art, try to place it more precisely in the context of an artist's overall corpus, the style system within which the work emerged, or the cultural milieu that constitutes its immediate environment.

Can we ever be certain of the intentions behind a given work? Certainly not—no more than we can be certain of the ultimate intentional complex out of which the behavior of our associates emerges (or, for that matter, of our own behavior—do we always know why we do what we do?). And yet it is invariably worth our while to attempt to fathom the reasons that provoke others to act as they do, as well as to plumb, through introspection, the motivational core of our own being. Certainty, while a guiding concept in the epistemological domain, is simply not all that relevant either to our real-life decisions or to our responses to works of art. Circumstances demand that we *act*, and that we do so within a definite (usually quite narrow) time frame. Consequently, people share secrets, take jobs, marry, board airplanes, all on the basis of the inferences they make about the intentions of others. Why, then, should we resist committing ourselves to a work of art until we are certain of its intentional structure?

However attracted we are to particular attributes that another person possesses—intelligence, a keen sense of humor, a graceful demeanor, or an optimistic outlook on life—what is of utmost importance in a friend and companion is sincerity. Any talent, when combined with insincerity, can positively become a lethal weapon, in service of no good end whatever. And as we have seen, Tolstoy regarded sincerity as the most important quality a work of art can possess. Collingwood deemed it to be absolutely essential (in the philosophical, that is, definitional sense of the term) to artistic activity properly so called: "If art means the expression of emotion, the artist as such ought to be candid; his speech must be absolutely free. This ... means that he is an artist only insofar as he is candid. Any ... decision to express this emotion and not that, is inartistic not in the sense that it damages *the perfect sincerity which distinguishes good art from bad,* but in the sense that it represents a further process of a non-artistic kind."[15]

Dewey judges that "Tolstoy's identification of sincerity as the essence of originality compensates for much that is eccentric in his tractate on art."[16] Whatever differences separate the theories of these thinkers—and there are many—they all seem to come to an accord over the need for sincerity in art, just as any number of moral theorists, with many and diverse axes to grind, would agree on the virtue of sincerity in the moral agent. In both cases, it may be naive to approach either works of art or people expecting to find this quality. But if we want the best from life, we should never abandon the search for sincerity in either.

— 6 —

Universality, Objectivity, and the Claim of Taste

We come at last to the issue of taste. Of all questions in aesthetics, this one is likely to have agitated more minds than any other. Whether taste is strictly an individual matter or whether aesthetic judgments passed by some people carry more weight than those made by others is a question that has all the ingredients necessary to be assured of philosophical longevity, and this it has indeed enjoyed.

For one thing, judgments of taste are made frequently, and often reflexively or unthinkingly, during the course of any day: in our choice of what to wear, what to say, where to go, what to do next, and so on; hence, matters of taste are rarely far removed from our ordinary consciousness. This contrasts, say, with the question of the ultimate constitution of matter, which, as crucial as it may be in science and technology, doesn't matter nearly as much to most people as does their choice of tie or scarf on a given day.

More important yet, though, is the fact that taste is an issue on which both principal points of view, pro and con, can obviously lay a strong claim to being right. All the enduring philosophical questions have this character about them: the skeptic tells us that there *can't* be genuine knowledge—there must always be some possibility of error—and yet so many are ready to reply that there *must* be genuine knowledge, otherwise we could never even know when we were in error. The determinist contends that there is no room anywhere in the physical universe for anything like a free will; and yet, the libertarian contends, our freedom proclaims itself in each and every choice we make. Taste (aesthetic judgment, aesthetic discernment—however we choose to label the activity) and its claim to validity seem to possess the same attributes as these other issues, in that a number of good reasons line up behind both poles of the debate.

The Problem

The Relativity of Taste

One is hard pressed, outside the aesthetic arena, to summon to mind an aphorism that can be thought to bear the weight of Philosophical Truth, but somehow aesthetics has come to be dominated by them. While no one would think of mounting a strenuous defense for such classic maxims as "A rolling stone gathers no moss" or "A watched pot never boils," everyone knows and hardly anyone ever bothers to call into question the dictum "Beauty is in the eye of the beholder." And this is as true of philosophers as it is of interior decorators and real estate agents, all of whose attention comes to focus on the great diversity in tastes across cultures, epochs, and persons. Indeed, it is a dictum with sufficient lineage to be able to boast of a Latin counterpart: "*De gustibus non disputandum est*" (there is no disputing matters of taste), and sufficient breadth to have other foreign language cousins: the French "*Chacun à son goût*" (each to his own taste), for example.

Judging from the common wisdom embedded in our traditional sayings, the questions of whether or not there are standards of taste or individuals especially qualified to make aesthetic judgments, or whether or not beauty (or any other aesthetic property) exists in the world, independent of this or that apprehension of it—three different slants on much the same position—have been settled to general satisfaction long ago. And the answer to the question in each of these formulations is negative: taste is not to be disputed; no one has any stronger claim to aesthetic sensitivity than anyone else; beauty resides not in objects but "in the eye of the beholder."

Of a Standard of Taste

Before simply awarding the victory to those who champion one or another of these relativistic aphorisms, however, it should be noted that a considerable inventory of facts, attitudes, and institutions speaks with equal vigor in support of standards of taste, the artistic authority of certain individuals, and the objective presence of beauty in the world.

1. We do, after all, have schools of art, and teachers in one artistic medium or another who attract students from near and far; and we have had such institutions and individuals for centuries. These schools and instructors do more than just instruct pupils on how to fabricate a likeness, assemble an intelligible sequence of chords, stand on their toes and execute leaps, or construct paragraphs free of grammatical errors—they strive to enable them to put these various skills to artistic use. Currently, anyone who desires to

attend such schools and receive whatever instruction they have to offer must be prepared to pay thousands of dollars for the opportunity; but what an utter waste of money and time this would be if each individual's taste were in some sense definitive, and no one's judgment could be thought to rule over anyone else's! For no matter how the prospective students should paint or dance or write, if it so happens that they are satisfied with their creations, then instruction would be superfluous. But that they see fit to place their talents in the hands of others suggests that they have a sense that they could do better, that better can be done, that better has been done; and of course once a term such as "better" is allowed to creep in, then the idea that each individual constitutes the final say in aesthetic matters comes into question.

One often hears (that is, I have often heard) art instructors themselves proclaiming that judgments of taste are purely individual; but then they select a syllabus, choose individual works to present to their students, focus on this artist rather than that one—and would they say "I choose the artists I like, I select the works and the readings I like, and my likes and dislikes are the sole determinants behind my choices"? Rather, one would expect them to say that these are the works or the artists that one ought to be familiar with in order to develop a proper sense of how a certain art form is practiced, has been practiced, perhaps even *ought* to be practiced. Art instructors who fancy that their likes and dislikes are the sole factors relevant to the making of curricular choices will be hard pressed to explain why they and not just anybody else ought to be teaching that course and drawing a salary for doing so.

2. Further, there are acknowledged masters and masterpieces within the domain of art: people travel thousands of miles to gaze at the Parthenon, stand in interminable and suffocating lines to get a glimpse of *La Gioconda;* we have read and revered Shakespeare's tragedies for centuries, while Bach's music continues to lead us to explore our emotional depths. Granted, many are left unmoved by some or all of whatever list of master-works we formulate: there is no shortage of grumbling emanating from the throngs who have waited and waited just for their twenty-second glimpse of Leonardo's masterpiece—"I spent all morning just to see *this*?"—or stood in crowds before the Parthenon—"If I'd'a wanted to look at ruins, I coulda stayed in da Bronx!" Rather than allowing these responses to discourage us from formulating such lists, however, it would seem more appropriate if we simply advised the insensitive individuals to learn a bit more about the artworks or styles in question, and in the interim to refrain from making ignorant and injudicious remarks. One might as soon question current accounts of planetary motion as speak deprecatingly of *War and Peace*.

3. In addition to teachers, artists, and masterpieces, the art world is also populated by critics or "experts." Critics are individuals engaged by newspapers, magazines, journals, networks, and the like to comment on works of art. All of them are disliked by someone; many, if not most of them misunderstand their task; not infrequently their pronouncements prove laughable in the long run; still, their very existence seems to speak against any notion of beauty being (merely) in the eye of the beholder. Why *their* eyes rather than just any other set? Why not select critics at random, from the population at large? Why not do away with the position entirely? Might the answer to these questions not be that the skilled critic is able to detect and articulate features of works of art that skip past the rest of us? And where they go noticeably wrong—the scorn, for example, heaped on the Impressionists by the first wave of critics ("Impressionism" itself being a pejorative term coined by one of these critics)—does not that very fact imply that there was a right interpretation, and that they simply missed it? But surely, where it is meaningful to speak of right and wrong we are in the domain of principles or universals or objectivity.

4. For certain types of art, most notably painting and sculpture, there is a market, and although this could be taken to constitute the crass side of the realm of art and beauty, market factors do contribute greatly to animating this realm. Indeed, for those individuals who otherwise have little interest in or involvement with the arts, the fact that there are people willing to spend millions of dollars for a painting (and there have to be more than one for this to occur—a work which only one person is interested in owning can be had for a song) is the kind of consideration that can make them sit up and take notice. And it makes us take notice because it is an instance where a value is placed on a work of art, where a community reaches some agreement about a work's value.

The range in prices for which works are sold may not and usually does not correlate extremely well with what we want to call their *artistic* value, due to a variety of nonaesthetic factors: (a) the relative scarcity of an artist's works—for example, those of van Gogh or Vermeer—can drive prices unnaturally high; (b) the reputation of an artist—Picasso, say—causes many of his less inspired works to bring exceptional prices; (c) a major exhibit of someone's work in a museum across town (or even across the Atlantic) can produce a flurry of enthusiasm that brings about a rise in prices; and these are but a few of such factors. Still, speaking quite imprecisely, great artists sell for large sums, mediocre artists for less. The correlation between monetary value and aesthetic value might be weak and uncertain, but if there is even the faintest correlation, it speaks against the pure relativity of aesthetic value.

5. Last, we might give a glimpse at the language we use in our "dealings" with works of art—surely not the last word in such a matter, but hardly irrelevant, either. When we pronounce something—a certain performance, for example—to be great, our words do not point toward ourselves and our feelings, but toward the performance: *it* is great. It is only when we run into heavy criticism for judging as we did that we may retrench and offer as a revised opinion, "Well, *I* liked it, anyway." That is to say, we have some expressions, such as the latter, that are explicitly designed to register our individual preferences, and which purport no further than that; then we have others that give every indication of offering judgments as to the presence of certain aesthetic qualities or the artistic merit of works of art themselves, and which implicitly solicit the agreement of others. The difference between these two modes of expression, and the contrast in attitudes that they underscore, makes it difficult to imagine that the one would merely collapse into the other; but that is what happens if there is no disputing matters of taste.

These are some of the principal desiderata that demand to be considered seriously before we entertain any thoughts of capitulating to the common wisdom and accepting as philosophical doctrine one or another or all of the aphorisms that assert the relativity or mere individuality of taste.

The issue can be and has been raised philosophically, in two different but not entirely distinct frameworks. One of these is concerned with the *scope* of our aesthetic judgments, the other with the *nature* of aesthetic quality itself. Regarding the former, when we judge something to be beautiful, does our judgment command the assent of everyone, or do we only reflect our own individual attitude? In other, somewhat more ponderous, philosophically charged words, are aesthetic judgments in any way, at any time, universalizable? And if so, under what conditions? (Perhaps we can even ask: in what universe?) If not, is the only alternative a complete relativism, reduced to the individual level, or might we not be able to establish some intermediate plateau standing somewhere between these two extremes?

The other principal means of framing our fundamental aesthetic question focuses on the nature of aesthetic quality itself, and asks whether beauty is a genuine property of the (beautiful) object, or if it is only a reflection of the mental or emotional state of the individual doing the judging. In philosophical terms, we are asking whether beauty is objective or subjective.

It is natural to see these two approaches as standing parallel to one another in the following fashion. Our judgments can be regarded as universal, the reasoning would go, when they are made with respect to some objective property of the world; but when we pass judgment only with respect to our own subjective states, such judgments are purely individual.

Any property that is objective is right out there for everyone to see—nothing is hidden in the recesses of individual consciousness. Thus if sphericity is an objective property of basketballs, anyone can determine that a basketball is spherical just by looking at it, handling it, or bouncing it. We would all feel it to be more than bizarre if someone were to say "Well, maybe you find it spherical, but I find it cubical." The person who said such a thing would stand in need either of advice on how to speak the language, or of some reasonably strong form of psychological counseling. In this manner, then, objectivity and universality seem to go hand in hand.

Subjectivity allies itself with individuality in that the way I feel toward anything is the way *I* feel about it; the way you feel toward it is the way *you* feel: I don't feel your feelings, and you don't feel mine. It can happen that we both describe our feelings about something—our hatred of racism, our admiration for a Gandhi—in the same terms, which suggests a similarity between these feelings; and yet I boil with rage and do nothing, you take to the streets and demonstrate; I end up with a headache when contemplating my rage, you too wind up with a headache, but it is produced by a policeman's billy club. However much we could be said to share certain feelings, a very important component of these feelings can never leave the confines of our private selves. And so if "beautiful" is indeed (merely) a sound we utter when moved in a certain way by some object or scene—if, that is, beauty is subjective in its reference—then it would seem to follow that it is individual in its scope.

The question of taste came of age in the eighteenth century, and the positions taken by certain of the most prominent philosophers of that era dictated the course the discussion would follow right up to our own time. In this chapter, let us examine the views of three of the most influential eighteenth-century thinkers, two of whom reflect the pairings of concepts just delineated (more or less—rarely do philosophers fit neatly into the pigeonholes we create for them), the third of whom seeks to establish some critical middle ground between them. Once we have seen the considerations brought to bear in establishing one position or the other, we can decide how much of the eighteenth-century reasoning is salvageable, or can be successfully introduced into our own intellectual and artistic framework.

The Scottish philosopher David Hume will be considered here as a representative of the subjective individualist position. Hume's essay "Of the Standard of Taste" has itself become something of a standard for essays on taste to measure up to. It will soon be apparent that placing Hume in this category stretches the truth a little, but only a little. Another Scot, Thomas Reid, will speak on behalf of objective universalism. The father of a school of thought known as *commonsense realism,* Reid's philosophical fame derives in large part from his incisive critique of Hume's philosophy. And occupying the ground between these two thinkers in a most enlightening way, as he sought to harmonize subjectivism with universalism, stands the great German philosopher Immanuel Kant.

Throughout this chapter our attention will appear to be directed almost entirely to the concept of beauty, or the beautiful, to the relative exclusion of other aesthetic predicates, such as the charming, the poignant, the dreary, the humdrum, and so on. In recent times, these other terms have come to occupy an important position in aesthetic analyses, while beauty has receded considerably in stature, becoming just one among innumerable predicates that can be applied to the furniture of the world. But in the eighteenth century, when Hume and Reid and Kant were writing, beauty was the preeminent aesthetic attainment, normally sharing the limelight only with the sublime, and standing in opposition to the ugly.

A variety of factors seems to have worked to produce this shift in emphasis, some artistic, some theoretical. Artistically, the urge to portray scenes of life that were anything but beautiful became increasingly prominent: Goya's horrific sketches of the Napoleonic battles in Spain, depictions of human impoverishment and desperation by Gorky, Dickens, and Dosotoevsky, to mention but a few examples. Artists came to see themselves less as creators of beautiful things and more as individuals possessed of the power to provide honest, expressive representations of many facets of human experience, much of which was not at all pretty.

Theoreticians of course responded to this tendency in the arts, but additional factors led to the "demotion" of beauty as the principal aesthetic predicate. For one thing, a closer examination of aesthetic experience itself led to the articulation of a richer set of categories in terms of which such experience could be understood. "Beautiful," it came to be recognized, was not the only complimentary term that could be applied to a work of art. Such terms as "poignant," "energetic," "insightful," and "warm" can easily be uttered in praise of a work or a performance—a performance that, nevertheless, one may not feel disposed to call "beautiful." Furthermore, as philosophy came increasingly to focus on language as either the source of or the solution to many of its problems, closer attention was given to the ways in which we use "beautiful," along with a host of other aesthetic terms. As a result, "beauty" and "the beautiful" lost their metaphysical majesty and became . . . just words.

But since the questions of objectivity and universality were initially posed in terms of whether beauty was an objective property of things, or whether our judgments regarding the beautiful were universalizable, I will remain faithful in the present discussion to these early formulations of the problem. At the very least, we can understand "beauty" not as describing a particular attribute or state of mind, but as merely holding place for any number of other terms of aesthetic significance.

The Subjective Approach: David Hume

David Hume presents a subjectivist position with admirable lucidity in his famous essay "Of the Standard of Taste."[1] Were he in any position to do so, he might actually express a certain surprise on finding himself treated as a subjective individualist, as I intend to do here, because he does suggest that some critics are more qualified than others to pass judgment on aesthetic matters, hence that the establishment of some standard of taste is at least possible. This is not a position that he sustains without qualification, however, and the list of qualifications he produces (a list that can easily be expanded in the same vein) could well prove sufficiently strong to overpower the affirmative thrust of his reasoning. Furthermore, Hume is known in philosophy as a skeptic, and it is most unusual to find someone being skeptical toward the pretensions of natural science yet indulgent where art and beauty are concerned. In short, it is my suspicion that his convictions concerning a standard of taste were not convictions that he would have clung to with bulldog tenacity.

Hume's subjectivism comes out clear enough in his essay, as he contends that "though it be certain that beauty and deformity, more than sweet and bitter, are not qualities in objects but belong entirely to the sentiment, internal or external, it must be allowed, that there are certain qualities in objects which are fitted by nature to produce those particular feelings."[2] Sweetness and bitterness are typically deemed to be subjective in nature, since they depend heavily on the nature and state of individuals' perceptual organs, and beauty, according to Hume, should be seen as more subjective even than that. He does allow that certain objective qualities are responsible for producing these feelings, an allowance that we shall see has more profound implications than Hume is prepared to countenance. Nevertheless, Hume ultimately judges that beauty is ascribed to an object not from the detection of certain qualities, but as a consequence of the arousal of certain feelings.

This emphasis on subjectivity is hardly unique to Hume; in fact, most of his contemporaries shared this belief. The reasoning behind the position seems to proceed in the following manner. That an object is spherical or nearly so, or some shade of red, is something that anyone with normal vision can apprehend. Even a more complicated entity—a horse, for example—is easily perceived for what it is by anyone familiar with the animal (and it is perceived as a "horse" by anyone conversant with the English language). But let someone follow the judgment that a certain animal is a horse with the interjection "Isn't it beautiful!" and it appears a new element has crept in. Now it is no longer familiarity with a certain species of animal that is at issue, but an attitude toward that animal: the phrase "Isn't it beautiful!" is not uttered in the same tone of voice as was the simple observation that it is a horse, but emerges instead with a certain warmth or passion clinging to it. However curious it is that people feel such passion toward an animal that snorts and smells and could at any moment rise up and deliver them a life-threatening blow with its hooves, it is nevertheless the case that some—many!—do feel that way. And the realm of feeling, it is often thought, is a very singular, individual realm, a realm that extends only as far as the consciousness of the person undergoing the feelings.

Some thinkers speak of beauty as producing a certain feeling of pleasure, others speak (perhaps more accurately) of some positive emotional experience; in either case, opinion has it that pleasures and emotions are both individual, idiosyncratic, *subjective* events. Hume's judgment that beauty is a more subjective matter than sweetness or bitterness would follow from the belief that emotions and pleasures are more deeply rooted in the consciousness of a particular individual, and are less capable of being shared than are judgments concerning, say, the taste of sugar or lemons.

Whether Hume and others are correct in deeming beauty to be a subjective matter, their affirmation brings to light an important truth, namely, that whether or not beauty turns out to be a purely subjective, individual matter, it is definitely the case that if no one, throughout all of history, was ever positively moved (pleased) by objects—be they natural or artificial—we would never have come to possess any concept of the beautiful. It would be as unknown to us as is the peculiar quality of the sensation of yellow to a person without sight. Outside of those people who have lived their lives in a state of mortal desperation, perhaps—and there are far too many such people in this most imperfect of worlds—I do not believe that there is anyone who fails to find something, at some time, beautiful. If ballet bores you, the current cinema offends you, serious music puts you to sleep almost as fast as reading does (which puts you to sleep immediately), then there is a postage stamp you crave, the thought of which changes the pace of your breathing, the sight of which widens your eyes as you exclaim "How beautiful!" Or perhaps it's that '57 Chevy, the black one with that silver streak across the rear fender. Or a thimble, a birdhouse, a Holstein. *Nobody* finds *nothing* beautiful.

From the indifference that we ourselves feel toward that thimble or that cow—the one that so entrances someone else—we can gain some insight into the indifference that certain others feel when forced to sit through a fugue that particularly enchants us. We can also see how, if the world were made up of nothing but thimbles and cows, the idea of the beautiful probably never would have occurred to *us*. And if that peculiar state of indifference that certain kinds of objects place us in were to become widespread, universal—indeed, if things had always been thus for everyone—beauty would be as irrelevant for humankind as thimbles and livestock are for some of us. So whatever that peculiar mental or emotional state may be that certain things—things that, consequently, we term "beautiful"—provoke in us, its occurrence does, I believe, stand as a necessary condition for the genesis and development of this most fundamental of aesthetic concepts. The employment of this concept in any particular instance, however, *may not* require the occurrence of such a state. This remains to be determined.

In short, aesthetics finds its ultimate grounding in aesthetic *response*. But it is quite another matter as to whether we are to honor each and every individual response. To do so would be to fall back into the "eye of the beholder" position, which is precisely the position under examination in this chapter. Thus for the moment we must remain suspended between these two positions: we grant that aesthetic response is fundamental to aesthetics; we aim to determine whether any collection of such responses can be woven into a larger judgmental fabric in which individual taste is not supreme.

The objective qualities responsible for producing the relevant feelings are not really the focus of Hume's attention in this essay, and he proceeds straightaway to an enumeration of the characteristics that ensure, not the beauty of any object, but the competence of a critic. He detects four such characteristics: (a) a certain delicacy of taste, (b) a freedom from prejudice, (c) practice in the matter of critical discernment (gained by making numerous comparisons among works of art), and (d) good sense.

Delicacy of Taste

This is perhaps the most interesting among these criteria. To illustrate such delicacy, Hume borrows an anecdote from Cervantes' *Don Quixote,* amending it in a slight but telling manner. He relates the story in the following fashion:

> It is with good reason, says Sancho to the squire with the great nose* that I pretend to have a judgment in wine: this is a quality hereditary in our family. Two of my kinsmen were once called to give their opinion of a hogshead,

---

*Of a monstrous size, crooked in the middle, studded with warts and carbuncles, tawny as a russet pippin, and hanging down some two fingers below his mouth." Miguel de Cervantes, *Don Quixote,* p. 529.

which was supposed to be excellent, being old and of a good vintage. One of them tastes it, considers it; and, after mature reflection, pronounces the wine to be good, were it not for a small taste of leather which he perceived in it. The other, after using the same precautions, gives also his verdict in favor of the wine; but with the reserve of a taste of iron, which he could easily distinguish. You cannot imagine how much they were both ridiculed for their judgment. But who laughed in the end? On emptying the hogshead, there was found at the bottom an old key with a leathern thong tied to it.[3]

Could there be a more perfect test of critical discernment? The tastes of leather and iron, which went undetected by all the others, could definitively be accounted for, certifying the acuity of taste possessed by the two gentlemen, and in turn encouraging us to accept their judgment as to the excellence of the wine.

The story as it occurs in *Don Quixote* is slightly different.[4] There, the wine is said by one to have a faint taste of leather, and by the other to have a similarly faint taste of iron. The difference is slight but telling, and it is easy to show why Hume's purposes required him to amend the anecdote as he did. The judgment passed in the original version is not a normative one—it merely comments on a certain aspect of the taste of the wine, but leaves us with no verdict as to its overall excellence. Hume, however, wants to link delicacy of taste with critical discernment, hence he is obliged to have the two men say both that the wine possessed a certain taste and that it was good. The judgment as to its goodness is aesthetic in nature (though Hume and most others in the eighteenth century would only say it was akin to an aesthetic judgment, leaving aesthetic judgment proper to the nontactile senses of sight and hearing—a matter for us to consider later), while the judgment as to the wine's being leathery stands independent of any question of its goodness: it is said to be both good *and* leathery, and presumably it could just as easily have been *bad* and leathery. The important point is that detection of the hint of leatheriness seems to lend a measure of certification to the further, normative judgment that it is good—somewhat like the judgment of an independent auditor that a company's finances are in order.

Freedom from Prejudice

There is both a denial and an affirmation contained in the idea of being free from prejudice. The denial is that we should *not* allow our own private interests and preconceptions to dictate to any work of art what questions it ought to address, what it ought to do. What that translates into, affirmatively, is that to do full justice to whatever work we are considering, it is desirable that we make every effort to understand sympathetically the conditions under which it came into being. To accomplish this, we should inform ourselves as fully as possible about these conditions: Who was the intended audience? What were the circumstances that prompted the work's creation? What, even, were the artistic idioms or conventions that prevailed at the time of creation? In effect, then, we are to broaden our artistic horizons in ways that will allow individual works of art to speak to us in their own voices, not to try to coax out of them what we want to hear, as a ventriloquist does to a dummy.

Practice, Practice, Practice

Here again, Hume is advising the potential critic to seek ever greater knowledge of a given artistic area by gaining ever greater exposure to works in that area. No one can speak with authority on modern sculpture without having looked at a good deal of modern sculpture, as well as sculpture leading into the modern period, Classical sculpture, and even "primitive" (that is, non-European!) sculpture.

Good Sense

Good sense, for Hume, involves a combination of such factors as intelligence, reasonableness, and stability (since, after all, no trustworthy critic— no trustworthy *person*—can be capricious, flighty). If a work of art offers complexities of any sort, we need the mental capability to make our way through these complexities, to apprehend the order in them, to see what events carry what implications, to remember what happened earlier in the same work, and so forth. In short, we should be mentally equal to whatever task a work of art poses in order to judge competently of its excellence.

Do we have, then, in the above list of qualifications, the formula for a sound critic, a critic to whom we can all look for help in steering us through the often brambly terrain of the art world? This question can be read in two different ways: (a) is Hume offering a description of the competent critic that he feels is capable of standing up to stern criticism? and (b) can his description stand up to stern criticism?

The Undoing of a Standard of Taste

There is reason to wonder if Hume intended his views on taste to be taken as rigorously as he did his more central philosophical convictions. As mentioned earlier, Hume is chiefly known in philosophy as a skeptic. He asserted that we could never really come to know the world as it is in itself, but could only know the *ideas* we receive from the world, and ideas are both qualitatively different from the things that produce them and ultimately private and individual. Of the concept of the self—one of humankind's most cherished notions—he denied being able to find anything more substantial to it than that the self is, in his words, a "bundle of perceptions," and he never even troubled to raise any questions as to the stuff composing such a bundle. Consequently, it is quite surprising to find him offering something more affirmative than a purely skeptical pronouncement with respect to the highly volatile realm of aesthetic experience. Given the qualifications he appends to his position, however, the assurance with which it can be pronounced appears to diminish considerably, for he goes on to say that "notwithstanding all our endeavors to fix a standard of taste, and reconcile the discordant apprehensions of men, there still remain two sources of variation, which are not sufficient indeed to confound all the boundaries of beauty and deformity, but will often serve to produce a difference in the degrees of our approbation or blame."[5] These two sources are "the different humors of particular men" and "the particular manners and opinions of our age and country."[6] When these various humors, manners, and opinions are enumerated, however—and it is easy to supplement Hume's list, which he keeps stylishly short—one is left wondering whether a large enough parcel of land remains on which a standard of taste may be planted. Hume suggests:

> A young man, whose passions are warm, will be more sensibly touched with amorous and tender images, than a man more advanced in years, who takes pleasure in wise, philosophical reflection, concerning the conduct of life, and moderation of the passions. . . . Mirth or passion, sentiment or reflection; whichever of these most predominates in our temper, it gives us a peculiar sympathy with the writer who resembles us.
>
> One person is more pleased with the sublime, another with the tender, a third with raillery. One has a strong sensibility to blemishes, and is extremely studious of correctness, another has a more lively feeling of beauties, and pardons twenty absurdities and defects for one elevated or pathetic stroke. The ear of this man is entirely turned toward conciseness and energy; that man is delighted with a copious, rich, and harmonious expression. Simplicity is affected by one; ornament by another. Comedy, tragedy, satire, odes, have each its partisans, who prefer that species of writing to all others.[7]

Clearly, such a list of variations in temperament can be stretched out indefinitely, especially if we wish to permute them in various ways, stir in gender differences, racial differences, the effects of climate, and so forth. Hume continues:

> For a like reason, we are more pleased, in the course of our reading, with pictures and characters that resemble objects which are found in our own age

and country, than with those which describe a different set of customs. It is not without some effort that we reconcile ourselves to the simplicity of ancient manners, and behold princesses carrying water from the spring, and kings and heroes dressing their own victuals. . . . For this reason, comedy is not easily transferred from one age or nation to another.[8]

And where the depiction of moral behavior is involved, Hume (seemingly unwittingly) evinces the very intolerance that he suggests ought to be overcome in an appropriately circumspect critic (though in his defense, it should be acknowledged that he never claims any special critical competence for himself):

> The want of humanity and of decency, so conspicuous in the characters drawn by several of the ancient poets, even sometimes by Homer and the Greek tragedians, diminishes considerably the merit of their noble performances, and gives modern authors an advantage over them. We are not interested in the fortunes and sentiments of such rough heroes . . . and whatever indulgence we may give to the writer on account of his prejudices, we cannot prevail on ourselves to enter into his sentiments, or bear an affection to characters which we plainly discover to be blamable.[9]

As it happens, each of us has a certain temperament, a certain gender; each is born into a particular family, in a certain environment, within a particular social framework, at a certain point in history, in a particular geographical location, and so on; and when all is said and done, it begins to appear as if no enumeration of these various factors that might purport to any reasonable degree of completeness will be the same for any two individuals. The subjectivity responsible for our aesthetic judgments seems poised here to collapse into a subjective *individualism,* in which each person's judgment speaks only for that person's state of consciousness.

We might glance again at Hume's list of qualifications the sound critic is to possess, to see if it contains any elements that can extricate us from this spiral toward subjective individualism. Interestingly, his list contains hints that subsequent thinkers endeavored to develop into more substantial grounds either for the objectivity of beauty or the universality of taste.

"Good sense," for example, could be seen as suggestive of the criterion of "rationality" that Thomas Reid employs (as we shall see in the next section) in characterizing beauty. Rationality is surely a notion that had been alive and well in philosophy long before Hume, and it had been regarded, at least since the time of the ancient Greek philosophers, as a definitive characteristic of the human being. Hume, therefore, could easily have appealed to it in order to ground the competence of the critic in a capacity readily recognized as universally human. But he chooses, instead, to speak merely of "good sense," and to use the term "reason" as equivalent not to "rational" but to our more informal term "reasonable."* No rigid aesthetic standard will be sustained by mere "reasonableness."

"Freedom from prejudice," or at least a notion very similar to it, as we shall see, becomes much more significant in the thinking of Immanuel Kant, and there leads to the hidden ground for the universality of aesthetic judgments. With Hume, though, it is little more than an invitation to be fair to works of art; no suggestion is made by him to any effect as grandiose as this: that if we pare away all our personal prejudices, we will reach some common mental framework that unites us.

In short, where Hume might have argued more strongly that the judgments of the competent critic are somehow exemplary for all of us, he turns instead toward a position both humbler and easier to maintain.

The charming "delicacy of taste" example—the cask of wine with the key in it—only tantalizes us with a prospect that can never be realized. The simplest work of art, say, a stroke of Japanese calligraphy, contains far more richness and depth, and requires far more in the way of studied discernment, than the detection of the taste of iron would. It might have been nice on Hume's part to suggest some test of art-critical discernment that could come close to matching this "taste test" for its simplicity and efficacy, but he offers none, for the simple reason, I suspect, that there is none to be offered.

Perhaps the most dismal of Hume's skeptical pronouncements is his characterization of the self as "a bundle of perceptions," lacking any central core or unifying element. His enumeration of the various factors that can cloud, or rather individualize, our critical pronouncements rings loudly of that characterization, and it does not appear that any of the criteria of critical aptitude that he specifies are strong enough to drag us away from this individuality and toward some measure of universality. His attempt to found a standard of taste on purely empirical grounds, as well-intentioned as it appeared at the outset, leaves us in the end despairing as to whether it is at all realizable.

A Case for Objectivity and Universality: Thomas Reid

Were it not for the skeptical views put forward by David Hume, it is unlikely that anything would be known today of Thomas Reid. He would

---

*If someone says, "Oh, Jonathan, be *reasonable!*" we can infer that Jonathan is inclining toward some excess, one that may lead to inconvenience of one sort or another. But if Jonathan is importuned to be *rational,* well, he has just totally gone off the deep end—one wonders if legitimate calls to rationality are ever heard by those to whom they are addressed.

have lived and died an unassuming Presbyterian minister and philosophy instructor—a fit subject, perhaps, for one doctoral dissertation, but nothing more. Faced with Hume's sweeping doubts, however—doubts that, because of their conduciveness to atheism, he found too alarming to pass unanswered—Reid was prompted to carve out his philosophy of commonsense, an approach that, as mentioned in Chapter Four, was to become the dominant philosophical movement during much of the nineteenth century not just in his native Scotland, but in America and France as well.

At the center of his rebuttal of skepticism stand his *first principles of commonsense*—principles the very doubting of which, he contended, would generate philosophical and practical problems far graver than those that supposedly led to the skeptical doubts in the first place. And among these principles are to be found first principles of taste, thereby offering a reply to, or a buttressing of, Hume's halfhearted defense of a standard of taste. Once we see the power attributed by Reid to first principles in general, it will be obvious that he is far more willing than Hume ever was to attribute unqualified universality to aesthetic judgments.

Reid combats Hume's subjectivism even more strenuously than his approach to standards of taste, arguing that it is entirely proper to attribute beauty to certain objects, and not just to the subjects who judge them. We see him returning again and again to this issue in his own "Essay on Taste,"[10] which suggests that it occupied a special place in his thinking. Let us therefore begin our examination of Reid's aesthetic views by considering his treatment of this latter issue. It will soon become apparent that to give it proper consideration, we must reflect seriously on a deeper question, namely, "What does it mean to say that something is a property of an object?"

Properties of Objects

As we saw earlier, while Hume alleged "that beauty . . . more than sweet and bitter, . . . belong[s] entirely to the sentiment," he did allow that there were certain qualities in objects "fitted by nature to produce those particular feelings." It is Reid's contention that any time we find some aspect of an object having a regular and predictable effect on human beings, it deserves to be treated as a genuine quality of the object itself, and not merely as the (insignificant) occasion for a (significant) subjective response.

In this respect Reid likens beauty to what has long been termed in philosophy a *secondary quality* (though he doesn't go so far as to treat it *as* a secondary quality). As his reasoning on this matter is quite interesting, it is worthwhile to give some consideration to the distinction drawn by philosophers between primary and secondary qualities. This distinction, especially in the eighteenth century, was perceived to be a very important one, although hardly any two philosophers supplied the same account for it. Nevertheless, they generally drew the distinction in a manner that placed the same properties, respectively, in each of the two categories, and they had much the same motives for doing so.[11]

Primary qualities (using Reid's enumeration) consist in "extension, divisibility, figure, motion, solidity, hardness, softness and fluidity," while secondary qualities include "sound, color, taste, smell, and heat or cold."[12] A close look at these lists should reveal that the primary qualities are taken to constitute bodies as they might have been treated within the framework of Newtonian physics—as possessing a certain shape and mass, as moving in a particular direction, and doing so with a certain velocity. Such objects were not taken to be of any particular color; their taste or odor was of no importance, nor did it matter whether they warmed us or cooled us. These latter qualities (the secondary qualities) were seen to live and die, so to speak, in the interaction between a body and an individual subject, while the former (the primary qualities) were viewed as being graspable for what they are in themselves, despite the variety of reactions produced in different individuals, or in the same individual at different times. In Reid's words, "Our senses give us a direct and distinct notion of primary qualities, but of the secondary qualities, our senses give us only a relative and obscure notion."[13]

Reid's point is this: the shape of a sphere communicates itself directly to us, through its visible appearance. What makes it appear spherical to us is its sphericity. And even though we become aware that pure sphericity may appear differently under different circumstances (when we attend to the visible appearance of the sphere in a manner common only to painters), nevertheless these different visible appearances are naturally understood by us, and are all immediately taken by us to be signs of the presence of a spherical object. Thus it makes perfectly good sense to say that the sphericity of the object is perceived by us because the object itself is spherical.

Contrast this with, say, our perception of a sound. We may hear a note produced by a flute, may immediately recognize the instrument to *be* a flute, may even (if we are burdened with absolute pitch) immediately recognize just what note it is. But this sound is in no way a constitutive element of the flute, in the way in which sphericity is constitutive of a sphere. It is produced by vibrations in a column of air, which are carried through the surrounding atmosphere to our ear. The sound and the sounding instrument are utterly dissimilar "entities." Our perception of the former is relative to a set of circumstances—the material of the instrument, the length of the column of air, the atmosphere through which it is carried, and our own hearing apparatus. No one of these factors *is* the sound proper, in the way in which the sphere is the sphere proper. If atmospheric or acoustic conditions were to be altered, so that the technique for producing a C were instead to lead us to hear a G, we would have no choice but to insist that the note in question actually was a G. If, on the other hand, a sphere appeared flat to us from a certain distance, we could easily adjust to this particular visual manifestation and judge, simply, "It's a sphere—that's the way spheres often look at this distance."

Color, in light of these considerations, is also relative and obscure in the sense that, while we know that we're looking at something red, we may well not know why it is red, and the reason why it is red, after all, *is* the quality of redness possessed by the object. Even if we should have an answer at hand—a scientific explanation of the phenomenon of color—it will have to mention the kind of sensory receptors we possess, which implies that redness, such as we conceive it, is a quality apprehended by "eyes like ours," and is not inherent in the object in the manner that sphericity is in spheres.

Given this characterization of the two types of quality, let us now consider Reid's account of how it is that both, secondary as well as primary, are legitimately attributable to bodies. When I handle a marble, my sensations enable me to discern its hardness and its sphericity; when I look at it, I perceive it to be a limpid blue in color. Reid claims that I detect the former pair of properties precisely because it *is* hard and it *is* spherical. The limpidity and the blueness, however, owe their appearance to some deeper set of causal circumstances acting on me in a certain way and leading me to attribute these properties to the object as well. These other, deeper causes are themselves genuine properties of the object, and they behave every bit as regularly as the primary qualities do; yet due to their peculiar manner of manifestation, my perception of the object that possesses them cannot capture anything of their essential nature.

If beauty is in any way akin to a secondary quality, it therefore seems appropriate, Reid concludes, to regard it as a genuine quality of the beautiful object: "To say that there is, in reality, no beauty in those objects in which all men perceive beauty, is to attribute to man fallacious senses,"[14] but one of the first principles of commonsense for which he argues holds "that the natural faculties, by which we distinguish truth from error, are not fallacious."[15] To imagine this principle being false would place us in more dire circumstances than even Hume's skepticism would, for after all, Hume, in establishing his position, requires that we be able to distinguish good reasoning (his) from bad (his opponents'). Thus even skepticism rests on this principle (and, Reid argues, others like it). Consequently, beauty can be taken to be a term designating a quality in much the same way that *"astringent, narcotic, epispastic, caustic* and innumerable others signify qualities of bodies, which are only known by their effects on animal bodies."[16]

No attempt is made by Reid to deny our involvement in judgments as to the beauty of this or that object. What he denies is that we are thereby obliged, merely because a certain subjective response is involved, to treat beauty *only* as subjective. And if he is right in this, then perhaps it is reasonable to speak of *recognizing* beauty without *feeling* it; although even at that, it may be wise to hold that the possibility of undergoing the appropriate experience under propitious circumstances must exist. Thus, suppose you are driving home in especially heavy traffic on an especially hot day on which your air conditioning has decided to malfunction (as it always does on hot days: it is a curious fact, one worthy of close study, that air conditioning never breaks down in the dead of winter), and suddenly there emerges from your car radio the languid, luxuriant opening measures of Debussy's *Afternoon of a Faun*. The chances of your being led to and deposited in the appropriate spiritual state are slim at best. Perhaps your irritation will be heightened: "Why did they have to play that *now?*" But you can still hear that it is a beautiful piece. And even if it was something you had never heard before, you could easily hear that it was a work that you would like to become more intimate with, in more propitious circumstances. A sunset viewed between storm clouds in an airplane could well have the same effect, or lack of one: the terror of the moment would crowd out any appropriate aesthetic response, and yet the beauty of the sunset would still stand forth for anyone to see.

A chemistry professor may well warn a student, "Be careful, that stuff is caustic," without having been burned by any of that particular batch of the stuff, or by any of it at all for a good thirty years, or perhaps never. And yet the stuff in question gives enough signs of being the caustic material the professor takes it to be, for his judgment and his admonition to be perfectly legitimate.

If the objectivity of beauty can be established by arguments such as these offered by Reid, there are still three qualifications that have to be recognized. First, it is worth recalling that Reid only *likens* beauty to a secondary quality: while there are important points of concurrence, there are likewise important differences. I find mention of at least two of these in his essay. For one thing, perception of beauty is dependent upon an individual's ability to perceive the full range of qualities, both primary and secondary, and merely to possess this latter ability still does not ensure that one will be able to see beauty where it exists: "It is impossible to perceive the beauty of an object without perceiving the object, or, at least, conceiving it."[17] To give an analogy, one must first be able to skate to play ice hockey, but just being able to skate in no way assures that one will be able to master all the other skills required of an ice hockey player. Normal powers of perception are thus necessary but not sufficient conditions for perceiving beauty. Many an individual has keen eyesight but no sense of the kind of proportions that make a scene beautiful, acute hearing but no capacity to appreciate the touching quality of a particular melody. Beauty, therefore, seems to be a quality once removed from both primary and secondary qualities.

The above consideration suggests this second difference, that while qualities, both primary and secondary, are simple, beauty is complex and relational. This, I take it, is what Reid has in mind when he asserts that "beauty and deformity in an object, result from its nature or structure,"[18] for natures do tend to be conceived of as complex (think, for example, of "human nature" and all that it implies), while structures are both complex and hierarchically ordered (the structure of a cell, a cathedral, an epic). It is when we start to think such thoughts as "too much red" or "the line on the left carries too far toward the center" that we are graduating from the level of merely perceiving an object and are coming to apprehend it as potentially beautiful. At this point we are becoming attuned to the relational properties the object possesses.

Thirdly, factors such as the above undoubtedly contribute to making judgments of beauty much more variable, from subject to subject, than even judgments of secondary qualities seem to be. After all, most of the world does agree that the sky is blue, gardenias smell sweet, and lemons taste sour. Perceptions of secondary qualities may vary somewhat from person to person, but the situation is ever so much worse where beauty is in question. Let us simply remind ourselves of those maxims mentioned at the beginning of this chapter, the ones asserting the indisputability of tastes or the radical individuality of each person's perception of beauty. People generally need to be argued into accepting that redness is not, strictly speaking, *in* the red object, but they usually need to be argued out of believing that beauty resides in the eye of the beholder. If there is a connection between objectivity, construed in Reid's manner, and universality, it is certainly not a universality that equates with unanimity.

Reason, First Principles, and Universality

Not all things that receive the label "beautiful," on Reid's account, deserve to be universally apprehended as beautiful. He distinguishes between two species of judgments in the aesthetic domain: the instinctive and the rational. Instinctive judgments of beauty are the sort that a child (or the child that dwells in any of us) would pronounce on catching sight, say, of a brightly colored pebble or a peacock feather. A pleasurable emotional response occurs, but no real reason can be given for it outside the fact that such things are pleasing.

"Suppose again that an expert mechanic views a well constructed machine. He sees all its parts to be made of the fittest materials, and of the most proper form; nothing superfluous, nothing deficient; every part adapted to its use, and the whole fitted in the most perfect manner to the end for which it is intended. He pronounces it to be a beautiful machine."[19] In this instance, Reid suggests, the judgment contains rational elements; in principle, anyone could perceive the beauty of the machine, but the word of the skilled mechanic is to be trusted above all others, since such an individual is best equipped to make that judgment. Furthermore, rationality is in a very important sense embedded in the machine. So the perception of beauty is in this instance something of a meeting of minds—our mind comes together with the creator's mind by way of the machine. There are two aspects to this meeting of minds that must be clarified in order to gain a proper sense of Reid's approach to the universality of beauty: the connection between beauty and expression, and the manner in which the first principles of commonsense control our experience of the world. Since we have given close attention to Reid's views on expression in the chapter devoted to that very issue, let us proceed directly to a consideration of his notion of first principles.

A first principle for Reid is a proposition that reflects a certain attitude that permeates human experience to its very core. When face-to-face with such propositions, he contends, we find that we have no choice but to affirm them. Even to argue for them is futile, for no evidence we could appeal to in pleading their case would be as secure and unquestionable as the principles themselves already are. The primary technique used to establish such principles is known in logic as the *reductio ad absurdum:* when the falsity of the principle is presumed, various absurdities follow, thus confirming the truth of the original principle.

Reid does suggest that there must be first principles of taste, for, among other reasons, "a fine taste may be improved by reasoning and experience; but if the first principles of it were not planted in our minds by nature, it could never be acquired."[20] Stronger yet is his suggestion that taste that is natural and rational, "may be true or false, according as it is founded on a true or false judgment. And if it may be true or false, it must have first principles."[21] But as to what these principles are, Reid never really offers any examples (just as Hume similarly neglected to supply an artistic equivalent of the "key in the cask" taste test). He mentions that a face without a nose or with a mouth askew could never be beautiful, but the presence of a nose or the alignment of the mouth constitute but the barest among necessary conditions for the beauty of a face. And even at that, if all body parts of all creatures capable of being called beautiful were to have their own first principles, that would make for a rather unwieldy catalogue.

We have seen in Chapter Four, however, that not only are beauty and morality connected in Reid's account, but it is in fact the morally upright soul that originally merits the description "beautiful." Therefore, the search for first principles of beauty ultimately leads us to the domain of morality, a domain where we should have little difficulty finding what Reid, at least, would take to be first principles. Surely loving one's neighbor, doing unto others as we would have them do unto us, refraining from senseless acts of violence, and the like would readily qualify as such principles.

What is more, the realm of morality is a realm in which reason should prevail. It is reason, after all, that is capable both of leading us to recognize first principles for what they are and indicating the path to proper moral conduct. It follows, then, that those who are beautiful must themselves be acting under the guidance of reason, and the works of art we deem beautiful have taken their shape under the watchful eye of reason. And since reason has so long been treated as definitive of the human being, Reid has no difficulty in granting that our judgments concerning beauty—*rational* beauty, at least—can hold universally.

What does it mean to "hold universally"? Clearly it doesn't mean that all humans will be of one mind, that we all will see beauty wherever it occurs. If that were a requirement, then nothing would ever count as beautiful, since no one thing has ever been found beautiful by everyone, throughout all time. What is implied is that when we truly apprehend beauty, we are entirely justified in demanding that others see it as well. Their failure to, or our failure to, is in principle ameliorable, since all of us, whether we realize it or not, live under the guidance of first principles, which establish the ultimate canons of rationality. Hence there is always a "court of appeals" before which judgmental differences can be tried and adjudicated. This is what an approach such as Reid's offers to replace subjective individualism. On the latter view, for me to demand that you see beauty where I see it is in effect to demand that you become me. On Reid's view, the only demand made is that you live up to your capabilities as a rational being; and I can count on your being rational.

Reflections

1. Near the beginning of this chapter, I suggested that a certain natural link existed between objectivity and universality—find one and normally you

will find the other. It is noteworthy that in Reid's case this link does not seem to hold, at least not very strongly. His position on the objectivity of beauty derives from the more general considerations concerning what is involved in being a quality of an object, while his approach to universality is grounded in our rational nature, especially as it participates in our moral life. The only point of accord between these two seems to reside in the first principles of commonsense, for each makes appeal at various points to such principles. Nevertheless, each appeals to different sets of principles, as those governing perception and predication are quite different from those governing our moral and intellectual life.

In short, then, we can welcome the one position without necessarily being committed to the other; and of the two, Reid's views on objectivity appear to have considerably more to recommend themselves—from them we gain genuine insight into the relation between language (especially the language of aesthetics) and the world. Serious questions, however, must be raised about his approach to universality.

2. For one thing, there has long been asserted—and there continues to be asserted—a strong bond between aesthetic qualities and morality. But Reid virtually collapses the aesthetic into the moral—the moral is the original source of beauty (or ugliness). And let us not forget, morality is a key to the universality of taste, since moral judgments "clearly" have first principles. But we may wonder whether all or even most aesthetic experience actually has direct moral implications. Is it not possible that the moralist in Reid has urged him to introduce moral significance into a domain that is not necessarily designed to receive it?

3. Or again, though we may grant that there exists some rational component to art and beauty (otherwise these concepts would not be uniquely applicable to the human domain), it is questionable whether this is sufficient for the universality we have been seeking. Since our attributions of beauty normally accompany some sensory experience (some would argue that they always do) and rarely accompany some purely ratiocinative process, we would do better to seek a universalizing feature in our cognitive makeup rather than in our power of reason. As it turns out, this approach is earnestly developed in the aesthetic theory of Immanuel Kant, to be considered next.

4. Finally, and perhaps most important, the model of aesthetic judgment that Reid provides simply seems out of line with the actual process itself as it occurs in the most important instances. To the extent that there are principles guiding our taste, then judgments of taste turn out to have nothing of the special character about them that we always fancied they had. Judgment in general involves confronting an object with a supply of concepts, and fitting the given object under one or another (or more) of the concepts; so it

seems that what constitutes a judgment of taste would be determined by what set of concepts a given object invites application of. We walk through the woods and are prompted to apply botanical categories; in a parking lot, automotive categories occur to us. So when passing through a museum, it would follow that we have an eye open for a certain set of aesthetic characteristics, which we find or fail to find embodied in this or that object. Somehow, this doesn't seem to do justice to the aesthetic process.

There seems to be an emotional involvement with a work of art, or a beautiful object, that can easily be absent from other areas of the judging process. We can identify trees all day, yet not interact with any of them with anything like the intensity that characterizes our interaction with a work of art. Of course, many a botanist may be positively moved by a tree—"Have you ever seen a cedar that broad?"—but the process of judging the breadth of a cedar requires no such reaction; indeed, such reactions could sometimes impede judgment, and furthermore, once we reach the stage of reacting in that fashion, it seems we have entered the domain of the aesthetic. In short, something more seems to be involved in aesthetic judgment than a simple (successful or unsuccessful) search for the embodiment of certain principles. When something is felt by us to be beautiful, its special nature, its individuality, impresses itself upon us: something in it reaches beyond the dimension of its being merely a particular token of a certain type. This too is an issue of great importance within the aesthetic theory of Kant.

Subjectivity Universalized: Immanuel Kant

A serious attempt was made to do justice to these various aspects of aesthetic judgment by the great German thinker Immanuel Kant, a late contemporary of Reid, and perhaps the most influential philosopher of the past two centuries. Kant described himself as having been awakened from his dogmatic slumbers by the philosophy of David Hume (the same could be said of Reid), the gist of this characterization being that he found himself both impressed by Hume's reasoning and shaken by its skeptical consequences. Could it be possible, as Hume seemed to be suggesting, that nature was essentially inaccessible to us—that what passed for science was a mere arrangement of our own ideas?

Upon running headlong into Hume, Kant's philosophical project became an effort to show that nature was in certain respects eminently knowable, precisely because its basic structure is inscribed upon it by the very cognitive apparatus through which we apprehend it. (This could be said of Reid's philosophical project as well, since his first principles and Kant's "cognitive apparatus" strongly resemble one another.)

Kant's aesthetic thought went through a transformation similar to that undergone by his theory of knowledge and reality. His early treatments of the subject remain entirely within the domain of empirical observation and offer no real hope that any principle could be discovered whereby it would be possible for a judgment passed by a particular individual to demand the assent of other individuals. But such an idea did eventually occur to him, and it is developed in his *Critique of Judgment.*

The uniqueness of Kant's approach consists in his effort to strike a harmony between, from one side, the singularly personal nature of aesthetic experience that led Hume (and so many others) to characterize it as subjective, and, from the other side, the sentiment accompanying this experience, prompting us to feel that others *ought* to be enjoying it as we are—that there is a universal element to aesthetic experience. Thus his *Critique of Judgment* aims to establish some ground for a universality quite unlike the universality that science seeks, or, for that matter, that Reid sought to attribute to aesthetic judgments. In these latter cases, a judgment is universal if it is either the articulation of a universally held principle or a valid inference from one or more of such principles. For Kant, the universality of aesthetic judgment involves, not principles and demonstrative proofs, but a universally communicable pleasure.

Now since most of our pleasures arise and terminate within ourselves, making no pretense at universal communicability, the central concern of Kant's project became one of specifying the determinants of this special type of pleasure. To anticipate in a word what will have to be expounded in a section, distinctively aesthetic pleasure is deemed by Kant to be *disinterested* pleasure, and it arises in a subject (you or me) through interaction with an object that evidences a peculiar purposive character.

To reach an understanding of Kant's theory of subjective universality, then, will require that we follow a tangled, sometimes thorny path. First, we must take a brief look at his basic theory of cognition. Then we will examine the concept of judgment and the important contrast between two different modes of judgment. Third, we will explain what is involved in the notion of disinterestedness. Fourth, we must clarify the role of purposiveness as it relates to our disinterested judgments. And finally—the last step necessary in accounting for universality—we will have to explain the nature and significance of the notion of disinterested pleasure. The going will at times be very rough, but the journey should prove well worth the struggle, leaving us in the end before a breathtaking theoretical landscape.

Cognition and Knowledge

Kant was disturbed by Hume's analysis of human experience, for he realized that indeed if the mind is merely the passive recipient of Nature's message, then we have no real means for testing or grounds for trusting what she communicates to us. For all we know, the Book of Nature may be one glorious fiction.

Kant was impressed, however, that certain features of our experience seem universal and unavoidable—objects appear in space and time, events are causally interrelated, anything that qualifies as a "thing" at all must be *one* thing. From these observations he reasoned that, since the contributions of external nature are always to some degree uncertain, any universal, unavoidable features of our experience must be supplied by the mind itself. His philosophical project in the major work *Critique of Pure Reason* thus became one of elaborating these peculiar features of our experience and demonstrating their necessity.

Sense experience, on Kant's view, involves an immediate synthesis effected by the mind between a certain sensory input and a conceptual framework. Two distinct faculties are responsible for this synthesis: the imagination, which somehow shapes the sensory data into (as we would expect) images, and the understanding, which supplies the appropriate interpretative concepts. We must not envision this as a sequential process; that is, neither unconceptualized images nor pure concepts devoid of sensory content are thinkable. Experience comes to us whole, and what Kant offers is an analysis, a distillation of its constituent parts. Thus the only world we know derives its shape in numerous vital respects from the activity of our own mind, from the interplay of our cognitive powers, principal among which are the understanding and the imagination.

Judgment

This act of putting things together, bringing (general) concepts to bear on (particular items of) sensory information, constitutes what Kant terms *judgment.* Thus, we judge something to be, say, a tree because we receive items of sensory information that make us impose certain categories and concepts (it is difficult *not* to make this process seem to unfold temporally, but Kant was generally quite emphatic in insisting on its immediacy).

Normally, when cognition occurs, our conceptual mechanism stands already in place, and is activated by the arrival of sensation. This "ordering of events" is what Kant terms *determinant judgment:* the concepts determine how the sensations are to be interpreted, as a certain machine sifts coins into their appropriate slots. But he also perceived a second form of judgment, termed *reflective judgment,* which in a sense proceeds in the direction opposite to determinant judgment. In reflective judgment the interpretive concepts are somehow incomplete, or entirely absent, and the task of the mind is to fabricate them or fill in around the existing (fragmentary) set. The incredible incident in the Apollo 13 saga, in which a pile of artifacts are dumped on a table before a team of scientists, who are then told, "This is what's on board. You have six hours: fabricate a carbon dioxide filtration device," shows reflective judgment at its most active.

Determinant judgment, in other words, follows the path laid out by our categories of interpretation, while reflective judgment hews the path. Clearly, on Kant's view judgment used reflectively is essential to the growth of scientific explanation and human understanding. And it just happens to be essential to aesthetic appreciation as well.

If this reflective use of judgment, Kant reasoned, is to uncover any real laws of nature (not just haphazard dicta), then it needs to be grounded in some principle; and the principle that best fits the circumstances holds that the particular laws of nature should be regarded as having a unity that only an understanding could supply. In other words, we should treat nature as if something akin to a divine understanding prescribed its laws (for our sake), because only by doing so will we have any hope of reaching some systematic understanding of it. Otherwise, chaos would be as likely as order, and scientific progress would be little more than an illusion. Thus the attribution of purposiveness to nature lies behind the reflective employment of judgment.

Now Kant contends that when judgment, used reflectively, leads to the realization "that two or more empirical heterogeneous laws of nature are allied under one principle that embraces them both," a distinct feeling of pleasure accompanies this realization.[22] In other words, it pleases us to solve a problem or make a discovery. A pleasure of this sort seems to be more intellectual in nature, yet it is undeniable that we do experience such feelings—the rush that accompanied the "Aha!" expressed in Archimedes's famous "Eureka!" This pleasure recedes as the new item of knowledge is incorporated into our basic cognitive framework, but it was definitely there at the outset.*

Disinterestedness

Pleasure likewise is at the very heart of our aesthetic experience, but Kant insists that it is a very special kind of pleasure—a *disinterested* pleasure.

---

*This is not exactly the Kantian view to the letter, but I believe the Kantian view, held to the letter, dissolves in contradiction. Kant holds that the pleasure does not wear off, and yet "it become[s] gradually fused with simple cognition, and no longer arrests particular attention" (Kant, *Critique of Judgment*, p. 28). It seems to me, though, that a pleasure that goes undetected is no real pleasure at all. Does it make any sense to say, "You're experiencing pleasure right now, though you may not realize it?" If it seems to, then substitute "pain" for "pleasure" and see how that sits.

This notion of disinterestedness turns out to be the key element leading to his contention that aesthetic judgments are universalizable, so let us consider it carefully.

To be disinterested does not mean to be uninterested, that is, bored or indifferent—quite the contrary, disinterestedness normally correlates with an intense, heightened state of mental attentiveness. The kinds of "interests" Kant aims to rule out by this specification include the following: (a) receiving the kind of physical pleasure that might be called "gratification," (b) experiencing that pleasure which accompanies the fulfillment of a particular goal or purpose, or (c) enjoying the singular pleasure that follows from doing, witnessing, or contemplating morally laudable behavior.

Physical pleasure is not aesthetic pleasure; or, as Kant is more likely to put it, pleasure in the beautiful is different from pleasure enjoyed by the senses. Across the centuries beauty has been consistently associated only with our visual and auditory senses (with the imagination mixed in, to account for our pleasure in the literary arts), as the other senses have been regarded as "base"—unworthy of the beautiful because some form of physical contact is required for their activation (obvious in the case of touch and taste, less so but still easily arguable in the case of smell, since presumably odors result from the impact of certain material effluvia upon our olfactory apparatus).

Kant accepts this division of pleasures, but carries it—quite cogently, and with a different rationale—even into the domains of sight and hearing. Some people take delight merely in the color yellow, or find a certain pleasure in the perception of pastel shades; some are touched by the simple throb of a guitar or the intonation of a violin, irrespective of whether these particular colors or sounds are arranged in any artistically interesting fashion. Even though preferences of this sort occur in the visual and auditory domains, they are still, Kant believed, more closely akin to the gratification derived from a good meal or a comfortable bed, than they are to the pleasure we take in the beautiful. Gratification, after all, is something we seek; the beautiful, on his account, finds us.

We are often pleased by the performance of a particular tool—a block plane, say—because it enables us to accomplish a certain goal, which in this case would be to level off and smooth out a surface of wood. Such pleasure is indeed genuine, Kant holds, but it is not aesthetic, due to its association with the fulfillment of a purpose. If at a given moment, however, we find ourselves contemplating the tool itself—the economical arrangement of its parts, the ingenious manner in which the blade can be raised and lowered securely, its streamlined shape—now we have moved into the domain of the aesthetic; we are appreciating not the utility of the instrument but its beauty. We set aside consideration of what it can do for us and admire it for what it is in itself. Similarly, if, while standing atop a mountain peak we look down upon a magnificent expanse of forest and tremble at the thought of its potential for timber production or how it might accommodate a resort hotel, we are not enjoying its beauty. That form of enjoyment comes only when we set aside any and all pecuniary considerations and delight in the mere contemplation of the forest—for the life it exhales and the mysteries it enfolds.

Morality, Kant believed, also constitutes a potential source of pleasure; but here too the pleasure is deemed by him to be an interested one—we are interested, quite simply, in seeing that the good is done, and we have definite ideas about how this is to be accomplished. Moral behavior necessarily involves setting and realizing goals, or at least striving to realize them; hence we consider a possible action, conceive of the rule that it would fall under, and act. How different this is from our enjoyment of something beautiful, where the intrusion of definite concepts and the realization of specific goals actually dissipates the experience and converts it into just another cognitive event in everyday life.

In characterizing this notion of disinterestedness, Kant actually suggests that we are not concerned even with the existence of the object under contemplation when we find it to be beautiful: something about the experience leaves us content merely to dwell on the idea that stands at the center of our consciousness at such a time, without seeking assurances of its objective grounding. What could this strange something be?

Purposeless Purposiveness

Kant's answer to this latter question is lamentably obscure, yet powerful in its suggestiveness. First, the pleasure associated with beauty derives from our apprehension of the *form* of the beautiful object. "Form" can of course be interpreted in a variety of ways, but many of these interpretations are irrelevant to the present context. Some involve a definite concept of what an object should be (the form of a hammer or a plough horse or a race horse), and Kant doesn't allow aesthetic judgment to follow from definite concepts; others involve a particular goal we might have in mind ("I need something *like this*"), and realizing or even striving after goals is similarly deemed antagonistic to the aesthetic process. The approach to form that Kant finds acceptable is one in which the object itself suggests a certain purposiveness, though without actually disclosing just what its purpose may be (and certainly without serving any of our own particular purposes). What does he have in mind by such purposiveness, and how does it contribute to the pleasure we associate with our experience of the beautiful?

To venture an answer to the first of these questions, purposiveness is plainly apparent in an automobile, for example—in the automobile taken as a single entity, and in the many different architectonic levels that make it up (although purpose, I must say, is not particularly apparent in any of the bucketful of parts that have fallen harmlessly off mine over the years). The purposiveness of a utilitarian object such as an automobile, in fact, collapses into the distinct purposes for which it was conceived. Purposiveness seems also to be readily discernible in the various organs that collaborate in constituting and sustaining a living organism: understanding a heart or a liver is understanding what it does for the organism in which it inheres— what purpose it serves. A certain purposiveness likewise seems to be exhibited by any organism taken as a whole, but there the matter begins to become hazy. For what is the purpose of a horse? We put horses to various uses, but dare we imagine that our uses constitute the purpose of the horse? An entire ecological system sometimes bears the appearance of an individual organism, given the intimate and necessary interrelations among its component organisms, but what might its purpose be? Here we seem to be approaching a domain in which purposiveness is detectable, and yet no particular purpose steps forward to declare itself.

Instances of this purposeless purposiveness also occur in the domain of art. A musical composition—a nocturne, perhaps—might be woven together in such a way that each of its melodic twists and turns, every rhythmic syncopation and harmonic modulation, seem to contribute perfectly to a sense of wholeness. But what purpose could this bare sense of wholeness be serving, beyond itself? Much music and art does, of course, serve definite purposes, from the arousal of patriotic fervor to the expression of individual sentiments to the financial enrichment of the artist. But often we are stopped short by the "rightness" of an artistic gesture that urges us to ask, "right for what?" and the only answer that offers itself is, "Right for what it is, where it is." Instances such as these may be what Kant had in mind in speaking of a purposiveness without purpose.

It is important to note, though, that purposiveness, as Kant understands it, is in no way part of the object, however loudly and clearly any object may seem to declare its purpose. A screwdriver may be eight inches long, have a silver-colored shaft and a red handle, weigh four ounces, be made of steel and plastic—all of these qualities could be said to be objectively present in the screwdriver. But that it is designed for the purpose of turning screws is not a constitutive property of its objecthood, however much such an intention might have led to its very existence, and however easy it may be to infer such a purpose from a consideration of its form. Instead, Kant argues, seeing things as purposive is an achievement of the subject, a certain state of mind in which we sometimes—often, perhaps—find ourselves, and in which our reflective judgment is set loose to render a fragment of our experience more intelligible.

Pleasure

As we have seen, anytime we take something to be exhibiting purposiveness, Kant believes our reflective power of judgment to be engaged in a pleasantly provocative way. In a manner of speaking, when reflective judgment is activated it sets out to negotiate a harmonious accord between imagination (the faculty of images, remember) and understanding (the faculty of concepts). And it is in this process, not in the actual achievement of any such accord, that Kant locates this peculiar feeling of pleasure. (As was mentioned earlier, the pleasure can even be seen to vanish once understanding comes to take possession of a concept or rule that can be put to use in subsequent cognition.)

Pleasure is a state of being that, if it had its way, would perpetuate itself indefinitely. It smacks of the absurd to say, "No, that's enough pleasure for me, thanks." What we might mean, even if we were to say such a thing, would be, "Any more of *this* would begin to displease me" (perhaps I have reached my popcorn-eating limit). I would then cease a particular action in the interest of maximizing pleasure. Now if the exercise of reflective judgment is, as Kant alleges, a pleasurable activity, and yet if the firm establishment of interpretive categories tends to obviate this activity (and the pleasure with it), then it would seem perfectly natural for us to be especially appreciative of those experiences in which our reflective judgment is set into motion, and yet is unable to lead us to any definite conclusion. In such experiences no unification of concepts is reached, no explanatory rule is generated, and yet the search for such devices is sustained. This is what occurs in the presence of the beautiful.

Where the beauty of nature is concerned, Kant appears to be suggesting that a flower, a fern, or a forest is perceived as beautiful because it sets us to musing, a form of musing that always leads us to pose the ultimate question "Why?" but that never quite allows us to formulate the one, precise answer that lays all further questioning to rest. Of course, to say "It is God's will" looks like one such simple answer, but this is hardly the case, for not only is our concept of God indeterminate, but our concept of God's purpose, such as it is embedded in the natural realm, is utterly inscrutable to us. Whenever we appeal directly to the "will of God" in explaining anything, our understanding of that phenomenon remains utterly stationary.

Beauty lies somewhere in that mysterious purposiveness that we can't restrain ourselves from attributing to nature but can't for the life of us account for with any degree of satisfaction. What else is there to that magnificent sequoia that stands so tall? Are we to say that big is beautiful? Isn't it that we marvel at its power to endure fires, storms, infestations; we wonder what it would tell us if it could speak; we wonder why it came to be in possession of such longevity (and we wonder this not without a trace of envy, for its longevity so greatly surpasses our own); indeed, we wonder *why*. Nature will never be seen as beautiful to any creature lacking an inquiring mind.

While Kant himself suggests that pure beauties are perhaps only to be found in nature, since there may always be some detectable purpose behind any human artifact, nevertheless it is possible to see something of this same reflective process at work in our responses to works of art. Certain artistic modes are better-suited to this approach than others: in painting and sculpture, works of the sort that have come to be known as "abstract," for their avoidance of any straightforward representationality;* in music, compositions with no text or title that likewise may create some representational purpose. In both of these media, well-formed works exhibit a certain structure and betray certain unifying tendencies, while resisting inclusion within any definite, formal scheme. In a great painting, as we saw in our discussion of artistic form, we won't be able to say, "All visual forces come to rest precisely here"; in a significant composition, we won't be able to say, "It follows precisely this set of rules, from start to finish." Where and when all visual forces do come to rest, we move on to the next painting, probably never to return to the previous one; the moment we realize that a particular composition has that cut-from-the-same-mold aspect, it likewise takes on the same allure as yesterday's crossword puzzle.

Works of art that are alive and beautiful for us are those that tantalize us with the suggestion that we might, if we live with them long enough, come to comprehend them; and yet the moment we seem to have them fully within our grasp, they evaporate. This interplay between mind and art may well be the process that Kant explains in terms of the harmonious interplay between imagination and understanding, touched off and sustained by reflective judgment.

---

*"Abstract" is an unfortunate term for nonrepresentational art, since abstraction, properly speaking, involves the distillation of certain pivotal elements from a scene, thus allowing for a drastically simplified representation. For some enlightening observations on abstraction, see David Morgan, "The Rise and Fall of Abstraction in Eighteenth-Century Art Theory," pp. 449–78.

Universality (At Last!)

In this characterization of the aesthetic experience is contained the grounding for Kant's contention that our aesthetic judgments are universalizable. He never deviates from his initial conviction that the judging process deserves to be regarded as a subjective matter, but he does contend, in effect, that not all subjective matters should be deemed personal, private, and idiosyncratic. And aesthetic judgment, properly viewed, is precisely one of those exceptional areas. From the considerations that have been presented here, two points emerge that together supply the rationale for this conviction.

First, these various faculties, whose harmonious interplay is essentially involved in aesthetic judgment—judgment in its reflective mode, imagination, understanding—are taken by Kant to be constitutive of human nature. Some of us may have richer imaginations than others, but all of us fabricate images from sensory data, all of us piece together pictures of the world that correspond to one another in certain salient respects. Some of us may have understandings endowed with a broader supply of empirical categories than others, but all of us share one fundamental set of categories—those that lead us to see events as causally connected, objects as substantial and unified, nature as a system of necessary interrelations, and so on. Some of us may be more prone to scientific inquiry than others, but all of us have at one time or another wondered, mused, noted similarities among certain elements of reality and formulated explanatory hypotheses, though they may have been quite bizarre or erroneous. And it is these very faculties that are quickened into activity by objects and events that we judge to be beautiful. It is by virtue of our like-mindedness, then, that we can expect others to be moved as we are in an encounter with something beautiful.

But this like-mindedness is not, in itself, quite enough to legitimize our expectation that others will see things as we do.* For to be sure, we have many inclinations and preferences that are distinctly our own, and with regard to which we feel no urge to extract a similar sentiment from others (indeed, we may at times be interested in discouraging it in others: where, for example, a friend and I are flying lazy circles over that Last Slice of Pizza). In short, where beauty is at issue, assurance is required not only that we humans share a common mental mechanism, but also that during this

---

*"Expectation" is used here in the strong sense, not merely to register a prediction of some sort. When we were told by our parents that they expected us to be home by eleven, it was understood that they were packing more into that assertion than a simple statement as to the likely time of our arrival.

particular experience our judgment is emerging directly and exclusively from the activity of that mechanism (and not from a similar but personal and idiosyncratic source: from the form of the painting, and not from the fact that it is a painting of a cat). This assurance is captured in Kant's notion of disinterestedness.

Circumstances in which we are truly disinterested are those in which we have set aside any and all of the considerations that pertain directly to us as beings concerned with our own comfort and well-being. It is our own personal cares, goals, interests, anxieties and so forth that set each of us apart from one another—that make of each of us a unique individual. But at those moments when we manage to transcend these practical concerns, we are all one, all cut from the same fabric: we shed the skin of individuality and emerge in all our humanness. When we are disinterested, then, we are solely *interested* in the delight provided by the free play of our cognitive faculties, an interest that, Kant believed, we have every right to impute to others—to all others who find themselves in possession of the same faculties, which on his view amounts to everyone.*

The self, for Kant, does not dissolve, as it did with Hume, into a bundle of perceptions; it possesses a distinct character, one that is both active and highly structured. Where we saw, with Hume, the power of taste threatening to crumble, as did the self, into a heap of humors, dispositions, social conditions, geographic determinants, and temporal restraints, and found him unwilling to secure it with anything stronger than Scotch tape (pun probably intended), we find Kant endeavoring to rescue this power by placing it in a necessary alliance with the very faculties that constitute the self *as* they constitute our world—a world shared by peoples across time and place, and amidst social and psychological differentiations. Universality is possible because our judgment is grounded in a common subjectivity.

---

*It astonishes me to see Kant's aesthetic theory thrown in among the heap of theories allegedly addressing themselves only to European males. If ever there was a theory that aimed to embrace all humankind, it is his. Quite likely Kant—the *man*—believed men to be intellectually superior to women, and white men to be superior to nonwhite men. These were not radical views in the Europe of his time; in fact, they were normal enough not even to merit pejorative terms to characterize them. But nowhere in the corpus of Kant's philosophy is there to be found the assertion that women or "savages" (as he probably would have put it) are devoid of imagination, understanding, or the power of reflection, or that they are inherently incapable of stepping back and taking delight in the interplay of these faculties. As it is, we all make our way through the same world, and since on Kant's view these various mental faculties bear the responsibility for constituting this world, it should be obvious that no human being is to be exempted, on grounds of sex or race, from the just claims of taste.

Critical Reflections

As valiant as Kant's effort is to establish the legitimacy of aesthetic judgment, it is hardly without problems. Let us mention some of the more serious ones.

1. There is plenty of room to wonder whether, in aesthetic experience, our mental mechanism is activated in anything like the manner Kant describes, or whether, for that matter, our mental mechanism itself resembles in any way his characterization of it.

While the Kantian approach to the question of our knowledge of the external world had been profoundly influential in this century, not just in philosophy but in cognitive psychology as well, it is doubtful that there are too many thinkers who would still apportion intellectual tasks among such faculties as the imagination, the understanding, and judgment (in fact, talk of "faculties" is somewhat dated). The idea that we ourselves structure experience rather than simply experience a prestructured world finds deep allegiances among many schools of thought; but that our understanding is armed with precisely that set of categories alleged by Kant, or that the interpretive frameworks are in some fundamental respect identical in all peoples—these are matters about which serious doubts have been raised over the years.

There are certain schools of thought, for example, that still accept some notion of a structure imposed by mind on experience, but locate it instead in our linguistic dispositions. This, of course, implies an interpretive pluralism far different from that envisioned by Kant—as many structures, it would appear, as there are language families. Others see interpretive structures varying from culture to culture, depending on the different sets of exigencies that each one faces: a pragmatic approach to the structure(s) of mind. Since Kant's time, in fact, the tendency among sociologists, anthropologists, and linguists has been to emphasize cultural differentiation, even at the level of "deep" structure, at the expense of homogeneity.

If there is any truth to these more recent approaches, it becomes difficult to hold that our aesthetic responses at base all derive from one single mode of experience, whether or not that experience should derive from the free play between imagination and understanding. Indeed, the emphasis on cultural variety can easily be carried into the aesthetic domain, such that artistic approaches and decorative styles constitute just one further point on which cultures can be seen to differ.

Interestingly, there is some flexibility built into the Kantian explanation of our aesthetic response, in that by virtue of its very nature, reflective judgment can lead different people at different times in different directions. Innovations in conceptual schemes and syntheses of principles are not at all bound to follow one and only one pattern: the mere conviction that an intelligible design has been imparted to the world imposes no precise constraints on the shape that design must take. But this is hardly a concession that is likely to allay all the doubts raised by the ever-deepening studies of cultural differentiation.

2. Even if we were to accept the whole of the Kantian account of beauty, there is room to wonder whether any one of us could ever actually be in a position to certify, "Yes, I have now set aside all personal, individuating concerns and have achieved a state of total disinterestedness." It may *feel* that way to us, and yet we may be overlooking the simplest of distractions or attractions that is responsible for the delight we are experiencing. Someone who knows us well could casually observe, "There you go again, doting on pastel colors—can't you see how insipid their arrangement is there?" or "You'd find something good to say about Andie MacDowell even if she delivered her lines like John Wayne!" (which some claim she does). In short, it seems that we need some criterion to enable us to distinguish, from within the framework of our own experience, between actually being disinterested and only fancying we are disinterested (for the feeling of universalizability wells up within us, as part of our subjective response).

Hume's "key in the cask" test, with one foot inside the aesthetic domain (pronouncing the wine good) and one outside ("were it not for a small taste of leather"), aimed to be such a criterion. But it has no known aesthetic equivalent, nor is it likely ever to have one. Reid's appeal to reason in aesthetic judgment, whereby such judgments were seen as being true or false, aimed at the same target, since truth and falsehood are objectively decidable; but a close look at aesthetic experience reveals that it has a quite different character from that experience which leads to truth or falsity. A presumption of like-mindedness such as Kant offers, as flawed as it is, appears to come closest to capturing the spirit of what is involved in demanding that others judge as we do.

Universality Revisited, and Revised

If the universe, or even the minuscule dot of it inhabited by humankind, appears too large and diverse to entertain any hope of attributing genuine universality to our aesthetic judgments; if it is improbable that there is any aspect of our nature, especially our cognitive nature, that we can expect to find both distributed generally throughout all humanity and centrally active in aesthetic experience, this may be because we were looking for too much to begin with. Perhaps there is some respect in which we can lessen the pretensions of our inquiry and, in so doing, increase our chance of achieving some success.

We could say, for example, that instead of specifying the conditions that *do* allow us to demand that everyone else respond to a work of art as we ourselves responded, what Kant offers is an account of what conditions *would* have to be met in order to utter such a demand. The slight but immensely significant shift in terminology that captures this distinction would be to move from saying, "Our judgments are universalizable *because* we are like-minded individuals," to saying instead, "Our judgments are universalizable *to the degree that* we are like-minded individuals." Even Kant himself suggests at one point that it could well be that no pure judgment of taste is ever made; still, these are the conditions that govern such a judgment. And after all, how are we to judge that a particular state of affairs is not realizable unless we have a clear sense of the parameters of that state of affairs? How can it be said that we can't "square the circle" until we know precisely what is involved in squaring the circle? How, then, can it be said we cannot universalize our aesthetic judgments until a clear picture of this act of judging has been drawn?

The shift from "because" to "to the degree that" could actually succeed in opening the door to the articulation of some subuniverses within which the demand for shared experience might meaningfully be met. Let us consider a few examples that tend to support this claim.

The culture responsible for hewing the statues that stand on Easter Island might well have found little to appreciate in classical Greek sculpture. But then those who dote on classical Greek sculpture are unlikely to look with any great favor on the megalithic Easter Island works. Undoubtedly the aestheticians of the eighteenth century—those from Europe, at any rate—would place great value on the classical sculpture and treat the other as crude, primitive, insufficiently evolved. But there are obvious limitations to their perspective, obvious respects in which it can be declared that they were not fit to judge of the Easter Island works, and obvious respects in which the culture responsible for producing these latter works was or would be eminently qualified to judge them. It is easy to envision people within that culture drawing distinctions, perceiving subtle differences, arguing among themselves over where to place the works, what direction to make them face, and so on. And it is also easy to imagine that certain people within that culture regarded such carvings as a massive waste of time and resented being obliged to participate in hauling them this way or that. All is not always copacetic in paradise.

These Easter Island malcontents, with their "deviant" ideas, spoke out, or, as is more likely, remained silent but unconvinced, within a framework that in its own way demanded obedience. Such a framework can be seen to constitute a distinct aesthetic perspective, or, shall we say, a universe of its own, unsullied by exposure to other competing universes, possessing its own set of priorities, its own rules of procedure, its own hierarchy of authority. Might we not say that the malcontents failed to judge things as they *ought* to be judged?

To continue this line of speculation, if a few Easter Islanders, fed up with the prevailing aesthetic, did actually leave the community, take to the sea, and establish a new society further to the west with a different set of sculptural priorities, we would have no alternative but to judge that a new culture—a new universe—had thereby been created. Where does this line of thinking lead us?

A plurality of universes should not be too alarming a notion. Our language contains the expression "universe of discourse," and use of this expression involves nothing more than the delimitation of the range of items potentially referred to in any given interchange, from "all there is" to, say, the class of animals or artworks. A few examples may clarify what is being suggested here.

Consider, to begin, the way certain musical parameters shape our listening consciousness. We in the West are principally accustomed to two modal systems, which are known as the diatonic major and minor scales. Others exist—others have existed in the West, even—but these two have come to dominate in the past three centuries. (The reasons for this are not entirely clear; they do perhaps conduce to drama in music more readily than other modes, but in any case we needn't engage the issue here.) As a result of this domination, our minds, for want of any significant exposure to other scale systems, have become patterned to respond to music written within our own, and unfit to deal effectively with music based on others.

Music written within the pentatonic scale—the scale on which much oriental music is based—sounds hollow to us, since the two half-intervals, from which so much of the drama of our music is wrung, are absent in it. But it is highly unlikely that an inhabitant of China or Japan would find such music to be hollow and undramatic. Music of India and the Near East, employing as it does quarter tones along with a considerable variety of different modes, "whines" at us, since we are accustomed to hearing intervals no narrower than the half tone, but again, it is unlikely that it whines at its own practitioners and devotees. Furthermore, the lack of a strong harmonic foundation in this music seems to have led to a corresponding richness of melodic and rhythmic elaboration—one that, perhaps, is a bit too rich for our comprehension. Since all music must be composed in one mode or another, it appears that from the very outset there is no real possibility of achieving any kind of aesthetic universality in that domain, but that the different modal systems provide an initial suggestion, at least, as to how we could set about to divide up the musical terrain in terms of competing universes.

In contrast to music, it is noteworthy that there are literary works that continue to offer satisfaction to readers across the centuries, and naturally these works and readers will come from widely divergent cultural backgrounds. Homer was relatively ancient even to Plato and Aristotle, he is three millennia removed from us, and yet his writing still is readily perceived as dramatic; his stories hold our attention as they unfold, and there is still much that an aspiring writer can learn from Homer about how to bring animation to a scene or a description. Yet undeniably much is lost to us: talk of the gods and their sallies into the human arena cannot possibly carry the significance for us that it did in ancient Greece; the moral system that we saw Hume faulting so strenuously may well not be our own; and even a modern Greek reader could not be moved by the poetry or the music of the language exactly as Homer's listeners must have been. Still, there remain some important dimensions of Homer's writing that overlap with our own dearest preferences.

An important element in Homer that is lost is, of course, the poetry. Lyric poetry especially resists translation (a French adage plays on the rhyme between *"traduire,"* to translate, and *"trahir,"* to betray), and is therefore accessible only to native, or at least fluent, speakers of a given language. An epic is more translatable, since, like a novel, it has characters, events, plot development, and the like, and is less dependent on linguistic sonority to achieve its effects. Indeed, when poetry is translated successfully, there is reason to wonder whether it wouldn't be better to say that a new poem has been created—some of Ezra Pound's translations of Chinese poetry occasion this reflection. Thus the relevant universe in the case of poetry just happens to coincide closely with a "universe of discourse": the linguistic framework within which a poem is created.

The visual arts seem more akin to prose works in their ability to span apparent temporal and cultural boundaries. Pre-Columbian statuary is held in high regard among many in our time, but who could pretend to fathom the mentality out of which such works emerged? Even medieval Western statuary, architecture, and stained glass meet with the fervent approval of many, yet few among these devotees share the religious faith to which so much art of that time gives testimony. In all these cases where works of drastically different cultures meet nevertheless with our approval, it *must* be judged that, however great the apparent differences in overall style of life may be, there are still certain grounds on which a genuine and deep sharing takes place. In these respects, then, we could perhaps think of certain cultures, certain universes, as coextending with one another.

Clearly, this manner of construing the notion of a culture is heavily infused with aesthetic determinants, which signals problems of the sort we saw Hume wrestling with not very successfully in his attempts to produce some noncritical criterion of good criticism. A self-contained culture—one that persists in relative isolation—might present itself to us as a whole entity of which one component is the aesthetic dimension. But just how would we go about characterizing American culture, where all the pathways of the world seem to crisscross in a dizzying jumble? Ethnic homogeneity will hardly get us far—better that we let people's aesthetic inclinations be our guide than to try to find some broader set of cultural determinants that will somehow, miraculously, match the aesthetic.

An image may be helpful in capturing the relationship among cultures being suggested here. Imagine one all-inclusive universe as a circle: the kind of universality sought objectively by Reid and subjectively by Kant could be represented by such a circle. Then picture a radical individualism, one in which each of us has our own taste and no one else's taste has any dominion over ours, as an indefinitely large collection of circles, no two of which coincide at any point. The alternative view I am suggesting here would then be captured by a collection of circles, each representing, in some loose sense of the term, a culture—a universe—certain of which overlap with one another to varying degrees, some entirely included in others, some perhaps extensive enough to include several circles concentrically or eccentrically within them, and so forth.

On this last account, each circle would represent a set of individuals, and within any given circle a judgment appropriately made (leaving aside, if you please, consideration of how to determine appropriateness) could lay claim to the assent of the other individuals contained within that circle, but only to those individuals—no demands could be made upon anyone from a circle entirely detached from the one within which a judgment was made. The order represented in this image is a far cry from that captured in the neat conception of universality dreamed of by the eighteenth-century thinkers, but it nevertheless offers more hope of accounting for the existence of critics, experts, teachers, schools, institutions, masterpieces, and the like than does the atomistic, individualistic view, which offers none whatever.

To bring this image to bear on a particular artistic domain, think of the musical parameters mentioned earlier, the modal systems employed in different cultures, for a start. They could be taken to establish various noncoextensive circles. Then within one of these, such as the one that has dominated in the West for several centuries, there are innumerable sub-circles—the music of the classical period, the baroque era, jazz, heavy metal rock, etc. Certain threads can be found reaching through all of these in various respects, such as the system of harmonic probabilities, techniques of melodic construction, or the like. Some styles are born and die out relatively quickly (disco, thankfully); others, while no longer serving as a source of composition, nevertheless persist in their appeal. Bach, for example, although dead for two and a half centuries, continues to impassion many listeners—more so now, without a doubt, than during his own lifetime. Jazz musicians forever find in him a kindred spirit (witness, for example, Keith Jarrett's recordings of Bach's keyboard works, Jacques Loussier's "loose" arrangements of various pieces); transcriptions of his works are made for whatever new instruments come along, and often they sit well on those instruments; compositions of his were reinterpreted during the Romantic period, and are now adopted and adapted to cinematic musical purposes.

We could even think that a criterion for greatness could be drawn from the ability of a single artist to touch and influence a great variety of artistic subcultures. Graphically, that would mean that any art that was central to or highly valued within the circle that included the richest variety of other circles could be deemed greater than that which has some appeal, however strong it may be, in one small, unencompassing circle.

Shakespeare, like Bach, spans the centuries—a couple more centuries, even, than Bach. His works are still performed and appreciated, though the language at times poses problems (perhaps it is time to consider translating Shakespeare into English!). Still, children can appreciate *A Midsummer Night's Dream;* Kurasawa's *Throne of Blood* largely dispenses with language and offers a purely cinematic version of *Macbeth,* brilliantly interpreting it within a feudal Japanese framework; *Romeo and Juliet* reappeared as a musical in *West Side Story,* and more recently, in Baz Luhrman's version, came complete with gun fights, car crashes, and Mercutio cast as a black drag queen; Ian McKellan provided a Nazi setting for *Richard III*—the possibilities of reinterpretation seem limitless.

On the other hand, *Oh, Calcutta!* came and went; it occupied a noticeable place in our culture for an amusing moment, but it will not exhibit any special longevity. That is to say, the subculture to which it appealed was small, and proved evanescent. It participates, therefore, in a circle that contains few other circles, though it may itself be contained by various others that capture more broadly the spectrum of stage works in the Western tradition.

The pseudonymous humor columnist Joe Bob Briggs has his own range of competence as a cinema critic, however restricted it might be. Through his uncanny ability to isolate what factors enable this slasher film, but not that one, to receive accolades from the demented public that dotes on such productions, he does indeed speak legitimately and articulately on behalf of a certain subuniverse. But this circle is a small one, and we can only pray that it will never become sufficiently mainstream to force Shakespeare and Chekhov to submit to it or be cast adrift.

On the present account, then, the number and variety of people an artist touches across time strongly influences that artist's claim to greatness. It says, in effect, that as an artist, you are free to do as you like, but you are also free to be ridiculed or ignored by all but your immediate family and friends. If that turns out to be the circle whose approval you solicit most, then it appears we are all happy: you find grounds for satisfaction within your drastically limited sphere of influence, while we freely exercise our right to ignore the eccentric works you create, and are justified in withholding any honorific judgments. So regardless of how deeply you succeed in pleasing this minute subculture, you mustn't think that you can thereby claim to be a great artist—to make this latter claim you must reach a wider and richer spectrum of humankind, and earn their approval over time.

Of course, compatible with this approach is the possibility, lamentable as it may seem at the moment, that Shakespeare and Bach will at some point in the future fall into an oblivion of noncomprehension and indifference (actually that already happened to Bach once: well into the nineteenth century Mendelssohn rescued him from near-complete eclipse, and the rest, as they say, is history). Given the manner, mentioned above, in which musical systems tend to exclude one another, one might expect Bach's hegemony to be somewhat the more fragile. If New Age music were to become prevalent, for example, then surely Bach and any other composer whose music followed a beginning-middle-end structure would be abandoned: such goal-directed creations could only offend ears acculturated to music that starts nowhere, goes nowhere, and merely continues, and continues, and continues.

Then again, we do seem to be on the threshold of becoming a postliterate society, dominated increasingly by fleeting images projected at us from the major foci of information and entertainment (the television, the computer); the relevance of a great playwright and wordsmith in such a world could well become precarious.

In either case, the disappearance of an artist now deemed great would imply, for our purposes, that the basic condition of like-mindedness ceased to join our culture to the one that succeeded it. In terms of the image I have been promoting, the artists in question would cease to enjoy dominion in any active circles; they would take their place alongside the Easter Island megaliths—towering monuments to God knows what.

It is my suggestion, therefore, that aesthetic judgment could well be seen to possess a certain range of applicability beyond being simply the brute utterance of the (momentary) preference of one individual, but that it is hardly reasonable to expect to find grounds for exacting agreement from all mankind where questions of taste are at issue.

A Final Thought

Philosophy has long represented itself as a quest for truth. "Love of wisdom" is what *"philo-sophy"* signifies in Greek, and wisdom is to be gained only through grasping certain fundamental truths (even if the most fundamental of all such truths should turn out to involve, as Socrates claimed, the recognition of his own ignorance). But truth, it appears, is not easy to come by; if it were, philosophy would have spoken its last word centuries ago.

The present study, as much as any other philosophical inquiry with a historical component about it, should make it clear that ideas and interpretive schemes succeed one another, if not rapidly, at least relentlessly. Philosophers never put forward theories that they take to be false, and yet none has ever put forward the theory that put to rest all subsequent theorizing.

It should hardly be concluded, however, that we have been engaged here in a pursuit of failure, for each theory considered has illuminated some facet of the aesthetic experience, even if none has shone with sufficient brilliance to efface all the others with its own light. Indeed, I myself confess that while I approach any theory first with the aim to understand it, then with the intent to confirm or disconfirm its claim to truth, I nevertheless can derive continued sustenance from a theory that I take to be effectively falsified. For even an incomplete or inadequate theory can call our attention to features of artworks the recognition of which will greatly enrich our experience of them.

In the end, then, if a theory of art can claim to have expanded our understanding and appreciation of some portion of the art world, then even though it may come to be questioned and ultimately abandoned, its edifying consequences are positive and permanent. It is in such a spirit that I offer the present book.

Notes

Notes to Chapter 1

1. Plato, *Meno*, p. 5.
2. Denis Diderot, *Oeuvres esthétiques*, p. 417. My translation.
3. Suzanne Langer, *Feeling and Form*, p. 60.
4. Clive Bell, *Art*, p. 7.
5. Ludwig Wittgenstein, *Philosophical Investigations*. The relevant discussion occurs in Sects. 65 to 77.
6. Morris Weitz, "The Role of Theory in Aesthetics," p. 30.
7. Ibid.
8. Ibid., p. 31.
9. Ibid.
10. Ibid., p. 27.
11. Wittgenstein, *Philosophical Investigations*, Sect. 124. The deep analyses that Wittgenstein engages in fall more into the category of metaphilosophy.
12. Maurice Mandelbaum, "Family Resemblances and Generalizations Concerning the Arts," pp. 219–28.
13. Ibid., p. 221.
14. Wittgenstein, *Philosophical Investigations*, Sect. 66.
15. Mandelbaum, "Family Resemblances," p. 222.
16. Ibid., p. 226.
17. Arthur C. Danto, *The Transfiguration of the Commonplace*, p. vi.
18. Arthur C. Danto, "The Artworld," p. 580.
19. Ibid., p. 581.
20. Ibid., p. 572. Emphasis mine.
21. George Dickie, "The New Institutional Theory of Art," p. 196.
22. Ibid., p. 203.
23. Ibid., p. 204.
24. Danto, *Transfiguration*, p. viii.
25. Danto, "Artworld," p. 581. Emphasis mine.
26. Danto, *Transfiguration*, p. 99.
27. Tom Wolfe, *The Painted Word*, p. 121.
28. Danto, *Transfiguration*, p. 111.

Notes to Chapter 2

1. Homer, *The Iliad*, p. 390. Emphasis mine.
2. S. H. Butcher, *Aristotle's Theory of Poetry and Fine Art*, p. 129.
3. Plato, *Republic*, p. 81.
4. Ibid., p. 324.
5. Ibid., p. 339.
6. Aristotle, *Poetics*, p. 33.
7. Ibid., p. 31.
8. Ibid., p. 30.
9. Ibid., p. 67.
10. Ibid., p. 44.
11. Plato, *Republic*, p. 337.
12. Ibid., pp. 337–38.
13. Ibid., pp. 338–39.
14. Ibid., p. 339.
15. Aristotle, *Poetics*, p. 40. Emphasis mine.
16. Butcher, *Aristotle's Theory*, p. 23. Emphasis mine.
17. This is a much-abbreviated version of the account Else offers, in the notes to his translation of the *Poetics*, in support of his interpretation.
18. Aristotle, *Poetics*, p. 40. Emphasis mine.
19. Ibid., p. 61. Emphasis mine.
20. Ibid., p. 39.
21. Ibid.
22. Ibid., p. 40.
23. Ibid., p. 29.
24. Rensselaer Lee, *Ut Pictura Poesis: The Humanistic Theory of Painting*, p. 11.
25. Ibid., p. 13.
26. This line of thinking can be found in his *Phaedo*, pp. 22–27.
27. Plato, *Republic*, p. 325.
28. See Lee, *Ut Pictura Poesis*, n. 49, p. 13; quote on p. 15.
29. An interesting challenge to this notion is posed by Nelson Goodman in his *Languages of Art*. Goodman contends that in truth, paintings represent objects purely by *denoting* them within certain symbol systems, and not by resembling them (this discussion occurs in Chapter One). I parried this claim some years ago, arguing that even resemblance is system and context dependent, which made it possible to speak meaningfully of a painting resembling its object. (See my "Representation, Relativism and Resemblance.")
30. Sometimes, of course, it can follow a cause, a movement, or even the development of an idea within a given social framework. The same point being made about the tragic hero applies equally well in these cases.

Notes to Chapter 3

1. Plato, *Philebus*, p. 400.
2. Aristotle, *Poetics*, p. 30.
3. Ibid., p. 30.
4. Ibid., pp. 30–31.
5. Kasimir Malevich, *The Non-Objective World*, pp. 67–68.
6. Bernard Bosanquet, *Three Lectures on Aesthetic*, pp. 40–41.

7. Le Corbusier and Amadée Ozenfant, "Purism," pp. 61–62, 67.

8. Bell, *Art,* pp. 16–17.

9. Ibid., p. 29.

10. Ibid., pp. 22–23.

11. Roger Fry, *Vision and Design,* p. 109.

12. Bell, *Art,* pp. 144–45.

13. Ibid., p. 148.

14. Ibid., p. 174.

15. Ibid., pp. 29–30.

16. Ibid., p. 31.

17. Ibid., p. 37.

18. John Dewey, *Art as Experience,* p. 89.

19. Aristotle, *Poetics,* p. 32.

20. Donald Francis Tovey, *Essays in Musical Analysis,* vol. 2, p. 15.

21. Ibid., p. 18.

22. Donald Francis Tovey, *The Forms of Music,* p. 125.

23. Ibid.

24. Tovey, *Essays,* vol. 2, p. 6.

25. Tovey, *Essays,* vol. 3, p. 23.

26. Tovey, *Essays,* vol. 2, p. 15.

27. Tovey, *Essays,* vol. 3, p. 59.

28. Edwin G. Boring, *Sensation and Perception in the History of Experimental Psychology,* p. 252.

29. This and the following six principles are from Boring, *Sensation,* pp. 253–54.

30. Rudolf Arnheim, *Art and Visual Perception,* p. 21.

31. Ibid., p. 9.

32. Leonard B. Meyer, *Emotion and Meaning in Music,* p. 14.

33. Ibid.

34. Ibid., p. 161.

35. Ibid., p. 92.

36. Ibid.

37. Meyer, *Emotion,* p. 200.

38. Rudolf Arnheim, *The Dynamics of Architectural Form,* p. 212.

39. Ibid., p. 210.

40. Ibid., p. 213.

41. Arnheim, *Art and Visual Perception,* p. 26.

42. Bell, *Art,* p. 49.

43. Ibid., pp. 53–54.

44. Ibid., p. 54.

Notes to Chapter 4

1. Thomas Reid, *Essays on the Intellectual Powers of Man,* p. 498.

2. Ibid., p. 501.

3. Ibid., p. 117.

4. Ibid., pp. 118–19. It does try the imagination a bit to wonder how an orator would fare if denied the use of articulate speech.

5. Leo Tolstoy, *What is Art?,* pp. 50–51.

6. Ibid., p. 51.

7. Ibid., pp. 51–52.

8. Ibid., p. 139.

9. Ibid.
10. Ibid., p. 140.
11. Ibid., p. 141.
12. R. G. Collingwood, *The Principles of Art,* p. 15.
13. Ibid., p. 141.
14. Ibid.
15. Dennis Corrigan, "The Evolution to Humor," p. 51.
16. Collingwood, *Principles,* p. 313.
17. Ibid., p. 315.
18. Ibid., p. 225. Emphasis mine.
19. Ibid., p. 226.
20. Ibid., p. 244. This too strongly recalls Reid's claim: "Abolish the use of articulate sounds and writing among mankind for a century, and every man would be a painter, an actor, and an orator."
21. Quoted in John Dewey, *Art as Experience,* pp. 85–86.
22. J.W.N. Sullivan, *Beethoven,* p. 19. This in turn is taken by Sullivan from Edmund Gurney's *The Power of Sound.*
23. René F.-A. Sully-Prudhomme, *L'Expression dans les beaux-arts,* p. 181. My translation.
24. Suzanne K. Langer, *Philosophy in a New Key,* p. 176.
25. The theory is developed in his *Tractatus Logico-Philosophicus,* Sections 2.1–3.01.
26. Suzanne K. Langer, *Feeling and Form,* p. 40.
27. Ibid., p. 27.
28. Alan Tormey, *The Concept of Expression,* p. 98.
29. Ibid., p. 106. First emphasis mine.
30. Ibid., p. 127.
31. Ibid., p. 128.
32. Ibid., p. 129.
33. Sullivan, *Beethoven,* p. 10.
34. Wittgenstein, *Philosophical Investigations,* Section 261.
35. Ibid., p. 20.

Notes to Chapter 5

1. Cited in Wimsatt and Beardsley, "The Intentional Fallacy," pp. 471–72.
2. Ibid., p. 470.
3. Ibid., p. 469, quoting Springarn (an intentionalist!).
4. Ibid., p. 477.
5. Ibid.
6. Ibid., p. 482.
7. John Dewey, *Art as Experience,* p. 127.
8. Ibid., p. 68.
9. Wimsatt and Beardsley, "Intentional Fallacy," p. 486 (n. 12).
10. Roland Barthes, *Image, Music, Text,* p. 146.
11. Ibid., p. 148.
12. Roger Fry, *Vision and Design,* p. 109. Emphasis mine.
13. Dewey, *Art as Experience,* p. 105.
14. Wimsatt and Beardsley, "Intentional Fallacy," p. 469.
15. Collingwood, *Principles of Art,* p. 115. Emphasis mine.
16. Dewey, *Art,* p. 190.

Notes to Chapter 6

1. David Hume, *Of the Standard of Taste and Other Essays.*
2. Ibid., p. 11.
3. Ibid., pp. 10–11.
4. I thank Ted Cohen of the University of Chicago for bringing this fact to my attention.
5. Hume, *Standard,* p. 19.
6. Ibid.
7. Ibid., p. 20.
8. Ibid., pp. 20–21.
9. Ibid., p. 22.
10. In Thomas Reid, *Essays on the Intellectual Powers of Man.* The "Essay on Taste" occurs in vol. 1, from pp. 490–508. See especially pp. 490, 492, 495–96, 499–500.
11. The terms primary and secondary qualities were coined by John Locke. The notion can be found in Descartes and others preceding Locke.
12. Reid, *Intellectual Powers,* vol. 1, p. 313.
13. Ibid.
14. Ibid., p. 500.
15. Ibid., p. 447.
16. Ibid., p. 236.
17. Ibid., p. 492.
18. Ibid.
19. Ibid., p. 501.
20. Ibid., p. 122.
21. Ibid., p. 453.
22. Immanuel Kant, *The Critique of Judgment,* p. 27.

Bibliography

Aristotle. *Poetics.* Trans. with intro. by Gerald F. Else. Ann Arbor: University of Michigan Press, 1973.

Arnheim, Rudolf. *Art and Visual Perception.* Berkeley: University of California Press, 1954.

———. *The Dynamics of Architectural Form.* Berkeley: University of California Press, 1977.

Barthes, Roland. *Image, Music, Text.* Trans. by Stephen Heath. New York: Hill and Wang, 1977.

Bell, Clive. *Art.* London: Chatto and Windus, 1914.

Boring, Edwin G. *Sensation and Perception in the History of Experimental Psychology.* New York: Appleton-Century, 1942.

Bosanquet, Bernard. *Three Lectures on Aesthetic.* London: Macmillan, 1915.

Butcher, S.H. *Aristotle's Theory of Poetry and Fine Art.* New York: Dover, 1951.

Cervantes, Miguel de. *Don Quixote.* Ozell's revision of the translation of Peter Motteux. New York: The Modern Library, 1930.

Collingwood, R.G. *The Principles of Art.* New York: Oxford University Press, 1958.

Corrigan, Dennis. "The Evolution to Humor." *The Artist's Magazine* 10, no. 7 (1993): 46–51.

Danto, Arthur. "The Artworld." *Journal of Philosophy* 61, no. 19 (1964): 571–584.

———. *The Transfiguration of the Commonplace.* Cambridge: Harvard University Press, 1981.

Dewey, John. *Art as Experience.* New York: Capricorn Books, 1958.

Dickie, George. "The New Institutional Theory of Art." In *Aesthetics: A Critical Anthology,* 2nd edition, ed. George Dickie, Richard Sclafani and Ronald Roblin, pp. 196–205. New York: St. Martin's Press, 1989.

Diderot, Denis. *Oeuvres esthétiques,* ed. Paul Vernière. Paris: Editions Garnier Frères, 1968.

Eddington, A.S. *The Nature of the Physical World.* New York: Macmillan, 1929.

Fry, Roger. *Vision and Design.* Cleveland: World, 1969.

Goodman, Nelson. *Languages of Art.* Indianapolis: Bobbs-Merrill, 1968.

Homer. *The Iliad.* Trans. by Richard Lattimore. Chicago: University of Chicago Press, 1967.

Horace. "The Art of Poetry." In *Latin Poetry in Verse Translation,* ed. L.R. Lind, pp. 129–42. Boston: Houghton Mifflin, 1957.

Hume, David. *Of the Standard of Taste and Other Essays.* Indianapolis: Bobbs-Merrill, 1965.
Kant, Immanuel. *The Critique of Judgment.* Trans. with analytical indexes by James Creed Meredith. Oxford: Oxford University Press, 1964.
Langer, Suzanne. *Feeling and Form.* New York: Charles Scribner's Sons, 1953.
————. *Philosophy in a New Key.* New York: Penguin Books, 1948.
Le Corbusier and Amadée Ozenfant. "Purism." In *Modern Artists on Art,* ed. Robert L. Herbert, pp. 58–73. Englewood Cliffs: Prentice-Hall, 1964.
Lee, Rensselaer. *Ut Pictura Poesis: the Humanistic Theory of Painting.* New York: W.W. Norton, 1967.
Malevich, Casimir. *The Non-Objective World.* Chicago: Paul Theobald, 1959.
Mandelbaum, Maurice. "Family Resemblances and Generalizations Concerning the Arts." *The American Philosophical Quarterly,* 2 (1965): 219–28.
Manns, James. "Representation, Relativism and Resemblance." *The British Journal of Aesthetics* 11 (Summer, 1971): 281–287.
————. "On Composing 'By the Rules.'" *Journal of Aesthetics and Art Criticism* 52 (Winter 1994): 83–91.
Meyer, Leonard B. *Emotion and Meaning in Music.* Chicago: University of Chicago Press, 1956.
————. *Music, the Arts, and Ideas.* Chicago: University of Chicago Press, 1967.
Morgan, David. "The Rise and Fall of Abstraction in Eighteenth-Century Art Theory." *Eighteenth-Century Studies* 27 (1994): 449–78.
Plato. *Meno.* Trans. by G. M. A. Grube. Indianapolis: Hackett, 1976.
————. *Phaedo.* Trans. by G. M. A. Grube. Indianapolis: Hackett, 1977.
————. *Philebus.* In *The Dialogues of Plato.* Trans. by Benjamin Jowett. New York: Random House, 1937.
————. *Republic.* Trans. with intro. and notes by Francis MacDonald Cornford. London: Oxford University Press, 1973.
Reid, Thomas. *Essays on the Intellectual Powers of Man,* and *An Inquiry into the Human Mind on the Principles of Common Sense.* In *Philosophical Works,* 2 vols., with notes and supplementary dissertations by Sir William Hamilton, and an introduction by Harry Bracken. Hildesheim: Georg Olms Verlagsbuchhandlung, 1967.
Sullivan, J.W.N. *Beethoven.* New York: Vintage Books, 1927.
Sully-Prudhomme, René F.-A. *L'Expression dans les beaux-arts.* Paris: Alphonse Lemerre, 1883.
Tolstoy, Leo. *What Is Art?* Indianapolis: The Bobbs-Merrill Co., 1960.
Tormey, Alan. *The Concept of Expression.* Princeton: Princeton University Press, 1971.
Tovey, Donald Francis. *Essays in Musical Analysis.* 7 vols. London: Oxford University Press, 1972.
————. *The Forms of Music.* New York: Meridian Books, 1964.
Weitz, Morris. "The Role of Theory in Aesthetics." *Journal of Aesthetics and Art Criticism* 15 (September 1956): 27–35.
Wimsatt, William Jr., and Monroe C. Beardsley."The Intentional Fallacy." *The Sewanee Review* 54, no. 3 (1946): 468–86.
Wittgenstein, Ludwig. *Philosophical Investigations.* New York: Macmillan, 1961.
————. *Tractatus Logico-Philosophicus.* London: Routledge and Kegan Paul, 1961.
Wolfe, Tom. *The Painted Word.* New York: Farrar, Straus and Giroux, 1975.

Index

Abstract Expressionism, 119, 127
Abstraction, 164n
Absurd, the 47–51
Achilles, 27, 35, 51
Alcibiades, 33
Allen, Gracie, 120
Antigone, 100
Antonioni, Michelangelo
 Blowup, 49–50
Arc de Triomphe, 121
Aristotle, 27–29, 171
 catharsis in, 36–38
 influence in the Renaissance, 38–43
 mimesis in, 29–31
 modern views on, 47–51
 theory of artistic form, 52–54, 61–63
 theory of dramatic representation,
  32–38
"Aristotle's rules," 41–42
Arnheim, Rudolf, 68, 70–74, 78
Ars, 6
Artworld, 11–18, 20–21, 24
Atonal music, 22, 75–76
Atreus, the house of, 33

Bach, Johann Sebastian, 7, 65, 76,
 135, 173–74
 B-minor Mass, 66
 "Es ist vollbracht" aria, 91
 St. John Passion, 51
Balance, 70–71
Balanchine, George, 7

Banta, Tony, 120
Barthes, Roland, 124–27
Baumer, Paul, 48
Bazaine, Jean, 119
Beardsley, Monroe, 109–19, 123–24,
 127–28, 131
Beauty, 3, 20
 in aesthetic theories, 139–40
 in human character, 85–87
 of a machine, 85, 153
 and morality, 85–87, 146, 154–55,
  161
 in nature, 85–89, 163–64
 the objectivity of, 148–52, 155
 the subjectivity of, 140–47
 the universality of,
  in Reid, 147–55
  in Kant, 155–68
Beethoven, Ludwig van, 18, 22–23,
 64–66, 124–25
 Missa Solemnis, 82–83, 109
 ninth symphony, 64
 piano sonata, Opus 111, 76–77, 107
Bell, Clive, 3–4, 71–72, 79, 102
 and formalism, 54–61
 and aesthetic emotion, 56–61
 and significant form, 56–61
Bellori, Giovanni Pietro, 41
Berra, Yogi. 18
Bissière, Roger, 119
Bloomsbury group, 54–55
Bond, James, 87

Bonnard, Pierre, 11
Bosanquet, Bernard, 55, 61
Bouguereau, William, 11
Braque, Georges, 11, 119
Briggs, Joe Bob, 173–74
Browning, Robert, 48
Bryce Canyon, 88–89
Bunker, Archie, 120

Cage, John, 6–7, 13
  "4 Minutes and 33 Seconds of
    Silence," 6, 13
Caesar, Julius, 33
Camus, Albert,
  The Plague, 48–49
Canaletto, 58
Caricature, 46–47
Carter, Jimmy, 47
Catch-22, 120
Catharsis, in tragedy, 36–38
Cervantes, Miguel de,
  Don Quixote, 142–43
Cézanne, Paul, 11, 58
  Mme Cézanne Seated in a Yellow
    Chair, 45, 78
Chairfalling, 16–17
Chopin, Frederic, 77, 108
  B minor prelude (Opus 28, No. 6), 82
Christo, 13
Clare, Angel, 48
Clinton, Bill, 47
Collingwood, R.G., 92–98, 107, 132
Communication, 83–84, 89–93,
  107–8, 126–27
Constable, John, 43
Corneille, Pierre, 41–42
Cotman, John, 58
Cousin, Victor, 84
Craft, as distinct from art, 92–94
Criticism, Hume's criteria of, 142–47
Crome, John, 58
Cubism, 44–45, 58, 60, 119

Dali, Salvador, 56
Dante, 7
Danto, Arthur, 11–15, 17–24
Debussy, Claude, 107, 120, 126
  Afternoon of a Faun, 151

Debussy, Claude (continued)
  string quartet, 120
Delta Kappa Epsilon, 16
Dewey, John, 60–62, 117–18, 126, 132
Dickens, Charles, 139
Dickie, George, 12–18, 24
Diderot, Denis, 3
Disney Corporation, 88–89
Donne, John,
  A Valediction Forbidding Mourning,
    116–17
Dostoevsky, Fyodor, 139
Dreedle, General, 120

Eddington, A.S., 4n
Eglise St. Philibert, 106
Eiffel Tower, 93
Electra, 33
Eliot, T.S.
  Four Quartets, 100, 130
  Mr. Eliot's Sunday Morning Service,
    111
El Greco, 45
  The Disrobing of Christ, 40
  Espolio, 26
Ellington, Duke, 124
Emotion, 156
  captured in artistic representation,
    27
  distinctly aesthetic, 56–61, 72–73
  emotionalism, 9
  expressed in art, 78–79, 81–84,
    89–100
  generated by artistic form, 27, 72
Entomology, 4–5
Expression
  and communication, 108
  different senses of the term, 80–83
    objective, 80
    subjective, 80–81
  and emotion, 99–100, 105–8
  etymology of the term, 83
  general theory of, 19–20, 26
  in nature, 84–85, 87–89
  and inner-outer distinction, 97–99
  Collingwood's theory of, 92–97
  Langer's theory of, 101–3
  Reid's theory of, 84–89

Expression *(continued)*
  Sully-Prudhomme's theory of,
    100–01
  Tolstoy's theory of, 89–92
  Tormey's theory of, 103–5

Family resemblances, 8–11
Farrakhan, Louis, 19
Fauvism, 58
Favre, Bret, 121
Flaubert, Gustave, 95
Form,
  artistic, 26–28, 64–67, 78
  significant,
    in Clive Bell, 56–61, 79
    in Roger Fry, 57
    in Suzanne Langer, 102–3
Formalism, 9, 26–28, 54–61
Forms, Plato's theory of, 31–33, 38–40
Forrest Gump, 117–18
Freedom,
  artistic, 5–6
  in moral behavior, 5–6
Fry, Roger, 54–55, 57, 60, 71–72,
    125

Gainesborough, Thomas,
  Blue Boy, 5
Gestalt theory, 54, 67–70
  in music, 74–78
  in the visual arts, 70–74
Giacometti, Alberto, 112
Giacometti, Diego, 112
Gioconda, La, 135
Giotto, 58
God,
  His goodness expressed in nature,
    84–85, 87–89
  in Neo-Platonism, 40
Gogh, Vincent van, 11, 99, 136
  Starry Night, 72–73
  Wheatfield with Crows, 121
Goldfinger, Auric, 87
Goneril, 125
Gorky, Maxim, 139
Gothic style, 58
Goya, Francisco de, 139
Grand Canyon, 88

Greenberg, Clement, 20
Guardi, Francesco, 58

Hamlet, 18, 62–63
Hardy, Thomas,
  Tess of the D'Urbervilles, 48
Hegel, G.W.F., 61
Hephaistos, 27
Hollywood, 38, 117–18
Holmes, Sherlock, 112
Homer, 27, 35–36, 40, 109, 171
  Iliad, 27
Horace,
  Ars Poetica, 42–43
Hume, David, 138–39, 150, 156
  skepticism, 140, 147–48, 156
  subjectivist theory of taste, 140–47,
    168, 172
  view of the self, 147, 166

Impressionism, 43–44, 136
Institutional theory, 12–18, 20–21, 24
Intellectualism, 9
Intentional fallacy, 109–13
Intentions
  of an artist, 57, 91, 110–13, 115–16,
    127–29
  and artist-audience communication,
    127–29
  and the internal-external distinction,
    113–18
  and the linguistic-cultural context,
    115–16, 123–27
  and originality, 118–23
Intentionality, 10
Intuitionism, 9

Jarrett, Keith, 173
Jazz music, 76, 173

Kant, Immanuel, 61, 139, 147
  concept of disinterestedness,
    160–61, 166
  concept of pleasure, 159–61, 163–64
  concept of purposiveness, 161–64
  judgment, reflective and
    determinant, 158–59, 163–66,
    167–68

Kant, Immanuel *(continued)*
  theory of cognition, 157–58, 167
  theory of the self, 166
  universality of aesthetic judgment,
    155–57, 160, 165–69, 172
Kingfish, the, 120
Koffka, Kurt, 68
Köhler, Wolfgang, 68
Kubrick, Stanley, 120
Ku Klux Klan, 19
Kurasawa, Akira,
  Throne of Blood, 173

Lake Wobegon, 124
Langer, Suzanne, 3, 101–4, 106
Leach, Robin, 131
Le Corbusier, 55
Le Moal, Jean, 119
Lessing, G.E.,
  Laoköon, 43
Liszt, Franz, 107
Locke, John, 68
Longinus, 109
Louis XVIII, 47
Loussier, Jacques, 173
Louvre, the, 73
Luhrman, Baz, 173

MacDowell, Andie, 168
Magritte, René, 56–57
Malevich, Kasimir, 55
Mandelbaum, Maurice, 9–11
Manessier, Alfred, 11, 119
McKellan, Ian, 173
Mendelssohn, Felix, 106, 174
Mercouri, Melina, 100
Mercutio, 173
Meyer, Leonard, 68, 72, 75–78
Michelangelo, 81
  Pietà, 91
Monet, Claude, 11, 15, 44
Moore, G.E., 110
Moran, Colonel Sebastian, 112
Mozart, Wolfgang Amadeus, 130
  A-major violin concerto, 66–67
  C-major piano concerto, 64
  Lucia Scylla, 66
  Requiem, 76, 131

Mussorgsky, Modeste,
  Pictures at an Exhibition, 125
Mystic Islands, 111
Mysticism, 59, 61

Naturalistic fallacy, 110
Natural selection,
  the Darwinian model, 88–89
Neo-Aristotelianism in aesthetics,
  39–43
Neo-Platonism in aesthetics, 39–41
Neo-Surrealism, 56
Never on Sunday, 100
New Age music, 174
Newman, Randy,
  Sail Away, 115
Nixon, Richard, 47

O'Connor, Frank, 118
Odysseus, 33
Oedipus, 33–34, 37
Oedipus, 100
Oh, Calcutta!, 173
"Old Man of the Mountain," the, 129
Open texture concepts, 9–10, 23–24
Orangutan art, 127–28
Organicism, 9, 54, 61–67

Panza, Sancho, 142–43
Parthenon, 135
Physics, 4
  Newtonian, 149
Picasso, Pablo, 11, 45, 47, 119, 136
  Demoiselles d'Avignon, 44
  Guernica, 91
  Still-life with Chair, 44
Pissarro, Camille, 44
Plato, 3, 42, 171
  influence in the Renaissance, 38–41
  Philebus, 52
  Republic, 31–32, 36, 39–40
  on representation, 27–28, 30–33,
    35–39
  theory of forms, 32–33, 35, 40
Pollack, Jackson, 7, 119
Polonius, 63
Pop Art, 20
Pound, Ezra, 171

Poussin, 45–46
The Lamentation, 40
Praxiteles, 7
Presley, Elvis, 124
Psychology, 4–5

Qualities,
the objectivity of, 15, 137–38,
148–52
primary and secondary, 148–52
the subjectivity of, 138

Racine, Jean, 41–42
Rap music, 77
Ravel, Maurice,
Pavane pour une infante défunte, 104
string quartet, 120
Regan, 125
Reid, Thomas, 91, 96, 98, 138–39,
146, 156
expression theory, 84–89
first principles of commonsense,
148, 153–54
on the objectivity of beauty, 147–52,
155
on the universality of beauty,
152–55, 172
Remarque, Erich Maria,
All Quiet on the Western Front,
48–49
Rembrandt, self-portraits, 41, 49, 60
Renoir, Auguste, 44
Representation, 11
Aristotle's theory of, 27–38
in modern aesthetics, 43–47
"natural" and "unnatural" modes of,
45–47
Plato's critique of, 27–28, 31–32, 39
relation to expression, 26–27
relation to formalism, 26–27, 164
relation of term to Greek *mimesis,*
29–31
in Renaissance aesthetics, 39–43
and the "ugly" truth, 47–51
Republic, of Plato, 31–32, 36, 39–40,
42
Rimski-Korsakov, Nikolai, 125–26
Rockwell, Norman, 56–57

Romanesque style, 58
Romanticism, 80, 109, 173
Rorschach inkblot test, 69
Rosenberg, Harold, 20
Rot, Dieter, 6

Salamis, sea battle at, 33
Saturday Evening Post, 56
Schoenberg, Arthur, 22, 124
Schubert, Franz,
unfinished symphony, 99
Shakespeare, William, 18, 135, 173–74
Hamlet, 62–63
King Lear, 125
Macbeth, 123, 173
A Midsummer Night's Dream, 173
Richard III, 173
Romeo and Juliet, 173
Signs,
arbitrary, 82, 86, 96, 98
as means to expressing inner states,
82–84, 89–90
natural, 85–89, 92
Sincerity in art, 91–95, 109, 132
Singier, Gustave, 119
Sisely, Alfred, 44
Sistine Chapel, 81
Smith, Tony, 21
Snoop Doggy Dogg, 124
Sociology, 4–5
Socrates, Plato's narrator, 31
Sophists, 27
Special effects in the arts, 38
Spielberg, Steven,
Schindler's List, 130
Staël, Nicolas de, 11, 47
Paysage de Sicile, 45–46
Star Wars, 122
Steinberg, Leo, 20
Stewart, Dugald, 84
Stoll, Avrum, 128
Strauss, Richard
Also Sprach Zarathustra, 120
Stravinsky, Igor, 124, 126
Sullivan, J.W.N., 99, 105–6
Sully-Prudhomme, René F.-A.,
100–101, 104
Suprematism, 55

Surrealism, 56–57
Süssmayr, Franz, 131
Symbolism,
   artistic, 78, 82
   expressing inner states, 84
   Suzanne Langer's theory of, 101–3
Symmetry, 52, 70, 73–74

Tabula rasa, 68
Taste,
   considerations favoring standards of,
      133–37
   Hume's theory of, 140–47
   the relativity of, 133–34, 145–47
   and subjectivity of beauty, 137–38,
      140–47
   the universality of, 152–54
Taxi, 120
Tolstoy, Leo, 18, 93–94, 96, 98, 100,
      107–9, 126, 130–32
   expression theory, 89–92
   War and Peace, 135
Tormey, Alan, 103–6
Tovey, Donald Francis, 62, 64–67
Trojan war, 33
Truth and representation,
   in Aristotle, 32–35, 37
   in narrative arts, 47–51
   in Plato, 31–33, 38–40
Turner, J.M.W., 43
2001: A Space Odessey, 120

Ugliness in nature, 88

Uniqueness, 63
Unity, as a formal concept, 53–54,
      61–67, 70–71
Ut pictura poesis, 39, 41–43

Variety, as a formal concept, 53–54,
      63, 66–67
Vermeer, Jan, 41, 136
Vieira da Silva, Maria, 11,
      46–47
Vinci, Leonardo da, 15
   La Gioconda, 135
Voluntarism, 9

Wagner, Richard, 22, 124
Wall Street, 129
Warhol, Andy, 11, 16, 18, 50–51
   Brillo Box, 11–14, 16, 20, 24
War and Peace, 135
War of the Roses, 34
Watergate, 50
Watteau, Antoine, 58
Wayne, John, 168
Weitz, Morris, 9–11
Wertheimer, Max, 68
West Side Story, 173
Wimsatt, William, 109–19, 123–24,
      127–28, 131
Wittgenstein, Ludwig, 7–11, 101–2,
      105
Wolfe, Tom, 20–21

Zeuxis, 40

About the Author

James W. Manns received his Ph.D. in philosophy in 1972 from Boston University. He is currently a professor of philosophy at the University of Kentucky. He has published numerous articles in the field of aesthetics and is the author of *Reid and His French Disciples* (1994).